Reconceiving Civil Society and Transitional Justice

Reconceiving Civil Society and Transitional Justice examines the role of civil society in transitional justice, exploring the *forms* of civil society that are enabled or disabled by transitional justice processes and the *forms* of transitional justice activity that are enabled and disabled by civil society actors.

Although civil society organisations play an integral role in the pursuit of transitional justice in conflict-affected societies, the literature lacks a comprehensive conceptualisation of the diversity and complexity of these roles. This reflects the degree to which dominant approaches to transitional justice focus on liberal-legal justice strategies and international human rights norms. In this context, civil society organisations are perceived as intermediaries who are thought to advocate for and support formal, liberal transitional justice processes. The contributions to this volume demonstrate that the reality is more complicated; civil society can – and does – play important roles in enabling formal transitional justice processes, but it can also disrupt them. Informed by detailed fieldwork across Asia and the Pacific Islands, the contributions demonstrate that neither transitional justice nor civil society should be treated as taken-for-granted concepts.

Reconceiving Civil Society and Transitional Justice will be of great interest to scholars of Security Studies, Asian Studies, Peacebuilding, Asia Pacific, Human Rights, Reconciliation and the Politics of Memory.

The chapters were originally published as a special issue of *Global Change, Peace & Security.*

Joanne Wallis is an Associate Professor in the Coral Bell School of Asia Pacific Affairs in the College of Asia and the Pacific at the Australian National University, Canberra, Australia. Her research focuses on peacebuilding and security in the Pacific Islands.

Lia Kent is a Visiting Fellow in the School of Regulation and Global Governance (RegNet) in the College of Asia and the Pacific at the Australian National University, Canberra, Australia. Her research focuses on transitional justice and the politics of memory in Southeast Asia.

Reconceiving Civil Society and Transitional Justice

Lessons from Asia and the Pacific

Edited by
Joanne Wallis and Lia Kent

Routledge
Taylor & Francis Group
LONDON AND NEW YORK

First published 2020
by Routledge
2 Park Square, Milton Park, Abingdon, Oxon, OX14 4RN

and by Routledge
52 Vanderbilt Avenue, New York, NY 10017

Routledge is an imprint of the Taylor & Francis Group, an informa business

British Library Cataloguing-in-Publication Data
A catalogue record for this book is available from the British Library

ISBN13: 978-0-367-46974-0

Typeset in Myriad Pro
by codeMantra

Publisher's Note
The publisher accepts responsibility for any inconsistencies that may have arisen during the conversion of this book from journal articles to book chapters, namely the inclusion of journal terminology.

Disclaimer
Every effort has been made to contact copyright holders for their permission to reprint material in this book. The publishers would be grateful to hear from any copyright holder who is not here acknowledged and will undertake to rectify any errors or omissions in future editions of this book.

Contents

Citation Information vi
Notes on Contributors vii

Introduction: Special issue on 'reconceiving civil society and transitional justice: lessons from Asia and the Pacific' 1
Joanne Wallis and Lia Kent

1 Reconciliations (Melanesian style) and transitional justice 11
Volker Boege

2 The role of 'uncivil' society in transitional justice: evidence from Bougainville and Timor-Leste 30
Joanne Wallis

3 Transitional justice and the spaces of memory activism in Timor-Leste and Aceh 51
Lia Kent

4 From transitional to performative justice: peace activism in the aftermath of communal violence 70
Birgit Bräuchler

5 Exploring the link between mine action and transitional justice in Cambodia 90
Dahlia Simangan and Rebecca Gidley

Index 113

Citation Information

The chapters in this book were originally published in the *Global Change, Peace & Security*, volume 31, issue 2 (June 2019). When citing this material, please use the original page numbering for each article, as follows:

Introduction
Special issue on 'reconceiving civil society and transitional justice: lessons from Asia and the Pacific'
Joanne Wallis and Lia Kent
Global Change, Peace & Security, volume 31, issue 2 (June 2019) pp. 129–138

Chapter 1
Reconciliations (Melanesian style) and transitional justice
Volker Boege
Global Change, Peace & Security, volume 31, issue 2 (June 2019) pp. 139–157

Chapter 2
The role of 'uncivil' society in transitional justice: evidence from Bougainville and Timor-Leste
Joanne Wallis
Global Change, Peace & Security, volume 31, issue 2 (June 2019) pp. 159–179

Chapter 3
Transitional justice and the spaces of memory activism in Timor-Leste and Aceh
Lia Kent
Global Change, Peace & Security, volume 31, issue 2 (June 2019) pp. 181–199

Chapter 4
From transitional to performative justice: peace activism in the aftermath of communal violence
Birgit Bräuchler
Global Change, Peace & Security, volume 31, issue 2 (June 2019) pp. 201–220

Chapter 5
Exploring the link between mine action and transitional justice in Cambodia
Dahlia Simangan and Rebecca Gidley
Global Change, Peace & Security, volume 31, issue 2 (June 2019) pp. 221–243

Contributors

Volker Boege is an Honorary Research Fellow with the School of Political Science and International Studies at The University of Queensland in Brisbane, Australia.

Birgit Bräuchler is a Senior Lecturer at the School of Social Sciences, Monash University, Melbourne, Australia.

Rebecca Gidley teaches at the College of Asia and the Pacific at the Australian National University, Canberra, Australia.

Lia Kent is a Visiting Fellow in the School of Regulation and Global Governance at The Australian National University, Canberra, Australia.

Dahlia Simangan is an Assistant Professor at Hiroshima University's Graduate School for International Development and Cooperation (IDEC) and Network for Education and Research on Peace and Sustainability, Japan.

Joanne Wallis is an Associate Professor in the Coral Bell School of Asia Pacific Affairs in the College of Asia and the Pacific at the Australian National University, Canberra, Australia.

INTRODUCTION

Special issue on 'reconceiving civil society and transitional justice: lessons from Asia and the Pacific'

Joanne Wallis and Lia Kent

ABSTRACT
This article, and the special issue it introduces, joins an emerging conversation about the role of civil society in transitional justice (TJ). Although civil society organisations play an integral role in the pursuit of TJ in conflict-affected societies, the literature lacks a comprehensive conceptualisation of the diversity and complexity of these roles. Building on an interdisciplinary workshop at the Australian National University in September 2016, the contributions to this special issue explore the forms of civil society that are enabled and disabled by TJ processes and the forms of TJ activity that are enabled and disabled by different kinds of civil society actors.

This special issue joins an emerging conversation about the role of civil society in transitional justice (TJ). Although civil society organisations (CSOs) play an integral role in the pursuit of TJ in conflict-affected societies, the literature 'lacks a comprehensive and rigorous conceptualisation' of the diversity and complexity of these roles.[1] This lacuna can partly be explained by the fact that TJ as a field is 'under-theorised.'[2] It is also a reflection of the degree to which dominant approaches to TJ focus on liberal-legal justice strategies and international human rights norms and take the 'state' as their key point of reference.[3] Based on these assumptions, CSOs are essentially viewed as gap-fillers or intermediaries; they are thought to play an 'indispensable role' in advocating for, and subsequently supporting, official, state-sponsored, TJ processes and ensuring their success.[4]

Based on our research on TJ in Asia and the Pacific we know that the reality is more complicated; civil society can – and does – play important roles in enabling formal TJ processes, but it can also disrupt them. Some groups may be engaged in struggles for 'justice'

This article has been republished with minor changes. These changes do not impact the academic content of the article.

[1]Paul Gready and Simon Robins, 'Rethinking Civil Society and Transitional Justice: Lessons from Social Movements and 'New' Civil Society', *International Journal of Human Rights* 21, no. 7 (2017): 956–975, 956.

[2]Ibid., 956.

[3]Thania Paffenholz and Christoph Spurk, *Civil Society, Civic Engagement, and Peacebuilding* (Washington: World Bank, 2006); World Bank, *Working Together: World Bank-Civil Society Relations* (Washington: World Bank, 2003); Catherine Barnes, *Agents for Change: Civil Society Roles in Preventing War & Building Peace* (The Hague: European Centre for Conflict Prevention, 2006); World Bank, *Civil Society and Peacebuilding; Potential, Limitations and Critical Factors* (Washington: World Bank, 2007); David Backer, 'Civil Society and Transitional Justice: Possibilities, Patterns and Prospects', *Journal of Human Rights* 2, no. 3 (2003): 297–313.

[4]Gready and Robins, 'Rethinking Civil Society and Transitional Justice', 956–957; David Crocker, 'Transitional Justice and International Civil Society: Toward a Normative Framework', *Constellations* 5, no. 4 (1998): 492–517, 492.

that diverge markedly from formal, liberal, TJ understandings and goals. The discourse and practice of TJ can also influence the nature, parameters and reach of civil society activity in any given society. Conscious that these complexities had been overlooked, and that Asia and the Pacific have been peripheral geographic regions in TJ scholarship, we convened an interdisciplinary workshop at the Australian National University in September 2016 with the goal of contributing to emerging debates on TJ and civil society. The workshop brought together leading and emerging international and Australian scholars to discuss numerous themes including: the heterogeneity of civil society in TJ; the roles of faith-based organisations vis-a-vie secular CSOs; the gender dimensions of civil society TJ efforts; the relationships (and tensions) between CSOs and the state; the influence of donor agendas on CSOs; and the significance of civil society-led TJ initiatives (including local reconciliation, art, memorialisation and community media initiatives).[5]

Although not part of the initial framing discussions, the theme of 'enabling and disabling' emerged during the lively workshop conversations as a useful way of capturing the complex dynamics of engagement between TJ and a diverse array of civil society actors.[6] This theme helped to capture what soon became apparent to workshop participants – that neither TJ or civil society could be treated as taken-for-granted static or stable concepts. From this starting point it seemed to make sense to explore the *forms* of civil society that are enabled and disabled by TJ processes and the *forms* of TJ activity that are enabled and disabled by different kinds of civil society actors. To put this differently, this theme allowed participants to reflect on the extent to which dominant TJ discourses and practices (which emphasise a 'tool-kit' of responses including criminal prosecutions, truth commissions, reparations packages and institutional reforms) socially construct certain kinds of civil society actors and activities – in particular human rights non-government organisations (NGOs) and liberal/legal TJ activity. How might this discourage or render invisible organisations and informal groups that engage in activities that do not conform to this mould? The theme of 'enabling and disabling' also allowed for a focus on the extent to which the activities of a diverse and often fluid collection of civil society actors and groups can promote or undermine the pursuit of TJ (broadly defined). How might close attention to civil society actors' 'modes of organisation' and 'repertoires of action' foster new ways of thinking about both TJ and civil society?[7] Underpinning much of the rich conversation that took place at the workshop was the idea that scholars need to be attuned to the complex historical, political and cultural realities of particular local contexts.

Building on these discussions, this special issue seeks to contribute to the literature on TJ, and peacebuilding more generally, by examining the diversity and complexity of civil society actors and activities in the Asia and the Pacific. Volker Boege challenges conventional approaches to civil society by highlighting the significance of locally-grounded reconciliation practices in the Melanesian sub-region of the Pacific Islands, particularly the Solomon Islands and the Bougainville region of Papua New Guinea. Joanne Wallis questions the presumed civility of CSOs in the conventional TJ literature in her analysis of 'uncivil society' groups in Bougainville and Timor-Leste. With a focus on Timor-Leste

[5]Several papers presented at the workshop are being published in Lia Kent, Joanne Wallis and Claire Cronin, eds., *Civil Society and Transitional Justice in Asia and the Pacific* (ANU Press, in-press).
[6]We are grateful to Professor John Braithwaite for coining this phrase.
[7]Gready and Robins, 'Rethinking Civil Society and Transitional Justice', 971.

and Aceh, Lia Kent highlights how the growing prominence of memorialisation within the TJ 'tool-kit' places high expectations upon local civil society 'memory activists' to promote the remembrance of the past in ways that have the potential to marginalise informal spaces and practices of memory. Birgit Bräuchler focuses on the potential of civil society-led arts and theatre projects in the Maluku region of Indonesia to contribute towards a broad and highly contextualised form of 'transformative justice' that prioritises local agency and responds both to past and present injustices. Dahlia Simangan and Rebecca Gidley also demonstrate the need for a wider understanding of how justice can be achieved in their discussion of the role of demining CSOs in Cambodia.

In the remainder of this introduction we explore the complexity of both 'civil society' and 'transitional justice', drawing on examples from this special issue. Woven throughout this introduction are examples of how TJ can both enable and disable forms of civil society activity and how civil society can both enable and disable forms of TJ. Our goal is not to articulate a definitive definition of civil society or of TJ but, rather, to broaden the reductionist understandings of both these terms that are found in the TJ and peacebuilding literature.

Reconceiving 'civil society'

One of the reasons why the role of civil society in TJ has been under-theorised is that the concept of civil society itself is ill-defined. It can potentially be applied to a range of non-state actors with 'varying values, issues of concern, animating philosophies, financial means and degrees of political, religious and/or ideological motivation'.[8] Despite this breadth, dominant understandings of civil society tend to reflect debates that have evolved in the context of western political thought. As such, civil society has largely come to be understood in a 'western liberal' guise: as an 'arena of voluntary – uncoerced – collective action around shared interests, purposes and values'.[9] Understood to be distinct from the family, the state and the market, this sphere is thought to enable the bringing together of 'citizens' [who are understood to be autonomous individuals] to take part in matters of public policy.'[10]

Within peacebuilding and development discourse the concept of civil society rose to prominence in the 1990s, as practitioners came to see the 'sponsorship and promotion' of CSOs as central to their interventions, and as key to achieving a liberal peace.[11] Civil society tends to be treated in this discourse as a 'floating signifier' that carries connotations of 'civility and virtue'.[12] It is often invoked to suggest ideas of 'autonomy, population participation and democratic validation'.[13] It is thought to act as a 'democratic counterweight to the power-brokers, economic, exploiters and warlords' that are said to dominate

---

[8]Lia Kent, Joanne Wallis and Claire Cronin, 'Introduction: Civil Society and Transitional Justice in Asia and the Pacific,' in *Civil Society and Transitional Justice in Asia and the Pacific*, ed. L. Kent, J. Wallis, and C. Cronin (forthcoming, ANU Press).

[9]Beatrice Pouligny, 'Civil Society and Post-Conflict Peacebuilding: Ambiguities of International Programmes Aimed at Building 'New' Societies', *Security Dialogue* 36, no. 4 (2005): 495–510, 497.

[10]Boege this issue. See also Renee Jeffery, Lia Kent and Joanne Wallis, 'Reconceiving the Roles of Religious Civil Society Organizations in Transitional Justice: Evidence from the Solomon Islands, Timor-Leste and Bougainville', *International Journal of Transitional Justice* 11, no. 3 (2017): 378–399, 379.

[11]Waibel, Ehlert and Feuer, *Southeast Asia and the Civil Society Gaze: Scoping a Contested Concept in Cambodia and Vietnam*, Routledge (2014), 5.

[12]Laura J. Shepherd, 'Constructing Civil Society: Gender, Power and Legitimacy in United Nations Peacebuilding Discourse', *European Journal of International Relations* 21, no. 4 (2015): 887–910, 893.

[13]Alex Jeffrey, *The Improvised State: Sovereignty, Performance and Agency in Dayton Bosnia* (Oxford, Wiley Blackwell, 2013), 113.

conflict-affected societies.[14] As the 'imagined agent of development' and peacebuilding, civil society is set up in opposition to a conflict-ridden and dysfunctional state.[15]

Understandings of civil society in the closely-linked discourse of TJ tend to be similarly anaemic, and are underpinned by what Paul Gready and Simon Robins refer to as 'normative idealism' – the idea that human rights are universal and that TJ will foster liberal democracy.[16] Part of the reason for this is that the TJ field has been heavily influenced by the civil society movements that emerged in Latin American and Eastern Europe during what is now referred to as the 'third wave' of transitions from authoritarian rule to democracy in the 1980s.[17] Many of the key players in these movements became involved in debates in the newly emerging field of TJ, bringing within them 'a set of agendas that emphasized, among other priorities, the pursuit of formal state-led responses to human rights violations'.[18] It therefore came to be assumed that CSOs were NGOs with a human rights focus: that they were secular, separate from the state, and supportive of a 'global' norm of accountability.[19] Civil society came to be understood, that is, as both 'civil' and in favour of 'global accountability norms' that stress liberal-legal accountability for perpetrators of mass atrocities.[20]

These reductionist interpretations are reflected in three problematic assumptions that are often made in peacebuilding and TJ scholarship. First, it is assumed that structures representative of 'the form that civil society has taken in modern western societies' – including NGOs and trade unions – exist in conflict-affected societies.[21] These structures are situated as part of a set of binary relationships that are often more imagined than real: 'governmental versus non-governmental, profit-making versus not-for-profit and public versus private.'[22] Challenging these conceptualisations, several contributions to this special issue recognise a heterogenous field of CSOs and civil society actors in Asia and the Pacific. Boege points to the significance of 'local-local' forms of community in Melanesia, which are 'embedded in local culture, custom, kin networks' and the churches. Bräuchler similarly argues that civil society in the Maluku context comprises a diverse collection of actors including 'special interest groups, faith-based organisations, traditional and community groups, researchers and research institutions, NGOs, women and youth groups, social and political movements, activists and artists, (non-profit) business associations or some combination thereof'. Focusing on artists and performers involved in documentary film making, blogging, IT, hip-hop, literature, theatre, tourism and environment, photography and painting, Bräuchler points out that civil society is not a fixed group of actors but a constantly changing field.

In her contribution, Wallis critically examines the presumed 'civility' of civil society and the assumption that CSOs share a commitment to TJ approaches based on liberal-legal

---

[14]Pouligny, 'Civil Society and Post-Conflict Peacebuilding', 496.
[15]Jenny Pearce, 'The International Community and Peacebuilding', *Development* 48, no. 3 (2005): 41–49.
[16]Paul Gready and Simon Robins, 'From Transitional to Transformative Justice: A New Agenda for Practice', *The International Journal of Transitional Justice* 8 (2014): 339–361, 343.
[17]Jelena Subotic 'The Transformation of International Transitional Justice Advocacy', *International Journal of Transitional Justice* 6, no 1 (2012): 119; Jeffery, Kent and Wallis, 'Reconceiving the Roles of Religious Civil Society'.
[18]Jeffery, Kent and Wallis, 'Reconceiving the Roles of Religious Civil Society', 382.
[19]Aaron P. Boesenecker and Leslie Vinjamuri, 'Lost in Translation? Civil Society, Faith-Based Organizations and the Negotiation of International Norms', *The International Journal of Transitional Justice* 5 (2011): 345–365.
[20]Jeffery, Kent and Wallis, 'Reconceiving the Roles of Religious Civil Society', 379.
[21]Beatrice Pouligny, 'Civil Society and Post-Conflict Peacebuilding', 498.
[22]Waibel, Ehlert and Feuer, *Southeast Asia and the Civil Society Gaze*, 5.

justice strategies and international human rights norms. Focusing on the cases of Timor-Leste and Bougainville region, she challenges the assumption that CSOs will necessarily act in ways that are conducive to reconciliation and peace, let alone favour liberal-legal processes of achieving this.[23] She finds that, in these contexts, where 'state institutions are fragile, illegitimate or absent', uncivil society groups can emerge, 'particularly as when seeking security people frequently strengthen their ethnic or language bonds; kinship, tribal, religious groups; and traditional political structures', rather than having broad-based memberships and interest in promoting the common good. These 'uncivil' society groups 'can be organised around societal divisions, oppose liberal democracy and liberal-legal TJ processes and engage in unruly behaviour, including violence and criminality'. Nonetheless, Wallis concludes that, while these groups 'would not necessarily be regarded as internationally legitimate by liberal peace standards ... [they] may nevertheless have strong local legitimacy'. Because of this, it is necessary for peacebuilding and TJ practitioners to take them seriously.

Of course, civil society in Asia and the Pacific also encompasses NGOs who are sympathetic to liberal-legal TJ mechanisms. These organisations face their own set of issues, particularly in terms of relations with the state, as Kent's and Simangan and Gidley's contributions highlight. Kent's discussion of the role of human rights NGOs engaged in 'memory activism' in Timor-Leste and Aceh highlights how these NGOs must not only negotiate delicate relationships with the state – which view them suspiciously due to their connections with western human rights advocacy groups – but also the expectations placed upon by TJ memorialisation frameworks. These frameworks assume that NGOs will stand outside of the state and 'challenge hegemonic narratives' *and* 'support and complement the state-building enterprise by fostering public participation and encouraging renewed forms of active citizenship'. In the context of Timor-Leste, where the state prioritises the 'remembrance of a heroic past and reconciliation with Indonesia' activists struggle in their efforts to achieve state sponsorship of memorialisation practices highlighting civilian experiences of violence. In Aceh, 'where the transition has been more partial than in Timor-Leste', the stakes of memory activism are high and there may also be personal risks to activists. Kent also argues that the orientation of NGO-led memory activism towards changing state policy and practice can inadvertently sideline local priorities and spaces for remembering and honouring the dead.

Simangan and Gidley focus on the challenges faced by NGOs operating in Cambodia, where there is an environment of 'shrinking freedom of expression and association'. These authors examine how one NGO, the Cambodia Mine Action Centre (CMAC), has facilitated the work of the Extraordinary Chambers in the Courts of Cambodia (ECCC). They show that CMAC has been able to operate effectively because it is engaged in what is perceived to be the politically neutral, but highly efficacious and practical, function of mine clearance. Because demining is a government priority, CMAC has a degree of latitude and freedom that CSOs focused on advocating for human rights protections do not have. This allows CMAC to provide 'opportunities for grassroots participation' that may serve as incubators for practices of deliberative democracy and participatory political

[23]Willemijn Verkoren and Mathijs van Leeumen, 'Civil Society in Fragile Contexts', in *The Handbook of Global Security Policy*, ed. Mary Kaldor and Iavor Rangelov (Chichester: John Wiley & Sons, 2014), 463–481; Sarah Crowther, 'The Role of NGOs, Local and International, in Post-war Peacebuilding', *Committee for Conflict Transformation Support Newsletter*, no. 15 (2001).

decision-making. At the same time, CMAC has to 'maintain a level of tolerance towards the government's authoritarianism and find issues of mutual concern'.

The second, related, consequence of anaemic accounts of civil society in the TJ literature is that problematic assumptions are made about the state. Civil society is assumed to operate in contexts where there is a legitimate state, a separation between state institutions and society, and between religious institutions and the state, and a population that identifies as citizens. Contributors to this special issue challenge this assumption by highlighting that post-conflict states generally do not conform to a liberal ideal of statehood. The state may have a limited presence in such contexts, or little local legitimacy. In Bougainville and Timor-Leste, for instance, the state is often perceived as remote from the lives of ordinary people, and people look to different, and often competing, sources of authority, including church and customary leaders (who are not necessarily distinct from the state). State-civil society dynamics are very different in Cambodia, which has a stronger presence in citizens' lives. Simangan and Gidley discuss how, in this context, an increasingly authoritarian state can restrict and seek to control civil society groups, including through requirements to register, make financial disclosures and demonstrate political neutrality. Civil society cannot be understood as separate from the state in this context either, as it is highly regulated and has to maintain a cooperative relationship with the government.

A third consequence of anaemic accounts of civil society in the TJ literature is that the ambivalent roles that international donors play in conflict-affected societies are overlooked or downplayed. This blind spot is at least also partly due to the fact that TJ has been depicted as an arena of 'technical expertise' rather than a set of discourses and practices that are deeply embedded in the political sphere. This has meant that, in general, the 'tensions between disparate policy agendas and conflicting transitional justice goals' have been overlooked.[24] Contesting this depoliticised depiction, there is a growing awareness amongst critical TJ scholars that Western states, donors and international NGOs can have a significant influence on the priorities and activities of 'local' civil society in conflict-affected societies.[25] The increasing professionalisation of the field of TJ further exacerbates these power differentials, as local and international NGOs face growing donor pressures to demonstrate the effectiveness and impact of their work.[26] Donors tend to gravitate towards, and fund, 'elite' civil society actors, who are often of a secular orientation and speak in 'an internationalised language of transitional justice' rather than those who 'may advance justice agendas and priorities that do not translate into that language because of indigenous (or other alternative) epistemologies'.[27] Indeed, as Kent argues, the TJ framework implicitly relies on, and fosters, 'a particular *kind* of civil society actor: a 'gentrified' civil society that is capable of negotiating with donors and state officials, writing project proposals in order to gain funding, and networking with international human rights organisations.'[28] This form of civil society organisation is not necessarily perceived as legitimate by local communities or as responsive to their core concerns.

[24] Lia Kent, *The Dynamics of Transitional Justice: International Models and Local Realities in East Timor* (Abingdon: Routledge, 2012): 31.
[25] Vasuki Nesiah, 'Transitional Justice Practice: Looking Back, Moving Forward', *Impunity Watch Scoping Study* (2016): 31.
[26] Jelena Subotic, 'The Transformation of International Transitional Justice Advocacy', *International Journal of Transitional Justice* 6, no 1 (2012): 119.
[27] Nesiah, 'Transitional Justice Practice', 44.
[28] Jeffrey, *The Improvised State: Sovereignty, Performance and Agency in Dayton Bosnia*, 110.

Several contributors to this special issue draw out these power dynamics. In relation to Cambodia, Simangan and Gidley suggest that concerns about government corruption mean that foreign donors often prefer to donate to CSOs than to government agencies. Boege describes how in Melanesia donor funding has encouraged the growth of CSOs that are 'modelled along the lines of Western liberal societies' and are 'usually presented as the 'local' voices of society', but which only survive because of international support. Indeed, Boege finds that in Melanesia 'this 'modern' civil society oftentimes is even positioned against the local-local and meant to supplant it'.

In a similar vein, Kent describes how, in Aceh and Timor-Leste, human rights-oriented NGOs focused on questions of accountability for human rights violations are comprised of 'a relatively small group of educated, urban, elites' who are interconnected via 'mutual participation in study tours, international conferences, and their connections, as part of transnational advocacy networks'. She notes that their advocacy for prosecutions does not not necessarily resonate with the priorities Timorese and Acehnese survivors, who are often subsistence farmers preoccupied with the concerns of everyday living. She also shows that these NGOs struggle due to the fact that, as international donors have deemed the 'post-conflict' peacebuilding phase over, funding for TJ activities has become increasingly scarce. This temporally limited external support for and funding of TJ 'sits uncomfortably with timescales for communities dealing with legacies of past violence and injustice that often cross multiple generations over decades and centuries.' Bräuchler is similarly critical of how donors have tended to treat civil society as 'partners in one-off peace or reconciliation events,' selecting participants and thus creating further inequalities. Writing against this 'instrumentalisation', she suggests that civil society needs to be 'reconceptualised as a constantly changing and diverse field'. Crucial to the success of the arts, music and theatre initiatives developed in Maluku to promote peace after communal mass violence, she argues, is the fact that they grew out the communities themselves rather than being the result of donor-driven agendas.

Reconceiving 'transitional justice'?

Just as conceptions of civil society in TJ need to be broadened, so too do understandings of TJ. While the TJ tool-kit has expanded in recent years beyond criminal prosecutions to encompass a wide range of other mechanisms – including truth commissions, reparations programs, lustration (the vetting of public officials), reforms to the police and military, curriculum revision, memorialisation and local justice mechanisms – the extent to which these developments have reshaped the field remains questionable.[29] It seems apparent that conventional TJ strategies and the mainstream TJ literature continue to prioritise liberal-legal justice mechanisms (in particular, criminal trials) and take the state as their key point of reference. Questions about the universality of international human rights norms and the disjunction between the 'distant justice'[30] offered by liberal-legal

[29]Eg see Rosalind Shaw and Lars Waldorf, 'Introduction: Localizing Transitional Justice', in *Localizing Transitional Justice*, ed. Rosalind Shaw, Lars Waldorf, and Pierre Hazan (Stanford: Stanford University Press, 2010), 3–26.

[30]Kora Andrieu, 'Civilizing Peacebuilding: Transitional Justice, Civil Society and the Liberal Paradigm', *Security Dialogue* 41, no. 5 (2010): 537–558, 554; Paul Gready, 'Reconceptualising Transitional Justice: Embedded and Distant Justice', *Conflict, Security and Development* 5, no. 1 (2005): 2–21.

international approaches to TJ and the often more locally legitimate and effective grassroots justice mechanisms in conflict-affected societies continue to be ignored.[31]

Contributors to this special issue join a growing body of critical TJ scholarship that seeks to broaden conceptions of justice grounded solely in liberal-legal frameworks by drawing attention to the diverse understandings of justice that may exist in conflict-affected societies. They are in broad agreement with Gready and Robins, who suggest that justice needs to be understood not as a 'singular concept', but as 'plural'. Moreover, rather than a 'set of objective, predetermined outcomes', justice is 'continually in the process of being constructed, and anchored in processes, perceptions and experiences'.[32] Contributors also recognise that justice can be pursued through a variety of strategies including memorialisation, grassroots reconciliation practices, arts and theatre initiatives and 'disruptive techniques' such as public meetings, rallies, occupations, strikes and demonstrations.[33] Influencing the state may not necessarily be the main goal of these strategies.

Narrow understandings of 'transition' that imply a definitive 'break' between the past and present orders are also challenged by contributors. These understandings can disguise the continuities of violence into the present, including the underlying economic, social and institutional legacies that affect the ability of many post-conflict states to become stable democracies.[34] A common thread underpinning the articles is that responding to complex legacies of violence requires a broad understanding of TJ that includes, yet also goes beyond, formal institutions with temporally limited mandates.[35]

Writing about peace activism in the Maluku region of Indonesia, Bräuchler observes that while the Indonesian government has created no formal TJ mechanism to respond to five years of communal mass violence, even if it had this would not have addressed the structural violence that helped to generate the conflict. She suggests, too, that liberal-legal TJ mechanisms focused on prosecution and punishment would 'not resonate with locally-grounded ways of peacebuilding' in Maluku. Drawing on the insights of Gready and Robins, Bräuchler proposes that the field of TJ needs to develop an understanding of justice 'not primarily as transitional, but as transformative'. This requires the need to move away 'from a sole focus on past (physical) violence' towards a focus also on 'addressing continuing injustices.' She demonstrates how, in the Maluku context, local CS actors see themselves as a social movement that seek to achieve transformation through 'performative justice' in the form of arts and music initiatives that highlight the 'long term social injustices' underlying the communal conflict. These initiatives make links to, and address, *continuing* injustices. For instance, through the 'Save Aru' movement key figures in the peace movement and young people have been able to bring their energy, networks and skills together to fight a 'plantation project that threatens one of

[31] Ali Wardak, 'Building a Post-war Justice System in Afghanistan', *Crime, Law, and Social Change* 41, no. 4, (2004): 319–341; Tracy Dexter and Phillippe Ntahombaye, *The Role of Informal Justice Systems in Fostering The Rule of Law in Post-Conflict Situations; The Case of Burundi* (Geneva: Centre for Humanitarian Dialogue, 2005), https://www.files.ethz.ch/isn/26971/CaseofBurundi.pdf.

[32] Gready and Robins, 'Rethinking Civil Society and Transitional Justice', 957.

[33] Ibid., 958.

[34] Lia Kent, 'Introduction: Transitional Justice in Law, History and Anthropology', *Australian Feminist Law Journal* 42, no. 1 (2016): 1–11, 3.

[35] Naomi Roht-Arriaza, 'The New Landscape of Transitional Justice', in *Transitional Justice in the Twenty-First Century: Beyond Truth Versus Justice*, ed. Naomi Roht-Arriaza and Javier Mariezcurrena (Cambridge: Cambridge University Press, 2006), 1–16, 2.

the poorest Moluccan districts and one of the main sources of Moluccan identity, adat land.' These movements are ongoing rather than confined to a temporally limited transition timeline.

Boege similarly argues for the need to prioritise 'local cultural context in the discourse and praxis of peace and justice.' In the Melanesian context, this means paying attention to the important role played by local reconciliation practices and to the interconnections between the 'material and spiritual realm.' Boege advocates understanding reconciliation in Melanesia using a 'relational ontology', which foregrounds 'relations and interactions, processes, dynamism, fluidity, giving priority to relations over entities'. By focusing on the 'relational-affective' dimensions of TJ, Boege challenges conventional assumptions about the legitimacy and effectiveness of liberal-legal TJ, by highlighting how these approaches do not provide space for 'addressing people's emotions and spirituality'. Kent makes a similar point in her article, which highlights the importance of locally grounded practices of mourning and care for the dead. She suggests that, in both Timor-Leste and Aceh, acknowledging and caring for the dead is a critical priority for those who lost loved ones during the conflict. These needs have a tendency to be sidelined in NGO-led memory-activism that is oriented towards prosecutions and changing state policy and practice.

The significance of the *socioeconomic* dimensions of justice are drawn out in Simangan and Gidley, Boege, and Wallis's contributions. Despite the fact that, for populations in post-conflict societies, the restoration of livelihoods and relationships may be prioritised above prosecutions, economic factors are often overlooked by TJ mechanisms driven by liberal-legal norms. As a consequence, as Simangan and Gidley observe, there has often been a failure to address the 'social and economic consequences' of conflict or meet local expectations of justice. For instance, as Boege remarks, in the Melanesian context conventional TJ approaches have underestimated the degree to which conflict-affected populations are preoccupied with the 'pragmatic' concerns of subsistence and survival. He argues that communities in Bougainville have a strong 'focus on material reparation (compensation) and a preference for restorative justice' rather than prosecution and punishment. Simangan and Gidley tell a more positive story in their discussion of how, in Cambodia, the work of demining CSOs provides vital 'physical rehabilitation and socio-integration services' to victims and survivors of land mines. The 'needs-based, locally-informed, victim-centred and development-oriented approaches' of demining CSOs facilitate TJ by assisting those affected by land mines to make sense of their past experiences and, by rehabilitating arable land, advance their future development.

At the same time, contributors do not romanticise the 'local' or 'customary' forms justice. Wallis observes that, in Bougainville and Timor-Leste, 'uncivil' society groups can rely for 'legitimacy on claims that they are advancing socio-economic development by providing public goods and, to differing extents, offering financial rewards to their followers, which is persuasive in the primarily subsistence barter economies.' Boege similarly observes that there are limits to local, customary reconciliation practices in the Melanesian context which arise, in part, from the risks of their commodification, their tendency to sideline women and questions about whether they can be upscaled or transferred. As he notes, in Melanesia customary reconciliation 'hinges on the existence of a community of relationships and values that are rooted in a common worldview and shared institutions'. All of this means that they have a utility when it comes to resolving disputes amongst 'intimate enemies' who are 'bound by some kind of relationship, a shared world-view and shared norms', but are less easily applicable to reconciliation between groups who lack these shared understandings.

Conclusion

By questioning the idea that TJ and civil society are taken-for-granted static and stable concepts, the contributors to this special issue have opened up existing understandings. Informed by rich, empirically grounded analysis, they provide a nuanced picture of the heterogeneity of civil society in Asia and the Pacific, which challenges many assumptions about the nature of civil society and its role in TJ. Collectively, they demonstrate that the universalist liberal-legal norms embedded in conventional understandings of civil society TJ do not capture the breadth and diversity of both civil society and TJ.

If there is an overarching suggestion to emerge from this special issue it is that there is a need for more empirically grounded accounts of civil society and its role in TJ that pay close attention to historical, social, political and cultural contexts. Rather than beginning with fixed, normative categories, scholars need to be open to the diversity of 'modes of organisation' and 'repertoires of action' that exist amongst a fluid and changing civil society.[36] They also need to recognise the plural nature of justice and the plurality of strategies for pursuing justice while, at the same time, acknowledging that globally-circulating discourses and assumptions about civil society and TJ can socially construct and constrain the parameters of local civil society action. Ultimately, by taking local knowledges, resources, actions and modes of organisation seriously, TJ practitioners and scholars might begin to imagine and develop more locally resonant responses to the continuing injustices experienced by conflict-affected populations. We hope that this special issue helps to inspire a desire to pursue this goal amongst its readers.

Disclosure statement

No potential conflict of interest was reported by the authors.

Funding

This work was supported by Australian Research Council: [Grant Number DP140102388].

[36]Gready and Robins, 'Rethinking Civil Society and Transitional Justice', 971.

Reconciliations (Melanesian style) and transitional justice

Volker Boege

ABSTRACT

This article examines *kastom* reconciliations as practiced in a Melanesian cultural context in the resolution of everyday disputes and as a means of peacebuilding after large-scale violent conflict. It explores Melanesian-style reconciliation in relation to the conventional international discourse on transitional justice, asking whether *kastom* reconciliations are – or can be – an alternative to, or a specific 'vernacularised' form of, transitional justice. Using examples primarily from post-conflict Bougainville and Solomon Islands, the article addresses some of the strengths and limitations of *kastom* reconciliation in comparison to those of transitional justice. In conclusion it is posited that protagonists of transitional justice could gain insights from the study of Melanesian reconciliations that would help them to reflect on their own taken-for-granted assumptions and consider avenues for developing the concept of transitional justice, making it more meaningful, effective and legitimate in a context such as Melanesia.

Introduction

This article sets out to challenge the Western transitional justice discourse and practice by examining Melanesian reconciliations, which operate in the same field as transitional justice, with the same aims – peace and justice. This is an ideal-typical juxtaposition of course, but for the purposes of sharpening the argument and the critique of transitional justice, some effort will be put into presenting the (potential) advantages of Melanesian reconciliations, in contrast to transitional justice.

The article builds a case for giving priority to local cultural context in the discourse and praxis of peace and justice, and for engaging with 'alternative understandings of justice'.[1] It situates the discussion of reconciliation(s) and transitional justice in a conceptual approach that takes the understanding of, and commitment to, local context as indispensable for peacebuilding, with the local(e) understood 'as a set of micro-level relationships between everyday people striving to get on with life, and along with each other, after mass violence'.[2]

This local is co-created and shared by a variety of interacting local, national, regional and international actors and institutions, and, accordingly, in the context of the locale,

[1] Aaron P. Boesenecker and Leslie Vinjamuri, 'Lost in Translation? Civil Society, Faith-Based Organizations and the Negotiation of International Norms', *The International Journal of Transitional Justice* 5 (2011), 345–365, 347.

[2] Erin Baines, 'Spirits and Social Reconstruction After Mass Violence: Rethinking Transitional Justice', *African Affairs* 109, no. 436 (2010): 409–430, 412.

institutions, concepts and arrangements of governance, security and peace are hybridised.[3] Melanesian reconciliations, though rooted in local context, are included in processes of hybridisation, as well as transitional justice, which has to thread itself into the locale, with a host of associated questions that arise when international liberal norms are imported into local contexts – questions with regard to

> the universal applicability of global justice norms and the mechanisms they underpin, the extent to which common practices can be adapted to fit local circumstances, the degree to which they resonate with target populations, and the ways in which they interact with local practices.[4]

This understanding of the local(e) is informed by a relational ontology, foregrounding relations and interactions, processes, dynamism, fluidity, giving priority to relations over entities.[5] The concept of relationality in a Pacific understanding embraces

> both individuality and communality, unity and diversity, visibility and invisibility, male and female, top and bottom, secular and sacred, heaven and earth, God and the world, (…), tangible and intangible. Relationality is a both/and way of thinking. It weaves and holds both together in a harmonious way (…) seemingly opposite realities cannot be separated or construed as opposite to one another.[6]

Being relational 'is about wrestling to understand the "individual" as part of the "community" and the "community" as imaged in the "individual" (…) it is about being able to have a fluid and holistic grasp of both'.[7] Affects, emotions, feelings are integral to such a relational understanding of self, community and, consequently, peace and justice.[8] A relational-affective approach facilitates engagement with unexpected and unfamiliar sources of peace, governance and justice, which are easily missed by the transitional justice discourse.[9]

Reconciliation Melanesian-style is fundamentally relational-affective, it takes emotions as 'important forms of knowledge and evaluative thought';[10] and it takes human beings not as isolated entities, as 'individuals', but as members of communities, defined through their relationships with other human beings, as well as with actors beyond the human sphere, in nature and the spirit world.[11] In Melanesia personhood is (understood

---

[3]Volker Boege et al., 'Challenging Statebuilding as Peacebuilding – Working with Hybrid Political Orders to Build Peace', in *Palgrave Advances in Peacebuilding: Critical Developments and Approaches*, ed. Oliver P. Richmond (New York: Palgrave Macmillan, 2010), 99–115.

[4]Renee Jeffery, 'Transitional Justice and the Tensions', in *Transitional Justice in Practice. Conflict, Justice and Reconciliation in the Solomon Islands*, ed. R. Jeffery (New York: Palgrave Macmillan, 2017), 1–36, 2.

[5]Charles T. Hunt, 'Beyond the Binaries: Towards a Relational Approach to Peacebuilding', *Global Change, Peace & Security* 29, no. 3 (2017): 209–227; Morgan Brigg, 'Beyond the Thrall of the State: Governance as a Relational-Affective Effect in Solomon Islands', *Cooperation and Conflict* 53, no. 2 (2018), 154–172.

[6]Upolu Luma Vaai and Unaisi Nabobo-Baba, 'Introduction', in *The Relational Self. Decolonising Personhood in the Pacific*, eds. U. L. Vaai and U. Nabobo-Baba (Suva: University of the South Pacific Press, 2017), 1–21, 11. See also Upolu Luma Vaai and Aisake Casimira, 'Introduction: A Relational Renaissance', in *Relational Hermeneutics. Decolonising the Mindset and the Pacific Itulagi*, eds. U. L. Vaai and A. Casimira (Suva: University of the South Pacific Press, 2017), 1–15.

[7]Upolu Luma Vaai, 'Relational Hermeneutics. A Return to the Relationality of the Pacific Itulagi as a Lens for Understanding and Interpreting Life', in Vaai and Casimira, Relational Hermeneutics, 17–41.

[8]Brigg, 'Thrall'.

[9]This means of course: unexpected and unfamiliar as seen from a Western point of view.

[10]Emma Hutchinson and Roland Bleiker, 'Emotional Reconciliation. Reconstituting Identity and Community After Trauma', *European Journal of Social Theory* 11, no. 3 (2008), 385–403, 393.

[11]On the relationality of reconciliation see John Paul Lederach and Angela Jill Lederach, *When Blood and Bones Cry Out: Journeys Through the Soundscape of Healing and Reconciliation* (St Lucia: University of Queensland Press, 2010). On relationality in a Melanesian context and the understanding of the Melanesian 'va' – 'the space between', that is: a relational

as being) genuinely 'relational and contextual'.[12] And community is not understood in an anthropocentric way, but in a holistic cosmic way, including people, land, ocean, ancestors, spirits, trees, villages, animals, language, mountains, God – who all exist only relationally.

This relational ontology is in contrast to a substantialist approach as reflected in the Western liberal transitional justice discourse that is concerned with the autonomous individual as a separate entity which can be treated in isolation – blamed, held to account, prosecuted, punished -, based on universalist notions of 'rights' and the 'rule of law', in particular the norm of individual criminal accountability. Moreover,

while a relational-affective approach aligns with the foregrounding of local cultural contextuality, transitional justice lays claim to universality and ubiquity, not reflecting on its own local ties as a 'Western' concept and its inevitable localisation – or vernacularisation – when entering a particular local social and cultural context.[13]

In the following, universalist assumptions will be challenged, and the problems with importing international liberal transitional justice mechanisms into local Melanesian contexts will be discussed, at the same time presenting cultural embeddedness not as an insurmountable barrier to transitional justice but 'as a context that defines relationships and meanings and constructs the possibilities of action'.[14] Thus, although this article does not assert that Melanesian-style reconciliations are per se superior to or incompatible with other forms, it builds a case for acknowledging their significance due to this cultural embeddedness.

The article will proceed as follows: first a brief overview is given over violent conflicts in Melanesia which necessitate engagement with discussions about transitional justice. The second section examines reconciliation in a Melanesian social-cultural context. This is followed, thirdly, by an exploration of reconciliation practice in Melanesia today, drawing on examples primarily from post-conflict Bougainville and Solomon Islands. In a final section some conclusions will be drawn, comparing transitional justice and Melanesian reconciliation.

Violent conflict and peacebuilding in Melanesia

In the post-colonial era, the island countries of Melanesia have been spared violent conflicts or violent regime changes on a scale as in other regions of the world.[15] Melanesia is a relatively peaceful region, albeit not totally free from violent conflicts.

Escalation of violent conflict mainly occurred due to a weak and ineffective state system, combined with the weakening of local customary systems of authority and social control. Often local conflict-prone issues became entangled with more 'political'

---

space that separates and joins, not least connecting the spiritual and the secular – see the contributions in Vaai and Nabobo-Baba, *Relational Self.*

[12]Unaisi Nabobo-Baba, 'In the Vanua. Personhood and Death within a Fijian Relational Ontology', in Vaai and Nabobo-Baba, *Relational Self*, 163–175, 163. For this relational understanding of personhood in a Melanesian cultural context see also Gordon Leua Nanau, '"Na Vanuagu". Epistemology and Personhood in Tathimboko, Guadalcanal' in ibid., 177–201. This understanding resonates with the African concept of Ubuntu, in the context of which "a person can only be a person through others" and personhood is understood "as rooted in a context of relationships" (Patrick Tom, 'A "post-liberal Peace" via *Ubuntu*?', *Peacebuilding* 6, no. 1 (2018): 65–79, 71).

[13]Jeffery, 'Transitional Justice'.

[14]Sally Engle Merry, *Human Rights and Gender Violence* (Chicago: University of Chicago Press, 2009), 9.

[15]Melanesia in the south-west of the Pacific region comprises of the political entities of Papua New Guinea (PNG), the Solomon Islands, Fiji, Vanuatu, New Caledonia/Kanaky, (West) Papua, and the Torres Straits Islands.

issues from different societal contexts (of state politics and political competition, and the modern economic sphere) so as to produce a dynamic which in some cases has led to large-scale and protracted violent conflict or even outright internal war.

Cases in point are the violent secessionist movement in Vanuatu in 1980; the violent conflicts between indigenous Kanaks and French settlers and French colonial state institutions in New Caledonia/Kanaky in the 1980s; the inter-communal violence and the military coups and coup attempts in Fiji in 1987, 2000 and 2006; the ongoing low-intensity violent conflict between indigenous Papuans and the Indonesian security forces in (West) Papua, or the endemic 'tribal' violence in the Highlands of PNG. Mention could also be made of a series of minor violent conflicts in all Melanesian countries. These incidents, however, were relatively short and locally confined, cost relatively few lives and did not pose a major challenge to the overall peace of the societies and states in question. By comparison, the civil wars in the Solomon Islands (1998-2003) and on the PNG island of Bougainville (1989-1998) were much more costly in terms of lives lost, infrastructure destroyed, people displaced, economies shattered. The negative impacts on people, society and state persist. These conflicts attracted international attention and led to international/regional interventions in support of peacemaking and peacebuilding – the Regional Assistance Mission to the Solomon Islands (RAMSI), and the Truce Monitoring Group/Peace Monitoring Group (TMG/PMG) and the United Nations Observer Mission on Bougainville. Even these - in a regional perspective: major - violent conflicts, however, have been modest in comparison to conflicts in other regions of the Global South. Anne Brown reminds us that 'most of Oceania, even in those countries that have been marked by periods of serious violence, is orderly and peaceful – this is almost entirely the work of local norms and justice practices'.[16] Even during the civil war in the Solomons, for example, most Solomon Islanders lived in peace (although they were not spared from indirect effects of the violence), because local non-state customary institutions were able to maintain peace and order in the communities, and actual fighting was confined to rather small pockets of the country's territory. The war on Bougainville was different, as it affected the entirety of Bougainville society (at the same time not directly affecting other parts of PNG, but with significant effects on PNG's overall politics and economy).

Hence although Melanesia is peaceful in comparison to other world regions, several violent conflicts occurred which necessitated post-conflict peacebuilding, in the context of which issues of transitional justice had to be addressed.

Civil society, which is generally attributed a prominent role in peacebuilding in general and in transitional justice in particular, plays a somewhat ambiguous role in peace processes in Melanesia. This is due to the fact that 'civil society' is mostly understood in its Western liberal sense: a sphere of organisations beyond the state which bring 'citizens' together in order to take part in matters of public policy, comprising NGOs, interest groups, business associations, faith-based organisations, trade unions, media, community-based organisations etc.. It is modelled along the lines of Western liberal societies, with prominence given to state-society, public-private, secular-religious dichotomies. Civil society organisations (CSO) are usually presented as the 'local' voices of society.

[16]M. Anne Brown, 'Security and Development: Conflict and Resilience in the Pacific Islands Region', in *Security and Development in the Pacific Islands. Social Resilience in Emerging States,* ed. M. A. Brown (Boulder and London: Lynne Rienner, 2007), 1–31, 10.

However, their relationship to the existing 'local-local' forms of community in a non-Western context such as in Melanesia is ambiguous.[17] 'Modern' civil society is introduced from the outside, while the 'local-local', which is embedded in local culture, custom, kin networks, is not seen as 'civil society'. Moreover, this 'modern' civil society oftentimes is even positioned against the local-local and meant to supplant it - because the local-local is perceived as being illiberal – for instance patriarchal, corrupt, backwards, inefficient, anti-women, neglecting human rights. There are numerous 'local' NGO/CSOs which only came into existence and can only survive because of external support from donors, international organisations and international NGOs, often based in the capital cities and with limited reach into rural areas. But of course there are also home-grown entities (many of which are also to a larger or lesser extent dependent on external assistance), and there are myriads of links tying CSOs and their personnel to the 'local-local'. Locals working for an (international) NGO, for example, while taking in the rationale and agenda of 'their' INGO, at the same time remain embedded in their kinship networks, with all the obligations that come with it. This makes Melanesian civil society different from Western civil society, although it might look the same from the outside.

Women's organisations are particularly strong elements of Melanesian civil society, and a considerable number of NGOs are led by women. Given that women often have problems to play prominent public roles in communities and even more so in the sphere of 'politics' and state structures, civil society offers them opportunities to make themselves heard and exert influence on the public affairs of their countries and communities. Influential women's peace organisations can be found in several Melanesian countries, and other peacebuilding NGOs have female leaders.

Some NGOs in Melanesia have specialised in peace and conflict studies and practical peace work. They are to a large extent dependent on support from INGOs and overseas donors. Some try to combine Western conflict resolution knowledge and local customary approaches, translating the language of liberal peace, human security and human rights into formats that fit the local cultural context and make it accessible to local communities.[18]

With regard to such 'vernacularisation'[19] of their cause, CSOs could take inspiration and learn from the churches, which are by far the most important 'civil society' institutions in Melanesia today - which is in marked contrast to the conventional understanding of civil society as a secular sphere. The churches were extremely successful in embedding the 'outside' Christian faith into Melanesian societies, winning them over to Christianity - the vast majority of Melanesians today are devout Christians. At the same time churches adjusted to local culture and customs. These customs and Christianity today are interwoven to such an extent that 'kastom' is generally understood as including Christianity. The interplay of Christianized customs and indigenised Christianity – in itself a specific

[17]The term 'local-local' was introduced into the peacebuilding discourse in order to differentiate a genuinely local sphere from exactly this kind of local liberal civil society which is introduced from the outside and emulates originally Western forms of civil society; of course, these spheres overlap, mix and blend to a certain extent; see Oliver P Richmond, 'A Pedagogy of Peacebuilding: Infrapolitics, Resistance, and Liberation', *International Political Sociology* 6 (2012): 1–17, 6.

[18]The Pacific Centre for Peacebuilding or Transcend Oceania (both Suva, Fiji) can be mentioned here.

[19]Vernacularisation refers to processes of transferring ideas, norms, concepts and practices (such as human rights or the rule of law) from the international sphere into specific local cultural contexts, carried out by intermediaries or bridge-builders capable to mediate between international and local institutions and actors. Sally Engle Merry, 'Transnational Human Rights and Local Activism: Mapping the Middle', *American Anthropologist* 108, no. 1: 38–51.

articulation of hybridity – was and is of major significance for peacebuilding and the understanding of peace and reconciliation in the region.

Churches are not institutions in charge only of a distinct religious sphere and of the spiritual wellbeing of their flock, but also influential social and governance actors. Churches can be found in (almost) every village; they are present everywhere, while 'the state' and 'civil society' are not. Often church leaders (together with customary leaders) take on governance ('state') functions in the local context. Churches and church-affiliated NGOs therefore are of major importance for conflict resolution and peacebuilding. Hence the liberal peace agenda in civil society is characterised by its combination with Christian values. On the other hand, local customary approaches to peacebuilding are imbued with Christian values. This double connection, with the churches as the interface between civil society and customary societal life, leads to a particular focus on reconciliation in peacebuilding. It can be said that reconciliation is at the heart of Melanesian peacebuilding, and one can argue that it is an alternative to – or a locally specific form of - transitional justice. In the following the concept and practice of Melanesian-style reconciliation will therefore be explored in more detail.

Kastom reconciliations

Kinship-based societal networks (of lineage, clan, tribe ...) underpin social order and wellbeing for most islanders and regulate the management of everyday life.

The local peace (and the local understanding of what peace is) is embedded in a close net of relations among people and between people and land. Land is communally owned by families, lineages, clans. It provides the basis for subsistence economies and food security of rural communities. Land is at the heart of the economic, social, cultural and spiritual life of those communities, with 'community' also comprising the non-human natural world (the land, animals and other aspects of nature) and the non-human spiritual world (the spirits of the ancestors, God). Kinship ties and village life are structured around the relationship to land. Land is crucial for identity, social security and the cohesion of everyday life. Without secure access to land there cannot be peace. Accordingly, disturbances of peace are linked to challenges to the land-people relationship. In fact, issues of land ownership, usage and degradation are the prevalent factors in local conflicts as well as in the region's large-scale violent conflicts.

Conflict was and is a normal feature of everyday social life in Melanesian communities, and at times conflicts can become violent and disruptive. Accordingly, communities have long-standing traditions of conflict prevention and resolution. Peace is understood in terms of harmony and balance in the life of communities, requiring reciprocity in relationships in all dimensions of life. Disturbance of community harmony and balance is disturbance of peace. It can take the form of physical violence, e.g. in conflicts over land, but also other forms, like swearing or sorcery, gossip and verbal insults, destruction of food gardens or property, and more often than not, a variety of conflictual issues are linked: a land dispute might be the trigger of a current conflict, but it becomes severe in the context of previous issues, e.g. adultery or swearing or accusations of sorcery, or a sorcery case might have its roots in previous land disputes, and so on. Such disturbances necessitate dispute resolution or peacebuilding activities which can restore reciprocal relations.

Only then the survival (both in the material and the spiritual sense) of the community can be secured for the future.

Relations are restored through reconciliations. Kastom reconciliations are locally specific and locally embedded, they vary from island to island, from region to region, from community to community. There are as many different types of reconciliation as there are different communities with a specific history and specific kastom.[20] This contextual cultural embeddedness is a decisive feature of customary approaches to conflict transformation and peacebuilding.[21] It marks a significant difference to 'modern' Western concepts – such as transitional justice – which lay claim to hegemonic universality and universal applicability.[22]

This cultural embeddedness puts into question any talk about 'Melanesian' reconciliations, as such talk is somewhat contrary to their very spirit. Nevertheless, for the purposes of Western academic conventions in general and the purposes of this article in particular, in what follows I'm going to present an ideal type (in Max Weber's sense) of Melanesian reconciliations in an abstracted manner, derived from Melanesian empirics - aware that this procedure is alien to the spirit of reconciliations in a Melanesian context.

Reconciliation is a long-term, complex and complicated multi-faceted process in which the wrongs of the past are acknowledged, responsibility is accepted and shared, and the basis for a common future is created.[23] Reconciliation breaks the cycle of pay-back (retribution), reconstructing relations and trust. It comprises of several stages, starting with an agreement between the sides to reconcile, followed by a series of meetings in which the issues at stake and the conditions for full reconciliation are talked through, leading to a final reconciliation ceremony.[24]

In the reconciliation process a common understanding of the causes and the history of the conflict has to be elaborated. Conflict parties have to negotiate a consensus regarding the interpretation of the past or, in other words, they have to establish the 'truth'.[25] Only

---

[20]Kastom, a Pidgin derivative of the English 'custom', is referred to by both people in the village and politicians in Melanesia today in order to stress their cultural heritage and the difference between their own ways and foreign ways of governance, economics, conflict resolution, peacebuilding etc., often depicting kastom as rooted in ancient pre-colonial traditions, a set of rules developed by the ancestors (Roger M. Keesing, 'Kastom Re-Examined', *Anthropological Forum* 6, no.4 (1993): 587–596, 589). Kastom governance is thus presented as the other of, or even alternative to, introduced state-based governance. At the same time, kastom is different from the customs of the pre-contact and pre-colonial past. It has developed since the times of first contact and colonization in the course of interaction and exchange of pre-contact custom and various external influences - Christian missions, colonial administrations, institutions of the nation state and the market economy. It continued to develop after the establishment of independent nation states, and it continues to change today. Kastom is not anachronistic, fixed and static, it changes all the time in the course of dealing with new challenges.

[21]Volker Boege, *Traditional Approaches to Conflict Transformation – Potentials and Limits* (Berghof Handbook for Conflict Transformation. Berlin: Berghof Research Center for Constructive Conflict Management, 2006), 6.

[22]This also applies to the term 'reconciliation' as used over the last decades in the parlance of peacebuilding and transitional justice – with an abstract generic de-contextualised understanding of reconciliation. By contrast, this article does not endeavor to present a general definition of 'reconciliation', instead it traces the understanding of the term by local people in a specific social and cultural context.

[23]For the following see in more detail Volker Boege and Lorraine Garasu, 'Bougainville: A Source of Inspiration for Conflict Resolution', in *Mediating Across Difference. Oceanic and Asian Approaches to Conflict Resolution*, eds. M. Brigg and R. Bleiker (Honolulu: University of Hawaii Press, 2011), 163–182.

[24]For an ideal typical traditional reconciliation process see James Tanis, 'Reconciliation: My Side of the Island', in *Weaving Consensus – The Papua New Guinea – Bougainville Peace Process*, eds. A. Carl and L. Garasu (Conciliation Resources Accord Issue 12/2002; London: Conciliation Resources, 2002), 58–61.

[25]This 'truth', however, can be different from the 'truth' strived for in transitional justice, e.g. via 'Truth and Reconciliation Commissions'. On different types of truth see Wendy Lambourne, 'Transformative Justice, Reconciliation and Peacebuilding', in *Transitional Justice Theories*, eds. S. Buckley-Zistel et al. (Abingdon and New York: Routledge, 2014), 19–39.

once such a consensus has been achieved reconciliation can take its course. Perpetrators are helped to see their roles in the conflict more clearly, so that they become capable and willing to take responsibility for their wrongdoings and for admitting guilt. They have to apologise to the ones they wronged and to ask for forgiveness. Victims must develop a willingness to accept the apologies and forgive. Heart-felt repentence and confession on the part of the offenders and heart-felt forgiveness on the part of the victims are the building blocks of reconciliation.[26] Reconciliation is not 'forgive and forget', but to remember without feelings of hatred and desire for revenge: To remember but without rancor, to live with the memories, but without the hatred.[27]

Such a kind of reconciliation is not a one-off event or a quick fix. It needs time. Slowness, breaks and 'time outs' are deliberately built into reconciliation processes to give parties time to calm down, assess the state of the process, re-formulate their position and to prepare themselves spiritually and emotionally to reconcile. The process is geared towards overall consensus and thus has to include all members of the community or the conflicting parties, and it has to reach an agreement which is accepted and adhered to by everybody. Reconciliation is holistic in the sense that it not only addresses a single conflict or incident or an isolated issue, but takes the overall relationships between conflict parties and their histories as well as the overall circumstances in which the conflict took place into account; moreover, it not only addresses the issues of the visible material world, but also the spiritual dimension, because in a Melanesian understanding peace it not only a 'political' or a 'justice' or a 'social' issue - is cannot be compartmentalised, it can only exist as an all-inclusive whole.[28]

Once solutions are found, they are ratified in highly ritual forms. Ceremonies mark the culminating points of the reconciliation process. Usually there is not just one reconciliation ceremony, but a series of ceremonies, according to the progress of reconciliation. The ceremonies vary from area to area[29], but generally they encompass rituals such as breaking spears and arrows, exchange of speeches, drinking and eating together from the same dish, singing and dancing together, or chewing betelnut together. These symbolic activities are expressions of commitment and trust and are more powerful than mere spoken or written words. Finally, gifts are exchanged (pigs, shell money, food, cash, or a combination of all these items). The whole community participates. So while some stages of the process

---

[26]Often there is no clear-cut boundary between victims and perpetrators. The victims of today might have been the perpetrators in the past, and vice versa. In wars like in Bougainville or Solomon Islands the phenomenon of victims-turned-perpetrators and perpetrators-turned-victims is quite common.

[27]Kimberly Theidon, 'Justice in Transition. The Micro-Politics of Reconciliation in Postwar Peru', *Journal of Conflict Resolution* 50, no. 3 (2006): 433–457, 453.

[28]Corbett, Jack, '"A Calling from God": Politicians and Religiosity in the Pacific Islands', *Global Change, Peace & Security* 25, no. 3 (2013): 283–297, demonstrates that analytic distinctions like state, society and religion are problematic in the Pacific societal context.

[29]In some places, for instance, people bury large stones. "The significance of the stone is that it is heavy and it does not move and it gives a sign of strong and unchanging reconciliation between the people" (Pat Howley, *Breaking Spears and Mending Hearts. Peacemakers and Restorative Justice in Bougainville.* London – Annandale: Zed Books – The Federation Press, 2002), 111. In other places the parties "would plant tangget plants on stone. This symbolised their promise to forget the past and remain as silent as stone. Anyone who violated this agreement would be cursed by the stone and any talebearer would be punished by its strength" (Tanis, 'Reconciliation', 59). Or: members of conflict parties chew betel-nut together, spit into a hole that was dug, and then a stone is planted on top of the hole, and people shake hands and share food. This ceremony "references a kastom belief that, once a reconciliation has been completed, one should remain silent as stone: the actions that caused the hevi will not be forgotten but they have been forgiven". Dwyer Paul, 'Peacebuilding Performances in the Aftermath of War. Lessons from Bougainville', in *Critical Perspectives on Applied Theatre,* eds. J. Hughes and H. Nicholson (Cambridge : Cambridge University Press, 2016), 127–149, 144.

can take place in 'private' or in a confined semi-public (e.g. only allowing the people who had been directly involved in the previous conflict and selected facilitators to participate), the reconciliation ceremony is an open public event (open and public in the community context, not necessarily completely open to outsiders). Church services and prayers and hymns are usually an integral part of these activities,[30] with priests and church ministers playing important roles in initiating and stabilising reconciliation processes.[31]

Reconciliation ceremonies are loaded with spiritual meaning. Reconciliation is a deeply emotional and spiritual experience. It is about deeply felt remorse, shame and the desire for forgiveness, about deeply felt grief, anger and sorrow and the desire to forgive.[32] It is about mending hearts.[33] It is about emotional healing, repairing broken relationships and restoring harmony so that people can live in peace not only with each other, but also with God and the spirits of the dead and their environment. There is no questioning of the existence of an invisible world, which is systematically excluded as a serious source of knowledge and agency in Western epistemologies. God is present in reconciliation, and so are the spirits of the dead. The worlds of the living and the dead, of the humans and the nonhumans, are closely interconnected. Whenever social relations break down, the spirit world is affected. This is why the nonhuman world has to be included in the restoration of relationships, and cleansing rituals that appease the spirits are linked to reconciliation.[34] Ceremony is an important vehicle for cleansing and purification. If such cleansing rituals are not performed, the spirits of the dead will not rest but come back and haunt the living, and all kinds of misfortune will befall the communities – illness, accidents, madness, death. Peacemaking through prayer is powerful in Melanesia.

In the context of reconciliation, justice is more restorative than punitive/retributive, although retributive elements can be part of kastom conflict settlements. The modern term restorative justice mirrors an understanding of justice that was and is an integral part of Melanesian customary conflict resolution. It is grounded in a fundamentally relational understanding of personhood, people and society – an understanding that necessitates and enables justice to be pursued as restoring relationships that were severed, disrupted or destroyed by violence and wrongdoing.[35] Not so much the punishment of individual offenders, but the restoration of social harmony within and between communities and the restoration of relationships between the communities of offenders and victims are the aim. The communities are always included in restorative justice, even if

[30]On the entwinement of kastom and Christianity and their complementary use see Debra McDougall, with Joy Kere, 'Christianity, Custom, and Law. Conflict and Peacemaking in the Postconflict Solomon Islands', in *Mediating Across Difference. Oceanic and Asian Approaches to Conflict Resolution*, eds. M. Brigg and R. Bleiker (Honolulu: University of Hawaii Press, 2011), 141–162.

[31]Renee Jeffery, 'Reconciliation and the Rule of Law in the Solomon Islands', in *Transitional Justice in the Asia Pacific*, eds. R. Jeffery and Hun Joon Kim (Cambridge: Cambridge University Press, 2013), 195–227, 213; Tanis, 'Reconciliation', 60.

[32]Cynthia Cohen, 'Creative Approaches to Reconciliation', in *The Psychology of Resolving Global Conflicts. From War to Peace. Volume 3: Interventions*, eds. Mari Fitzduff and Chris E. Stout (Westport, Conn and London: Praeger Security International, 2006), 69–102. She also makes the point that 'purposeful rationality is inadequate to the task of reconciliation" (69).

[33]See the title of Pat Howley's book, Howley, 'Breaking Spears and Mending Hearts'.

[34]Lisa Schirch, *Ritual and Symbol in Peacebuilding* (Bloomfield, CT: Kumarian Press, 2005), 148–149. Lederach and Lederach, 'Blood and Bones', 163–165. For Peru Theidon, 'Justice'.

[35]On restorative justice and reconciliation as relational conceptions of justice as opposed to a liberal individualist notion with its focus on individual offenders and their punishment see Jennifer Llewellyn and Daniel Philpott, 'Restorative Justice and Reconciliation: Twin Frameworks for Peacebuilding', in *Restorative Justice, Reconciliation, and Peacebuilding*, eds. J.J. Llewellyn and D. Philpott (Oxford: Oxford University Press, 2014), 14–34 . They also make the point that the term restorative justice should not be taken literally – restoration encompasses an improvement in the quality of relationships so as to make them more sustainable in order to prevent relapse into conflict or violence.

the issue at stake is between an individual offender and an individual victim, as these are seen as embedded in their communities.

Reconciliations which comprise restorative justice are future-oriented and thus in contrast to the Western more backward-looking punitive and retributive justice approach, which also underlies transitional justice. In Melanesia, reconciliation and restorative justice are 'twin frameworks for peacebuilding'.[36] In this context, accountability is also thought of more in restorative terms (and not so much in terms of blame, prosecution and punishment), geared towards restoring the victim(s), reintegrating the offender(s) who have accepted responsibility, admitted guilt and apologised, and repairing the harm done to the community at large. This can include retributive elements, hence in kastom reconciliations restorative and retributive justice are interdependent – with a preponderance of the restorative aspect. Melanesians do not have problems with the combination of restorative justice in the customary context and punitive justice in the context of the legal system of the state: sometimes they want offenders to be put into prison.[37] There can, however, remain a 'gap between the international accountability norm and local practice.'[38]

In this understanding of accountability, restorative justice and reconciliation, the exchange of gifts plays an important role. Gifts to compensate for damage done and wrongs committed serve to cement reconciliation and restore relationships. Reconciliations thus not only aim at spiritual and emotional healing, but they also have a material side. Reparations are signs for and part of restoring relationships. Traditionally gifts were items held precious by the communities such as shell money, pigs, mats and food. Nowadays cash and modern goods are also exchanged. The exchange is an outward sign of reconciliation.

These days people more and more often complain that the 'true' customary meaning of the exchange of material goods is being lost, with compensation - meaning in particular the payment of cash – taking centre stage. This is a growing concern: people trying to use reconciliation and accompanying compensation to make money. In the following examples of reconciliations in practice will be considered.

Post-conflict reconciliations

In the aftermath of the violent conflicts in Bougainville and the Solomon Islands, kastom reconciliations became an important element of peacebuilding. In both cases, the parties fighting each other were not anonymous mass armies, but mostly people who knew each other – they were 'intimate enemies'.[39] As such, building peace between them lent itself to kastom ways. Local reconciliations took place in many places all over Bougainville over the last two decades, and this continues at the time of writing, with women often playing leading roles. These 'local reconciliation efforts have done more to consolidate popular

[36]Llewellyn and Philpott, 'Restorative Justice', 14.

[37]See the discussion about the relationship between retributive and restorative justice in Wendy Lambourne, 'Transformative Justice, Reconciliation and Peacebuilding', in *Transitional Justice Theories*, eds. S. Buckley-Zistel et al. (Taylor and Francis, 2013), 19–39. She recommends "a more syncretic transitional justice mechanism that combines retributive and restorative elements" (21).

[38]Boesenecker and Vinjamuri, 'Lost in Translation', 347.

[39]Theidon, 'Justice in Transition'.

commitment to peace than any other aspect of the process'.[40] They were the means to restore social networks and relations that had broken down during the fighting, and to restore social trust and a sense of moral order.

This was also the case in the Solomon Islands. Here too kastom ways have been used to deal with the effects of 'the tensions' at the local level in many places.[41] As was also the case in Bougainville, the churches and church-based networks and groups such as the Solomon Islands Christian Association and its Peace Committee, the Tasiu (the Melanesian Brotherhood) or CARITAS, as well as women leaders and women's NGOs[42] such as Women for Peace, were prominently involved.[43] Both the Solomon Islands and the Bougainville case show that those CSOs which are engaged in the process in locally grounded ways are for the most part close to the churches, faith-based and guided more by Christian understandings of reconciliation and forgiveness than by secular transitional justice norms. Civil society in Melanesia thus is not necessarily a stronghold and advocate of transitional justice in its liberal secular individualistic sense.

In the Solomon Islands, kastom reconciliations were overshadowed by the establishment and the activities of a national Truth and Reconciliation Commission (TRC). Local reconciliations and the TRC very much operated separately. This disconnect was a problem for peacebuilding and transitional justice; many Solomon Islanders were critical of the TRC, as it was seen as an alien concept and going against local kastom.

The Solomon Islands TRC was established mainly upon initial requests from the churches, but then implemented by the government, supported by international donors.[44] The TRC followed the principles and agenda of the conventional international transitional justice approach, with mixed results at best.[45] Mainly funded by international donors and committed to alien 'Western' ways of operating and the universalist human rights language, it was strongly criticised for ignoring – or even violating – local kastom and falling short of locals' expectations.[46] The TRC 'was not adequately contextualized

[40]Anthony Regan, 'Why a Neutral Peace Monitoring Force? The Bougainville Conflict and the Peace process', in *Without a Gun. Australians' Experiences Monitoring Peace in Bougainville, 1997–2001*, eds. M. Wehner and D. Denoon (Canberra: Pandanus Books, 2001), 1–18, 15.

[41]For examples see McDougall, Christianity'.

[42]John Braithwaite et al., *Pillars and Shadows. Statebuilding as Peacebuilding in Solomon Islands* (Canberra: ANU e Press, 2010), 82. - There are some women chiefs, particularly in the matrilineal communities of Guadalcanal and Isabel provinces, and women at times are engaged (mostly invisibly) in kastom dispute resolution; Matthew Allen et al. *Justice Delivered Locally. Systems, Challenges, and Innovations in Solomon Islands* (Washington DC: The World Bank, 2013), 41–43.

[43]Renee Jeffery, 'Enduring Tensions: Transitional Justice in the Solomon Islands', *The Pacific Review* 26, no. 2 (2013), 153–175 (particularly 164–166); John Maebuta and Rebecca Spence, *Attempts at Building Peace in the Solomon Islands: Disconnected Layers.* Reflecting on Peace Practice Project Cumulative Impact Case Study. Cambridge, MA: CDA Collaborative Learning Projects, 2009, 23–27.

[44]The TRC was established under the Truth and Reconciliation Commission Act 2008. It was publicly launched to great fanfare by Archbishop Desmond Tutu from South Africa in April 2009, but only commenced operations in 2010. It presented its final report to the Prime Minister in February 2012. This report was unofficially released electronically in April 2013 by the report's editor, Bishop Terry Brown, who had become frustrated by the government's inaction regarding publication. - On the debate about the TRC see Braithwaite et al., *Pillars*, 86–91: Jeffery, 'Enduring Tensions', 168–171. For a critical assessment see Louise Vella, *Translating Transitional Justice: The Solomon Islands Truth and Reconciliation Commission* (SSGM Discussion Paper 2014/2. Canberra: Australian National University, 2014); Holly L. Guthrey 'Local Norms and Truth Telling: Examining Experienced Incompatibilities within Truth Commissions of Solomon Islands and Timor Leste', *The Contemporary Pacific* 28, no.1 (2016), 1–29; Holly L. Guthrey, *Victim Healing and Truth Commissions. Transforming Pain Through Voice in Solomon Islands and Timor-Leste* (New York and London: Springer, 2015), and the contributions in Jeffery, *Transitional Justice.*

[45]Jeffery, 'Enduring Tensions'.

[46]"Ironically, as the human rights discourse has largely been promoted by foreigners through the delivery of foreign aid, it has come to be regarded by many Solomon Islanders as a form of neocolonialism that threatens to undermine cultural values and norms." Claire Cronin, 'Subjectivities of Suffering: Human Rights in the Solomon Islands Truth and

or integrated with local approaches to reconciliation and peacebuilding and therefore fell short of its ambitious mandate'.[47] Claire Cronin reports that during her fieldwork she 'was often presented with the argument that the TRC had failed to "touch" the people, that is, that it had failed to connect with the heart and soul of Solomon Islanders, that by which they defined themselves as human'.[48] Public 'truth-telling' for its own sake (and the accompanying assumption that there is a universal notion of 'truth'), in particular, encountered resistance, as disclosure about personal and sensitive topics in public or to outsiders can contradict kastom.[49] Guthrie found, for example, that people who had given public testimony before the TRC 'took issue with what they perceived to be an incompatibility between their own sociocultural values and expectations and the work of their country's truth commission'.[50] The TRC 'was limited to hearing a certain truth, framed by particular questions centred on human rights as defined in international law but not yet frequently adopted or accepted by Solomon Island communities'.[51] The inclusion of the term 'reconciliation' contributed to misunderstandings as it 'might have been confusing for the local population who expected a stronger relationship between their notion of reconciliation – which is usually held on the village level and involves the exchange of compensation – and the work of the TRC'.[52] As a result, the TRC was seen as an alien endeavour, of not much use for the needs of the people on the ground (who had expected to get something, not least material benefits, in return for giving their statements, according to the kastom understanding of reconciliation).[53] Hence the TRC remained 'a minor player on a crowded stage'.[54]

In neighbouring Bougainville a different path was taken in relation to transitional justice. Here the Bougainville Peace Agreement (BPA) granted amnesty and pardon 'for all persons involved in crisis related activities or convicted of offences arising out of crisis related activities' (BPA, clause 33).[55] Immunity regulations were incorporated into the PNG and Bougainville constitutions. This approach was complemented by the decision to deal with human rights abuses and other wrongs committed during the war through kastom reconciliation. As a consequence, no TRC was established. Whether to have one

Reconciliation Commission', in *Transitional Justice in Practice: Conflict, Justice and Reconciliation in the Solomon Islands*, ed. R. Jeffery (New York: Palgrave Macmillan, 2017), 37–62, 50.

[47]Vella, *Justice*, 1.

[48]Cronin, *Subjectivities*, 54.

[49]Vella, *Justice*, 10. "Sexual violence, or other human rights violations such as killings, torture and ill-treatment, (...), were not topics that could be discussed easily, if at all" (ibid., 11). Asking direct questions on such sensitive issues in a Solomon context usually leads nowhere.

[50]Guthrie, 'Local Norms', 2.

[51]Vella, *Justice*, 11.

[52]Guthrey, 'Local Norms', 10: see also Guthrey, 'Victim Healing', 163; Vella, Justice, 13. Lambourne, 'Transformative Justice', makes the point that it is "critical to analyse how language and culture affect the interpretations and expectations of local populations and governments in the negotiation and implementation of transitional justice mechanisms" (34).

[53]Louise Vella, 'What Will You Do With Our Stories? Truth and Reconciliation in the Solomon Islands', *International Journal of Conflict and Violence* 8, no. 1 (2014), 91–103; Holly L. Guthrey and Karen Brouneus, 'Peering into the "Black Box" of TRC Success: Exploring Local Perceptions of Reconciliation in the Solomon Islands TRC', in Jeffery, *Transitional Justice*, 85–111. Locals criticised the "disconnection between the concept of reconciliation used by the SI TRC and traditional notions of reconciliation based on Solomon Islands *kastom*" (105).

[54]Vella, *Justice*, 1.

[55]The BPA states in clause 341 (d) that "the arrangements for pardon and amnesty are intended to reduce tensions and divisions that could continue to flow from the conflict" (Bougainville Peace Agreement (30 August 2001), in: A. Carl, and L Garasu eds. *Weaving Consensus*, 67–85.

or not was discussed, but no consensus could be reached, and the debate about pros and cons of a TRC continues even today.[56]

With the immunity from prosecution regulations in place, without a realistic option to take cases to the courts and without a TRC, kastom reconciliation became the main avenue for transitional justice. Hundreds of local reconciliations have been conducted over the last two decades. However, there are problems. Some reconciliation processes have been dragging on for a long time, and others have not started yet. Particularly in light of the upcoming referendum on independence (scheduled for June 2019) there is a growing sense of urgency with regard to outstanding or unfinished reconciliations, and efforts are intensifying to speed up reconciliations. For instance, more recently so-called 'mass reconciliations' have taken place, in which different cases in one region are grouped together and dealt with in one process. It is not clear how effective and legitimate this will be. It is definitely a deviation from what has been seen as kastom reconciliation so far.

Then there is the issue of monetisation. Reconciliations are costly, and they can be used as a money-making device. Bringing people together for reconciliation ceremonies and feeding them, and providing the gifts/compensation items, often costs a lot of money. This is why parties who want to reconcile increasingly ask for outside assistance, mainly in the form of cash. This was a serious problem in post-conflict Solomon Islands, where the custom of compensation (replacing the tit-for-tat of violence through the reciprocity of exchange of gifts) became increasingly commercialised, with monetary compensation replacing exchanges of customary forms of wealth (e.g. shell money, pigs, food), and with demands being made way above what used to be common kastom practice, thus using the custom of compensation as a pretext for extorting money, not least from the government.[57] The traditional function of compensation, namely restoration of relationships, then easily gets lost. 'Competition for state compensation crushes reconciliation as something that can build peace by touching people's hearts'.[58]

In Bougainville it also became more and more common that outsiders would provide the resources which make reconciliations possible, and for conflict parties to demand such outside support.[59] Sometimes this even goes as far as parties demanding the money they have to pay as compensation from outside sources. As mentioned previously, compensation is increasingly in cash – in addition to or instead of traditional items such as pigs or shell money. Locals have a tendency to blame outsiders for the commodification of reconciliations – these outsiders brought the money in and thus distorted the true meaning of kastom reconciliation, undermining its legitimacy.

Despite this trend, many of today's reconciliations remain non-commercialised; conflict parties deliberately abstain from monetary compensation (or with money only as a minor element in the mix of gifts exchanged), and they themselves provide the food, cover the

[56] Joanne Wallis, *Constitution Making During State Building* (New York: Cambridge University Press, 2014), 294.

[57] Demands for compensation have at times turned into a lucrative business for some, and this has contributed to the discrediting of kastom reconciliation. This "corruption of *kastom*" was taken to extreme levels in the early stages of peacebuilding in the Solomon Islands, where "unscrupulous politicians co-opted *kastom* and customary practices including compensation for their own purposes" (Joanna R. Quinn, '*Kastom* in Dispute Resolution: Transitional Justice and Customary Law in the Solomon Islands', in R. Jeffery, *Transitional Justice*, 63–84, 80). See at length Jon Fraenkel, *The Manipulation of Custom: From Uprising to Intervention in the Solomon Island* (Wellington: Victoria University Press, 2004); "a government compensation culture has evolved as a shallow and quick fix" (Braithwaite et al., *Pillars*, 148).

[58] Braithwaite et al., *Pillars*, 148.

[59] UNDP, *Peace and Development Analysis. Findings and Emerging Priorities.* Port Moresby: United Nations Development Programme Papua New Guinea Country Office, 2014), 12.

costs of transport and so on. People are very proud of these – as they see them – 'true' reconciliations, contrasting them with so-called phoney reconciliations which are criticised as superficial, hollow tokenism or a way to make money.

Another significant problem in addition to the commodification of reconciliations is how to upscale or transfer an approach that works in the community context to other contexts, without that approach becoming instrumentalised and thus losing legitimacy and effectiveness.[60] This is a fundamental question which points to the limits of kastom reconciliation. Kastom reconciliation hinges on the existence of a community of relationships and values that are rooted in a common worldview and shared institutions. It works within and between relatively small groups in the local context. Conflicts among the members of the 'we-group' can be addressed this way. Conflicts between neighbouring communities pose relatively minor problems, because some overarching customary principles can usually be developed and applied that forge common ground. In other words: kastom reconciliation works for 'intimate enemies', people bound by some kind of relationships, a shared worldview and shared norms. Dealing with outsiders is much more difficult. Conflicts between 'us' and 'them', who do not share 'our' culture, are much harder to tackle. If 'they' do not understand, do not respect, or are unwilling to participate in 'our' ways of conflict resolution, reconciliation might become impossible.[61]

In the Bougainville case, for example, this problem became obvious in the attempts of locals to reconcile with Rio Tinto/BCL (Bougainville Copper Limited), the company which operated the huge Panguna copper and gold mine and was seen by many Bougainvilleans as responsible for the war. Bougainvilleans expect BCL to apologise and 'make both material and symbolic reparations'[62] in the course of a reconciliation process; over the last years BCL had indicated that it was willing to come in for reconciliation. A lot of thought and effort from various sides was put into making 'bel kol' possible.[63] 'Bel kol' (cooling of the heart) is the very first symbolic step in a longer reconciliation process. Various dates for a bel kol ceremony were announced, but the ceremony had to be postponed again and again. Stakeholders could not agree on the content, form and meaning of bel kol, and some remained opposed to it. The consensus necessary for reconciliation could not be reached and hence relationships could not be rebuilt.

Another fundamental question concerns the capacity of kastom reconciliation to deal with 'modern' forms of violence which had not been part of traditional societal life and conflict,[64] in particular gang rape and other forms of sexual violence against women that were a feature of the wars in Bougainville and Solomon Islands. However, the transitional justice approach has its problems too. Sexual violence is a taboo subject in Melanesian societies that is not talked about in public,[65] and if it is – as was the case with the

---

[60]Bloomfield discusses the tension between bottom-up interpersonal reconciliation and top-down political reconciliation. David Bloomfield, *On Good Terms. Clarifying Reconciliation*. Berghof Report No. 14. (Berlin: Berghof Research Center for Constructive Conflict Management, 2006), 27–28.

[61]Boege, 'Traditional Approaches'.

[62]Kylie McKenna, *Corporate Social Responsibility and Natural Resource Conflict* (London and New York: Routledge, 2016), 193.

[63]Kylie McKenna, 'Mining and Reconciliation: Negotiating the Future of the Panguna Mine in Bougainville', *SSGM In Brief* 2015/35.

[64]Joanne Wallis, Renee Jeffery and Lia Kent, 'Political reconciliation in Timor Leste, Solomon Islands and Bougainville: the dark side of hybridity', *Australian Journal of International Affairs* 70, no. 2 (2016), 159–178, 174.

[65]Louise Vella, *Translating Transitional Justice: The Solomon Islands Truth and Reconciliation Commission*. SSGM Discussion Paper 2014/2 (Canberra: Australian National University, 2014). This is similar to East Timor, see Lia Kent 'Engaging with 'The Everyday': Towards a more dynamic conception of hybrid transitional justice', in *Hybridity on the ground in*

Solomon Islands TRC – it can lead to serious problems: the re-traumatisation and re-victimisation of women and the resurgence of violent conflict.[66] Talking in public is not necessarily healing and not always conducive to reconciliation. It can be harmful, and it can open the circle of pay-back violence.[67]

The question of women's voices in reconciliations is closely linked to the problem of power relations. Power imbalances play out in reconciliation processes, with questions arising such as who decides on the need for reconciliation in a specific case, whose needs are addressed and whose interests are served, and whose not. For example, there can be pressure on victims to accept apologies by perpetrators and to forgive, although they are not ready (yet) to do so. Imbalances with regard to age, kinship networks or resourcefulness play a role, but the most prominent imbalance in Melanesia is gender-related. Although it would be misleading to think of women in Melanesia as generally powerless or less powerful than men, in certain contexts gendered power relations are significant, and this can affect the position of women in reconciliations.[68] Furthermore, young people generally have a lesser status than the old. The very old, old widows in particular, can also be powerless (if they lack family support); and there are clans or extended families that are more powerful than others. All these power asymmetries can affect reconciliations.[69]

Reconciliations Melanesian-style thus are not without problems. It is questionable whether they can lead to 'justice' in the transitional justice's emphatic normative sense. Nevertheless, they can address fundamental needs of people and communities trying to cope with the effects of violent conflict. They can be seen as an alternative to transitional justice, but they can also be seen as a culturally sensitive form of transitional justice. They are not per se incompatible with transitional justice, nor would it be appropriate to present them – in a de-contextualised manner – as superior to other forms of reconciliation.

Conclusion

Reconciling Melanesian understandings of reconciliation with the mainstream Western civil society and transitional justice discourse, although not impossible, has its difficulties. Although both Melanesian reconciliations and transitional justice pursue the overarching

peacebuilding and development. Critical conversations, eds. Joanne Wallis et al. (Canberra: ANU Press, 2018), 145–161, 157–158. On the "perceived incompatibility between cultural norms and publicly airing sensitive stories" (Guthrey, 'Victim Healing', 5) see Guthrie, 'Victim Healing', 161-162.

66Guthrey, 'Local Norms', 13: " … interviewees from Solomon Islands spoke about their sense that issues of sexual violence should not be discussed in mixed company, and thus some aspects of the TRC's work were perceived to be incongruent with local norms". " In Solomon Islands, strong cultural taboos limit women's ability to discuss rape or sexual experiences. Doing so would contravene cultural practices and risk further violence, shame or other repercussions" (Vella, '"What will you do with our stories' 99).

67Guthrey and Brouneus, 'Peering into the 'Black Box'', 100–103. They found strong criticism of the TRC as it was perceived as a foreign concept going against kastom, particularly ignoring the dangers of public story-telling – if people told their stories publicly "the old wounds opened up by their stories will reignite anger and spur violent revenge" (103).

68Most communities in Bougainville or on Guadalcanal (the main island of Solomon Islands), for example, are matrilineal, with a relatively strong position of women in the customary social context. Women were highly influential actors in peacebuilding in Bougainville and Solomon Islands.

69For a critique of 'ethnojustice' (as well as transitional justice), including customary reconciliation, see Adam Branch, 'The Violence of Peace: Ethnojustice in Northern Uganda' *Development and Change* 45, no. 3 (2014), 608–630 who argues that this type of justice consolidates "a patriarchal, gerontocratic order" (616) and "empowers older men at the expense of youth and women" (619).

goal of rebuilding a 'just peace' after violent conflict, the actors, methods, scope, specific aims and, in fact, the very understanding of 'justice' and its relationship with 'peace' differ considerably.

Melanesian approaches are highly context-specific, grounded in the social fabric and culture of the locale, with the locale understood not as an abstract space, but relationally, as the network of relations between humans as well as non-human actors. These actors are bound together by a shared (at times violent) history and obliged to shape a shared future. Reconciliations thus are relational endeavours, dealing with the sphere of the 'in-between', geared towards the restoration of relationships between 'intimate enemies', and of relationships with the spirit world and God. By contrast, the conventional Western understanding of reconciliation which underlies the transitional justice discourse is grounded in substantialism and universalism, with the principles of transitional justice applied to separate entities, to individuals as criminally accountable. It is geared towards serving the victims and punishing the perpetrators, claiming general validity and applicability beyond the specifics of a certain locale, with a tendency to see the local merely 'as a space for intervention, not comprehension, not knowledge, not capacity'.[70] Accordingly, that discourse does not pay much attention to historical, social and cultural contexts. 'International and national policy makers have imposed a uniform approach on justice after conflict, ignoring the complex local dynamics that are most relevant to people's lives'.[71] As 'a highly normative formula with universalist claims', the conventional Western discourse 'tends to make context a blind spot'.[72] This can lead to serious negative consequences, as, for example, with the TRC in the Solomon Islands where 'a strong sense that the TRC did not belong to Solomon Islands and was merely a creation by foreigners to address local problems without considering local ways' prevailed.[73]

The transitional justice approach is not free from the dangers that Sally Engle Merry pointed to with regard to the human rights discourse in general, namely that this discourse

> contains implicit assumptions about the nature of civilized and backward societies. Concepts of civilization and savagery, rationality and passion, that were fundamental binaries of thinking during the imperialist era creep back into debates over human rights (...). The practice of human rights is burdened by a colonialist understanding of culture that smuggles nineteenth-century ideas of backwardness and savagery into the process.[74]

Transitional justice is prescriptive, normative, outcome-oriented, aiming at an end-state ('justice'), positing linear cause-and-effect chains, both with regard to the issues that have to be dealt with through 'transitions' (violence, oppression, injustice) and the transitional process towards 'justice' itself. It is substantialist, based on an individual rights (and accountability) concept and the assumption of clear demarcations of 'victims' and 'perpetrators'. Its focus is on the individual victims and their needs. Kastom reconciliations, by

---

[70]Baines, 'Spirits', 430.
[71]Baines, 'Spirits', 415.
[72]Marita Eastmond, 'Introduction: Reconciliation, Reconstruction, and Everyday Life in War-torn Societies', *Focaal – Journal of Global and Historical Anthropology* 57 (2010), 3–16. 5, also Sally Engle Merry, *Human Rights and Gender Violence* (Chicago: University of Chicago Press, 2009), 226, who criticizes that "those promoting universal standards tend to see local context as irrelevant or even a hindrance".
[73]Guthrey, 'Local Norms', 14.
[74]Merry, 'Human Rights', 226.

contrast, are guided by the insight that 'relational transformation' is 'the heart of peacebuilding.'[75] They are relational, process-oriented, community-oriented, complex and open-ended, acknowledging that to be a 'victim' is not the only marker of people's relational identities, and that there can be a broad spectrum of different experiences of 'victimhood', depending on specific contexts. This kind of reconciliation purports a relational conception of justice.[76] Melanesian reconciliations are community-centred rather than victim-centred (assuming that this also serves the needs of the victims). They aim at reintegration of offenders so as to restore relations. They do not necessarily lead from point A – violence, conflict – to point B – conflict resolution, harmony – in a linear way; rather, they are circular, repetitive, itinerative and iterative - long and windy roads of conflict transformation, with frequent detours, dead ends and fresh starts.[77] 'Final settlements' are not 'final' at all, but are open to renegotiation at some time in the future. The past is not past: it can resurface (or be made to resurface) at any time; 'resolutions' therefore are not really 'resolutions'. But the process enables people and communities to get on with life (for the most part).

And this is an important point not to underestimate: People want to get on with their 'normal lives', and reconciliations matter only inasmuch as they (hold the promise to) make this possible. Protagonists of transitional justice have a tendency to overestimate the significance of their cause (and the importance of what they think can be achieved through pursuing that cause) for the 'objects' of their efforts, the people on the ground.[78] People prefer restorative justice, understood 'as a compensation for loss, not as a retribution for offense'.[79] Transitional justice can be found wanting in this regard, because of its focus on prosecution and punishment and its rather narrow understanding of reparation –backward-looking reparative justice concerned with 'historical reparations', not so much forward-looking distributive justice concerned with the socioeconomic needs of victims and their communities (employment, healthcare, education, ...).[80] In the context of conflict transformation, restoration of livelihoods and relationships is more important for the future wellbeing of communities than punishment of offenders. This also means that 'forgetting' and 'silence' can have space in Melanesian reconciliations.[81]

---

[75]Schirch, Ritual, 151.

[76]Llewellyn and Philpott, Restorative Justice.

[77]On the circular character of reconciliations see Lederach and Lederach, 'Blood and Bones'.

[78]Eastmond, 'Introduction', points to the "gap between the aspirations of transitional justice and the experiences and needs of local communities" (6) and reminds us that the everyday problems of people in post-conflict communities might be more urgent than issues of transitional justice.

[79]I. W. Zartman, 'Conclusions: Changes in the New Order and the Place for the Old', in *Traditional Cures for Modern Conflicts. African Conflict "Medicine"*, ed. I.W. Zartman (Boulder, Co.: Lynne Rienner, 2000): 219–230, 222.

[80]Lambourne, Transformative Justice, 29–31.

[81]On 'forgetting' and silence as coping mechanisms, particularly for women, see Guthrie, 'Victim Healing' (158-159), Vella, Justice, 10–11; on the significance of silence in peacebuilding Tarja Vaeyrynen 'Silence in Western Models of Conflict Resolution' in *Mediating across difference. Oceanic and Asian approaches to conflict resolution,* eds. M. Brigg and R. Bleiker (Honolulu: University of Hawaii Press), 38–56. Her findings resonate well with Melanesian experiences as she posits that "silence forms invisible relational and interactive links and bonds in communities among people who have experienced the trauma of violence. Silence can create networks of trust, care and communal solidarity for those who have become isolated during conflict. By binding communities together silence can produce a countermemory vis-à-vis official narratives. It can normalise everyday life after violence" (50). In a Melanesian context, 'truth-telling' does not necessarily have the healing and liberating effects that proponents of transitional justice, coming from a Western cultural background, take for granted, and "silence does not just indicate the impossibility to speak or the impossibility to encounter the unspeakable, but it can generate a sense of community" (ibid., 51). Braithwaite goes even a step further: he cites cases from Indonesia where 'non-truth' (lying) was integral to and conducive to reconciliation (John Braithwaite, 'Traditional Justice' in *Restorative Justice, Reconciliation, and Peacebuilding,* eds. Jennifer J. Llewellyn and Daniel Philpott (Oxford: Oxford University Press, 2014).

This approach goes hand in hand with attention to the affective, emotional and spiritual dimensions, with emotions seen as 'both part of the social fabric and as forms of knowledge and judgement'.[82] Peace cannot be built, and justice cannot be restored, without addressing people's emotions and spirituality. Reconciliations Melanesian style do not separate the material and spiritual realm, everyday life is imbued with spirituality. Transitional justice largely fails to recognise the spiritual dimension. Instead, its focus is on (statutory) law, legality, legally sound processes and outcomes. Kastom reconciliations, by contrast, do not pay much attention to legal concerns. They are definitely not the functional equivalent of legal procedures. Legal, normative and institutional questions are of little relevance to these reconciliations, which are embedded in Melanesian worldviews and cosmologies, with profoundly different constructions of community and personhood, nature and the sacred, and hence of peace and justice.

Finally, the fact that people can implement kastom reconciliations themselves is another significant advantage: they have voice and agency, they are in control. Reconciliations are socio-cultural mechanisms at people's immediate disposal, they are familiar with the process, and they know what outcomes can be expected. This marks an important difference to the transitional justice focus on formal institutions, TRCs, trials and other top-down formal institutionalised mechanisms which are not at the disposal and under the control of ordinary community members; processes and outcomes often are not well understood, and victims and perpetrators are largely objects of external mechanisms.

This is not to say that transitional justice mechanisms and procedures cannot be valuable and necessary in a Melanesian context. Rather, the argument is that culturally specific, locally grounded reconciliations can substantially contribute to peacebuilding, because they address needs, cover issues and pursue practices which cannot adequately be addressed, covered and pursued by transitional justice. Whether such reconciliations are an alternative to or can be productively combined with transitional justice remains to be seen; again, it will very much depend on the specific context. What seems to be clear, however, is that transitional justice is no substitute for reconciliations, and that in a Melanesian context there cannot be sustainable peace without reconciliation. Frictions and tensions between the different approaches 'can be approached conversationally rather than coercively', most notably by local intermediaries with a 'double sensibility'.[83] Such intermediaries can be crucial for finding ways to bridge the gap between international and local understandings and expectations with regard to justice, truth and reconciliation. In fact,

> further attention to the role of actors engaged in negotiating the boundaries between international norms and local practice is crucial to understanding norm adoption and transformation. Study of those actors who remain under the radar screen of international practice and largely disconnected from international civil society networks but whose role is crucial to local practice may be especially important.[84]

---

[82]Hutchinson and Bleiker, 'Emotional Reconciliation', 396.

[83]Braithwaite, 'Traditional Justice', makes this point with regard to tensions between restorative and traditional justice; it is even more valid with regard to reconciliation and transitional justice. On the importance of such intermediaries also Merry, Human Rights, 229.

[84]Boesenacker and Vinjamuri, 'Lost in Translation', 364.

Protagonists of transitional justice could gain insights from the study of Melanesian reconciliations that would help them to reflect on their own taken-for-granted assumptions and consider avenues for developing the concept of transitional justice, making it more meaningful, effective and legitimate in a context such as Melanesia.

Disclosure statement

No potential conflict of interest was reported by the author.

ORCID

Volker Boege http://orcid.org/0000-0003-1337-5525

The role of 'uncivil' society in transitional justice: evidence from Bougainville and Timor-Leste

Joanne Wallis

ABSTRACT

Transitional justice (TJ) scholarship and practice often pins much hope on civil society. It generally assumes that civil society organisations demonstrate 'civility', have broad-based memberships, support liberal democratic values and promote TJ approaches based on liberal-legal justice strategies. Yet there is nothing inherently virtuous about civil society and in conflict-affected societies it often lacks these desired properties; it can be underdeveloped, unruly and disruptive. So, what role do, and should, 'uncivil' society groups play in TJ processes? To answer this question this article uses comparative case studies of the role of uncivil society groups in Bougainville and Timor-Leste. These cases exhibit similar broad cultural, socio-political and socio-economic characteristics. In both cases uncivil society groups are organised around societal divisions, attempt to operate as alternatives to the state, oppose liberal democracy and liberal-legal TJ processes and engage in unruly behaviour, including violence and criminality. These uncivil society groups are not regarded as internationally legitimate, but they nevertheless have strong local legitimacy, particularly when the state is absent or weak. Consequently, this article concludes that in conflict-affected societies it is necessary to engage with groups regarded as both civil and uncivil to promote locally legitimate and effective TJ, and peace more broadly.

Introduction

Transitional justice (TJ) has emerged as a central component of liberal peacebuilding. TJ is said to support the institutionalisation of the key tenets of the liberal peace in conflict-affected societies by helping to reform state institutions, support democratisation, establish the rule of law and build a human rights culture.[1] In this process, TJ scholarship and practice increasingly envisages a role for civil society, broadly defined as the 'arena of un-coerced collective action around shared interests, purposes and values'.[2] This is because civil society is seen to play important roles in building trust and

[1]Kora Andrieu, 'Civilizing Peacebuilding: Transitional Justice, Civil Society and the Liberal Paradigm', *Security Dialogue* 41, no. 5 (2010): 537–558; Rama Mani, 'Rebuilding an Inclusive Political Community After War', *Security Dialogue* 36, no. 4 (2005): 511–526.

[2]Centre for Civil Society, *Report on Activities, July 2005–August 2006* (London: London School of Economics and Politics Science, 2006) http://eprints.lse.ac.uk/29398/1/CCSReport05_06.pdf.

providing public goods in the absence of the state,[3] in promoting and strengthening democracy and good governance,[4] in advocating for human rights[5] and in highlighting and collecting evidence of human rights violations.[6] Civil society is also said to have driven much of the global human rights and TJ agenda,[7] to have advocated for, and helped to implement and monitor, TJ mechanisms,[8] and to have instigated community-led TJ processes when the state has been unable or unwilling to adequately do so.[9] Consequently, civil society is often perceived to play an 'indispensable role' in the success of TJ processes.[10]

These claims assume that civil society organisations (CSOs) demonstrate 'civility', understood to mean public spiritedness, tolerance and a sense of obligation towards the whole society.[11] Reflecting their focus on institutionalising the liberal peace, they also assume that CSOs have characteristics that are seen to support liberalism, including broad-based memberships that cut across societal (such as ethnic or sectarian) divisions, an ideological preference for liberal democratic values and a commitment to TJ approaches based on liberal-legal justice strategies and international human rights norms.[12]

But the TJ literature 'lacks a comprehensive and rigorous conceptualisation of the role that civil society plays' in TJ processes[13] and consequently overlooks that there is 'nothing inherently virtuous' or 'civil' about civil society.[14] In many conflict-affected societies the challenge for peacebuilding, including TJ, is 'not that civil society does not exist but that it is the wrong kind, at least from the point of view of the international community'.[15] 'Uncivil' society groups can be organised around societal divisions, oppose liberal democracy and liberal-legal TJ processes and engage in unruly behaviour, including violence and

---

[3]Benjamin Gidron, Stanely N. Katz, and Yeheskel Hasenfel, *Mobilizing for Peace: Conflict Resolution in Northern Ireland, Israel/Palestine, and South Africa* (Oxford: Oxford University Press, 2002); Thania Paffenholz and Christoph Spurk, *Civil Society, Civic Engagement, and Peacebuilding* (Washington: World Bank, 2006); World Bank, *Working Together: World Bank-Civil Society Relations* (Washington: World Bank, 2003).

[4]Catherine Barnes, *Agents for Change: Civil Society Roles in Preventing War & Building Peace* (The Hague: European Centre for Conflict Prevention, 2006); Robert Putnam, *Making Democracy Work: Civic Traditions in Modern Italy* (Princeton: Princeton University Press, 1993); World Bank, *Civil Society and Peacebuilding; Potential, Limitations and Critical Factors* (Washington: World Bank, 2007).

[5]Kathryn Sikkink, *The Justice Cascade: How Human Rights Prosecutions are Changing World Politics* (New York: W.W. Norton & Company, Inc., 2011).

[6]Pablo de Greiff, 'Transitional Justice and Development,' in *Transitional Justice and Development: Making the Connections*, ed. Pablo de Greiff and Roger Duthie (New York: Social Science Research Council, 2009), 9.

[7]David Backer, 'Civil Society and Transitional Justice: Possibilities, Patterns and Prospects', *Journal of Human Rights* 2, no. 3 (2003): 297–313.

[8]David Crocker, 'Transitional Justice and International Civil Society: Toward a Normative Framework', *Constellations* 5, no. 4 (1998): 492–517, 493.

[9]Kieran McEvoy, 'Beyond Legalism: Towards a Thicker Understanding of Transitional Justice', *Journal of Law and Society* 34, no. 4 (2007): 411–440, 434.

[10]Crocker, 'Transitional justice', 492.

[11]Edward Shills, 'The Virtue of Civil Society', *Government and Opposition* 26, no. 1 (1991): 3–20; Benjamin R. Barber, *A Place for US: How to Make Society Civil and Democracy Strong* (New York: Hill & Wang, 1998).

[12]Aaron P. Boesenecker and Leslie Vinjamuri, 'Lost in Translation? Civil Society, Faith-Based Organizations and the Negotiation of International Norms', *The International Journal of Transitional Justice* 5, no. 3 (2011): 345–365.

[13]Paul Gready and Simon Robins, 'Rethinking Civil Society and Transitional Justice: Lessons from Social Movements and 'New' Civil Society', *International Journal of Transitional Justice* 21, no. 7 (2017): 956–975, 956.

[14]Michael W. Foley, 'Cautionary Tales: Soft Intervention and Civil Society', in *Strengthening Peace in Post-Civil War States: Transforming Spoilers into Stakeholders*, ed. Matthew Hoddie and Caroline Hartzell (Chicago: University of Chicago Press, 2010), 163–188, 164.

[15]James Mayall, 'The Legacy of Colonialism', in *Making States Work: State Failure and the Crisis of Governance*, ed. Simon Chesterman et al. (Tokyo: United Nations University Press, 2005), 36–58, 56.

criminality.[16] Therefore, this article addresses the question: what role do, and should, uncivil society groups play in TJ processes?

I adopt a broad understanding of TJ activities as including 'the full range of processes and mechanisms associated with a society's attempts to come to terms with a legacy of large-scale past abuses, in order to ensure accountability, serve justice and achieve reconciliation'.[17] This may include formal institutions such as truth and reconciliation commissions and criminal trials aimed at violations of human rights and humanitarian law,[18] as well as other less formal activities that seek to respond to legacies of past violence, such as memorialisation and grassroots reconciliation practices.

Building on a nascent critical literature seeking to rethink civil society and its role in TJ, I identify an underappreciated aspect of the TJ literature relating to the role of uncivil society groups. I argue that conventional conceptions of CSOs and their roles in peacebuilding and TJ rely too uncritically on assumptions regarding their nature, function and ideological preferences. This overlooks the fact that in conflict-affected societies civil society often lacks these desired properties; it can be underdeveloped, unruly and rely on 'disruptive techniques'.[19]

Therefore, I argue that the peacebuilding and TJ literature needs to adopt a more nuanced and contextual understanding of civil society, which pays attention to the cultural, historical and political conditions in the conflict-affected society in question.[20] This understanding will likely reveal the presence of uncivil society groups which 'lie outside or jar with civil forms of civic and democratic engagement' and which would not necessarily be regarded as internationally legitimate by liberal peace standards, but which may nevertheless have strong local legitimacy.[21] This may help to inform more 'contextualised visions of justice and rights'.[22] This implies that, if peacebuilding and TJ processes are to reach an entire conflict-affected society to achieve justice and enduring peace, they will need to 're-imagine and model alternative approaches' to understanding civil society, including balancing their concern with international liberal-legal legitimacy with achieving local legitimacy by engaging with these uncivil society groups.[23]

To support my argument, I examine case studies of the role played by uncivil society groups in two conflict affected-societies, Bougainville, an autonomous region of Papua New Guinea, and Timor-Leste. I use the 'structured, focused comparison' research method, whereby I adopt the same framework for analysis of each case.[24] I have selected these cases for analysis and comparison for four reasons. First, they fall within the geographical and cultural area known as 'Melanesia' and consequently exhibit similar broad

[16]Marina Ottaway, 'Democratization in Collapsed States', in *Collapsed States: The Disintegration and Restoration of Legitimate Authority*, ed. I. William Zartman (London: Lynne Rienner Publishers, 1995), 235–250, 240.

[17]UN, *Report of the Secretary-General on the Rule of Law and Transitional Justice in Conflict and Post-Conflict Societies*, UN Doc. S/2004/616, 24 August 2004, 3.

[18]Naomi Roht-Arriaza, 'The New Landscape of Transitional Justice', in *Transitional Justice in the Twenty-First Century: Beyond Truth Versus Justice*, ed. Naomi Roht-Arriaza and Javier Mariezcurrena (Cambridge: Cambridge University Press, 2006), 1–16, 2.

[19]Gready and Robins, 'Rethinking civil society', 958.

[20]Christopher M. Hann, 'Introduction: Political Society and Civil Anthropology,' in *Civil Society: Challenging Western Models*, eds. Christopher M. Hann and Elizabeth Dunn (London: Routledge, 1996), 1–26.

[21]Alex Shankland, et al., 'Unruly Politics: *A Manifesto*', mimeo (Brighton: Institute of Development Studies, 2011): 1.

[22]Gready and Robins, 'Rethinking Civil Society', 959.

[23]Ibid.

[24]Alexander L. George and Andrew Bennett, *Case Studies and Theory Development in the Social Sciences* (Cambridge: MIT Press, 2005).

cultural, socio-political and socio-economic characteristics, including relatively small (Bougainville has a population of approximately 300,000 people, Timor-Leste of 1.17 million people), primarily rural, subsistence populations. Second, both have similar histories; after decolonisation large portions of the populations of both attempted self-determination, but in 1975 Bougainville was incorporated into Papua New Guinea and Timor-Leste was occupied by Indonesia. Both were then engaged in long – and bloody – independence struggles.[25] These self-determination struggles concluded in 1997 in Bougainville and in 1999 in Timor-Leste, both of which then engaged in peace and TJ processes. Third, in both cases centralised statehood is a relatively recent phenomenon, state institutions have struggled to achieve control over, and the loyalty of, their fragmented and divided societies, and liberal democracy is not yet consolidated. Instead, local socio-political institutions and practices remain influential. Fourth, in both cases there are uncivil society groups that have played a role in challenging peace and TJ processes. The similarities between the two cases make it possible to hold variables constant and to identify implications from the empirical findings for scholarly and practitioner discussions of the role of uncivil society in TJ.[26]

This article begins by outlining the conventional liberal understanding of civil society and its role in peacebuilding and TJ processes. I then build on a nascent critical literature which challenges the liberal assumptions on which this conventional understanding is based. I critically examine the assumed civility of civil society and argue that we need to account for the role of uncivil society in peacebuilding and TJ processes. I then analyse the role of uncivil society groups in Bougainville and Timor-Leste, before comparing the two cases and identifying lessons for TJ scholars and practitioners in the conclusion.

'Civil' society and TJ

As noted, I adopt a broad definition of civil society, intended to reflect that civil society is often diffuse and fragmented. While some narrow definitions require that CSOs be actively involved in political deliberations,[27] a broader definition captures the reality that people also 'meet, communicate, and organise' for purposes beyond controlling state institutions or exercising political power.[28] It can also be difficult to clearly demarcate what constitutes a political issue, or distinguish between the private and public spheres, particularly in conflict-affected societies with little tradition of strong state institutions.[29] Some definitions are also normative, holding that civil society consists only of 'formal, nongovernmental organisations that are generally presumed to "do good"'[30] and embody

---

[25] Anthony J. Regan, *Light Intervention: Lessons from Bougainville* (Washington: U.S. Institute of Peace Press, 2010); CAVR, *Chega! The Report of the Commission for Reception, Truth and Reconciliation in Timor-Leste: Executive Summary* (Dili: Commission for Reception, Truth, and Reconciliation Timor-Leste, 2005).

[26] Adam Przeworski and Henry Teune, *The Logic of Comparative Social Inquiry* (New York: John Wiley, 1970).

[27] Victor Perez Diaz, *The Return of Civil Society: The Emergence of Civil Society in Spain* (Cambridge: Harvard University Press, 1993).

[28] Camilla Orjuela, 'Building Peace in Sri Lanka: A Role for Civil Society?', *Journal of Peace Research* 40, no. 2 (2003): 195–212, 196; Juan J. Linz and Alfred Stepan, *Problems of Democratic Transition and Consolidation: Southern Europe, South America, and Post-Communist Europe* (Baltimore: Johns Hopkins University Press, 1996).

[29] Petr Kopecky, 'Civil Society, Uncivil Society and Contentious Politics in Post-communist Europe', in *Uncivil Society? Contentious Politics in Post-communist Europe*, ed. Petr Kopecky and Cas Mudde (London: Routledge, 2003), 1–17.

[30] Orjuela, 'Building Peace in Sri Lanka', 196.

'certain aspirations about the organisation of modern society'.[31] In contrast, a broad definition includes any social network,[32] ranging from 'internationally operating development organisations to very localised initiatives and traditional forms of association'.[33]

The idea that civil society is inherently civil had its roots in the work of Mario Salamonio, a 16th century Roman jurist who argued that kingdoms and princedoms were instituted 'by agreements of men' to leave the 'state of nature'. This agreement would be generated by the political community, who would form a *civilis societas* (with *societas* the Roman word for partnership) made by free contract among the individual partners.[34] The idea was developed during the Enlightenment, when Locke and other contractarians used it to describe the way in which populations put '*on the bonds of Civil Society*' [emphasis in original] in order to form a political community and consent to being governed.[35] Interest in the concept was revived in the context of opposition to communism and totalitarianism Eastern Europe. During the transition to democracy, civil society was seen as potentially nurturing civic initiatives to act as check on state institutions.[36]

Building on this liberal interpretation and influenced by 'normative idealism',[37] much of the TJ and peacebuilding literature has tended towards a somewhat monolithic view of civil society, which assumes that it is both civil and favours the liberal peace, including liberal-legal justice strategies. Over the last 20 years civil society has come to be treated as the 'imagined agent of development'[38] during liberal peace interventions. Indeed, civil society is sometimes presented as an effective alternative to government in conflict-affected societies because it is seen as more representative, more legitimate, less corrupt and closer to grassroots populations.[39] As noted, many TJ scholars and practitioners have assumed that CSOs in conflict-affected societies will advocate for the international norm of seeking accountability for perpetrators of human rights violations and assist in diffusing that norm within their society. Reflecting this view, the conventional peacebuilding and TJ literature assumes that local CSOs should be empowered and promoted in conflict-affected societies.[40]

'Uncivil' society and TJ

By tending to treat civil society as a monolithic and inherently positive entity, the conventional peacebuilding and TJ literature may have invested disproportionate confidence in the civility of many CSOs in conflict-affected societies, their broad-based memberships

---

[31] Kopecky, 'Civil Society, Uncivil Society', 7.

[32] Putnam, *Making Democracy Work.*

[33] Willemijn Verkoren and Mathijs van Leeumen, 'Civil Society in Fragile Contexts', in *The Handbook of Global Security Policy*, ed. Mary Kaldor and Iavor Rangelov (Chichester: John Wiley & Sons, 2014), 463–481, 465.

[34] M. Salamonio, *De Principatu* (Milan: Giuffre Editore, 1955), 27–29.

[35] John Locke, *Two Treatises of Government* (Cambridge: Cambridge University Press, 1960), 95; John Keane, *Global Civil Society?* (Cambridge: Cambridge University Press, 2003).

[36] Kopecky, 'Civil Society, Uncivil Society', 5.

[37] Paul Gready and Simon Robins, 'From Transitional to Transformative Justice: A New Agenda for Practice', *The International Journal of Transitional Justice* 8 (2014): 339–361, 343.

[38] Jenny Pearce, 'The International Community and Peacebuilding', *Development* 48, no. 3 (2005): 41–49.

[39] ECCP, *European Conference on the Role of Civil Society in the Prevention of Armed Conflict*, Report of a conference held at Dublin Castle, Dublin, 31 March–2 April (Utrecht: European Centre for Conflict Prevention, 2004); Verkoren and van Leeumen, 'Civil Society in Fragile Contexts'.

[40] UN Secretary General, *In Larger Freedom: Towards Development, Security and Human Rights for All*, UN Doc. A/59/2005, 21 March 2005; Foley, 'Cautionary Tales'.

and interests, and their support for liberal democracy, including liberal-legal TJ processes. Consequently, there is a nascent critical literature which recognises a more diverse field of CSOs and challenges the assumption that they will necessarily act in ways that are conducive to reconciliation and peace, let alone favour liberal-legal processes of achieving this.[41] This emerging critique suggests there is value in critically examining civil society when considering its role in TJ and the broader liberal peacebuilding project. A useful starting point for this analysis is the frequently unacknowledged fact that 'all known forms of civil society are plagued by endogenous sources of incivility'.[42] Consequently, a new understanding of civil society is emerging which recognises that it can be 'unpredictable and more diverse'[43] than previously acknowledged and that it can frequently engage in 'unruly politics'.[44] Consequently, even in consolidated democracies civil society can range 'from democratic to undemocratic actors and from peaceful to violent agents'.[45] Therefore, we need to account for the role of 'bad civil society',[46] or 'uncivil society' and ask what role it does and should play in TJ processes.

Analyses of uncivil society in the TJ, peacebuilding or wider political science literature are relatively rare. Most attempts to identify uncivil society are based on what it is not, that is, that it does not resemble civil society. For example, Larry Diamond's definition of civil society states that:

> A third distinguishing mark is that civil society encompasses *pluralism* and diversity. To the extent that an organisation – such as a religious fundamentalist, ethnic chauvinist, revolutionary, or millenarian movement – seeks to monopolise a functional or political space in society, claiming that it represents the only legitimate path, it contradicts the pluralistic and market-oriented nature of civil society. Related to this is a fourth distinction, *partialness*, signifying that no group in civil society seeks to represent the whole of a person's or a community's interests.[47]

Some explicit definitions of uncivil society focus on its nature, with Kofi Annan highlighting that it includes groups 'who undo the good works of civil society'.[48] Others on its function, including in their definitions mafia-like groups, paramilitaries, terrorists, criminals, drug dealers and human traffickers.[49] Others focus on its ideological preferences, holding that uncivil society groups 'advocate hate and bigotry', as they fail to recognise other citizens as 'moral agents deserving civility'.[50] Common to all definitions is an agreement that uncivil society lacks civility, that is, that it demonstrates negative traits of interpersonal

[41] Verkoren and van Leeumen, 'Civil Society in Fragile Contexts'; Sarah Crowther, 'The Role of NGOs, Local and International, in Post-war Peacebuilding', *Committee for Conflict Transformation Support Newsletter*, no. 15 (2001); Gready and Robins, 'Rethinking Civil Society'; Orjuela, 'Building Peace in Sri Lanka'.
[42] John Keane, *Civil Society: Old Images, New Visions* (Stanford: Stanford University Press, 1998), 135.
[43] Gready and Robins, 'Rethinking Civil Society', 959.
[44] Shankland et al., 'Unruly Politics'; see also Akshay Khanna, 'Seeing Citizen Action through an 'Unruly' Lens', *Development* 55, no. 2 (2012): 162–172.
[45] Roberto Belloni, 'Civil Society in War-to-democracy Transitions', in *From War to Democracy: Dilemmas of* Peacebuilding, ed. Anna K. Jarstad and Timothy D. Sisk (Cambridge: Cambridge University Press, 2008), 182–210, 186–187.
[46] Simone Chambers and Jeffrey Kopstein, 'Bad Civil Society', *Political Theory* 29, no. 6 (2001): 837–865, 838.
[47] Larry Diamond, 'Rethinking Civil Society: Toward Democratic Consolidation', *Journal of Democracy* 5, no. 3 (1994): 4–17, 6.
[48] Kofi Annan, 'Address at the Opening of the Signing Conference for the United Nations Convention Against Transnational Organized Crime', Palermo, December 12, 2000, http://www.unodc.org/unodc/en/about-unodc/speeches/speech_2000-12-12_1.html; Keane, *Civil Society: Old Images*; Leigh A. Payne, *Uncivil Movements: The Armed Right Wing and Democracy in Latin America* (Baltimore: Johns Hopkins University Press, 2000).
[49] Belloni, 'Civil Society in War-to-democracy Transitions', 183; Annan, 'Address at the Opening of the Signing Conference'.
[50] Chambers and Kopstein, 'Bad Civil Society', 839–840; Ami Pedahzur and Leonard Weinberg, 'Modern European Democracy and its Enemies: The Threat of the Extreme Right', *Totalitarian Movements and Political Religions* 2, no. 1 (2001): 52–72.

behaviour,[51] and that it reflects narrow interests, which challenges liberal democracy and the rule of law that rely on a broad-based social contract. This forms the basis of the definition I adopt in this article. While this broad definition can include armed groups, what distinguishes armed uncivil society groups from bandits or gang violence is that they pursue a political agenda which is legitimate (at least to their supporters) and is 'deeply rooted in … [their supporters'] own understanding of what is right and just'.[52] While these groups' actions might be 'politically transgressive' or even criminal, they also 'have a potency' and 'make things happen'.[53] That such groups are not usually contemplated by conventional accounts demonstrates the need to explore this underappreciated aspect of the TJ literature.

It is surprising that conventional peacebuilding and TJ accounts do not pay much attention to the role of uncivil society, given that, during conflict, 'anti-civic and violent forms of associationism prevail over those pro-democracy organisations celebrated by advocates of civil society'.[54] Even after conflict, 'the warring parties typically continue to contest the state',[55] and often have little regard for, or oppose outright, liberal democratic values.[56] This can weaken the state and undermine TJ processes driven by liberal-legal approaches.

One reason that the conventional peacebuilding and TJ literature often overlooks the role of uncivil society is that it has been strongly influenced by an understanding of civil society generated in consolidated liberal democracies. These accounts rely on the presence of a legitimate state, a separation between state institutions and society, and on a population that identifies as citizens. Yet in conflict-affected societies the state is often weak, with a limited presence and little legitimacy at the local level. Consequently, there can be no clear distinction between civil society and the state, particularly as CSOs frequently deliver public goods typically expected to be provided by the state and consequently both present themselves and act as alternatives to the state.[57] Therefore, these societies may not have coalesced a social contract in the form understood by liberalism. Relationships between state actors and the population tend not to be guided solely by the impartiality and sense of common good on which liberalism relies, but at least partly on self-interest, patronage, personalised leadership and clientism,[58] which can represent, at least to some, a locally legitimate 'moral economy of entitlement and obligation'.[59]

When state institutions are fragile, illegitimate or absent this 'provides an opportunity for uncivil groups to thrive', particularly as when seeking security people frequently

---

[51] Laurence Whitehead, 'Bowling in the Bronx: The Uncivil Interstices Between Civil and Political Society', *Democratization* 4, no. 1 (1997): 94–114.

[52] Shankland, et al., 'Unruly Politics', 1.

[53] Ibid.

[54] Roberto Belloni, 'Civil Society in War-to-democracy Transitions', 187.

[55] Ibid., 188.

[56] Nelson Kasfir, 'Civil Society, the State and Democracy in Africa', *Commonwealth & Comparative Politics* 36, no. 2 (1998): 123–149.

[57] Beatrice Pouligny, 'Civil Society and Post-Conflict Peacebuilding: Ambiguities of International Programmes Aimed at Building 'New' Societies', *Security Dialogue* 36, no. 4 (2005): 495–510; Verkoren and van Leeumen, 'Civil Society in Fragile Contexts'.

[58] Verkoren and van Leeumen, 'Civil Society in Fragile Contexts'; Mathijs van Leeuwen and Willemijn Verkoren, 'The Complexity of Civil Society Building: Key Challenges for Enhancing Post-conflict Civil Society Approaches', *Journal of Peacebuilding and Development* 7, no. 1 (2012): 81–94.

[59] Shankland, et al., 'Unruly Politics', 1.

strengthen their ethnic or language bonds; kinship, tribal, religious groups; and traditional political structures.[60] Therefore, rather than having broad-based memberships and interest in promoting the common good, uncivil society groups can form around 'ascriptive criteria', such as race, ethnicity, language, religion or military service and pursue narrow interests.[61] While such uncivil society groups can play a positive role,[62] they can also undermine peacebuilding, including TJ processes, by sustaining societal divisions or enforcing 'intra-ethnic private and illegal rule'.[63] Indeed, most conceptions of civil society in the peacebuilding and TJ literature underestimate the role that conflict, economic decline, social stress, violence and ethnic fissures plays in generating uncivil society groups and in reinforcing the power and social structures that support them.[64] For example, this can provide space for 'ethnic entrepreneurs' to draw upon purported ethnic identities to take advantage of economic opportunities and build groups around them.[65] It also explains why many uncivil society groups are focused more on socio-economic development than on the civil–political rights prioritised by liberal-legal TJ practices.[66]

International peacebuilding interventions can also have unintended consequences that can decivilize CSOs. For example, interveners can enhance the power of certain CSOs by favouring them as local partners, foster conflict through competition for funding and destroy local markets.[67] Interveners can undermine the legitimacy of CSOs by requiring that their programming reflect the values of Western donors, rather than local populations.[68] Compounding this, interveners have been encouraged to incorporate local CSOs into their operations with little attempt to analyse their local legitimacy.[69] Instead, interveners focus primarily on the legitimacy of CSOs assessed against their compliance with international norms. While many uncivil society groups would not be regarded as internationally legitimate, they may nevertheless have strong local legitimacy, that is, local populations may regard them as 'proper, or appropriate within some socially constructed system of norms, values, beliefs and definitions'.[70]

In this regard, conventional accounts of the role of civil society in peacebuilding and TJ have overlooked questions about the universality of international human rights norms and

---

[60]Belloni, 'Civil Society in War-to-democracy Transitions', 188.

[61]Ibid., 190.

[62]Kathleen Collins, *The Logic of Clan Politics in Central Asia: The Impact of Regime Transformation* (New York: Cambridge University Press, 2006); Perviz Mullojanov, 'Civil Society and Peacebuilding', in *Politics of Compromise: The Tajikistan Peace Process*, ed. Kamoludin Abdullaev and Catherine Barnes (London: Conciliation Resources 2001), http://c-r.org/resources/politics-compromise-tajikistan-peace-process; Nat J. Colletta, Markus Kostner, and Ingo Wiederhofer, 'Disarmament, Demobilization, and Reintegration: Lessons and Liabilities in Reconstruction', in *When States Fail: Causes and Consequences*, ed. Robert Rotberg (Princeton: Princeton University Press, 2004), 170–181; Peter Uvin and Charles Mironko, 'Western and Local Approaches to Justice in Rwanda', *Global Governance* 9, no. 2 (2003): 129–231.

[63]Belloni, 'Civil Society in War-to-democracy Transitions', 190.

[64]Christoph Spurk, 'Understanding Civil Society', in *Civil Society and Peacebuilding: A Critical Assessment*, ed. Thania Paffenholz (Boulder: Lynne Rienner, 2010), 3–28.

[65]Thierry Volery, 'Ethnic Entrepreneurship: A Theoretical Framework' in *Handbook of Research on Ethnic Minority Entrepreneurship*, ed. Leo-Paul Dana (Cheltenham: Edward Elgar, 2007), 30–41.

[66]Gready and Robins, 'Rethinking Civil Society'; Gready and Robins, 'From Transitional to Transformative Justice'.

[67]Mary Anderson, *Do No Harm: How Aid Can Support Peace or War* (Boulder: Lynne Rienner, 1999); Roberto Belloni, 'Civil Society and Peacebuilding in Bosnia and Herzegovina', *Journal of Peace Research* 38, no. 2 (2001): 163–180.

[68]Pouligny, 'Civil Society and Post-Conflict Peacebuilding', 499.

[69]Randall Pulijek-Shank and Willemijn Verkoren, 'Civil Society in a Divided Society: Linking Legitimacy and Ethnicness of Civil Society Organisations in Bosnia-Herzegovina', *Cooperation and Conflict* 52, no. 2 (2017): 184–202.

[70]Mark C. Suchman, 'Managing Legitimacy: Strategic and Institutional Approaches', *Academy of Management Review* 20, no. 3 (1995): 571–610, 574.

the disjunction between the 'distant justice'[71] offered by liberal-legal international approaches to TJ and the often more locally legitimate and effective grassroots justice mechanisms in conflict-affected societies.[72] Indeed, many uncivil society groups in conflict-affected societies can subvert formal TJ processes in favour of local justice mechanisms which may violate international human rights norms, but be legitimate according to local socio-political practices and norms.[73] As noted, they also tend to pursue an agenda that prioritises socio-economic development rather than civil–political rights.

Uncivil society in practice

I now examine case studies of two conflict affected-societies, Bougainville and Timor-Leste, which provide illustrative examples of the role that uncivil society groups play in transitional justice processes. As noted, the similarities between the two cases make it possible to hold variables constant and suggests that my common findings relating to the role of uncivil society groups in both cases have implications for scholarly and practitioner discussions of the role of uncivil society in TJ. I undertook field research in Bougainville and Timor-Leste, primarily utilising semi-structured interviews and participant observation, as well as analysis of secondary sources and media reports.

In both cases I have selected the most significant uncivil society groups for analysis. Reflecting the structured, focused comparison research method, to aid the comparison of my two cases, I adopt the same framework for analysis in each. To contextualise my discussion of the formation and role of the uncivil society groups being analysed, I begin by providing a brief background on the conflict and peace process and describe the TJ processes that have been attempted. Guided by the literature reviewed above, I then identify the sources of legitimacy and support of the uncivil society groups under analysis, and describe the uncivil ideological preferences and beliefs that they promote and the uncivil behaviour in which they engage, including how they challenge the state and disrupt peacebuilding and TJ.

Uncivil society in Bougainville

Between 1989 and 1997 Bougainville experienced a civil war that was sparked by grievances relating to the massive Panguna copper and gold mine located in the centre of Bougainville Island, but which expanded to become a secessionist struggle and intra-Bougainvillean conflict. Only a 'light' international intervention was embarked on to end the war; near neighbours Australia and New Zealand provided small, unarmed truce and peace monitoring teams and the United Nations a minute observer mission.[74] In 2001 a comprehensive political settlement granted Bougainville extensive political autonomy and the right to vote on its political future (with the option of independence) between

[71]Andrieu, 'Civilizing Peacebuilding', 554; Paul Gready, 'Reconceptualising Transitional Justice: Embedded and Distant Justice', *Conflict, Security and Development* 5, no. 1 (2005): 2–21.

[72]Ali Wardak, 'Building a Post-war Justice System in Afghanistan', *Crime, Law, and Social Change* 41, no. 4, (2004): 319–341; Tracy Dexter and Phillippe Ntahombaye, *The Role of Informal Justice Systems in Fostering The Rule of Law in Post-Conflict Situations; The Case of Burundi* (Geneva: Centre for Humanitarian Dialogue, 2005), https://www.files.ethz.ch/isn/26971/CaseofBurundi.pdf.

[73]Kieran McEvoy and Lorna McGregor, eds., *Transitional Justice from Below: Grassroots Activism and the Struggle for Change* (Portland: Hart Publishing, 2008).

[74]Regan, *Light Intervention*.

2015 and 2020. A constitution-making process was undertaken between 2002 and 2004, and by 2005 Bougainvilleans had established the Autonomous Bougainville Government (ABG). However, the ABG had limited capacity, with many public goods continuing to be provided by the Papua New Guinea government or local socio-political institutions at the village and hamlet levels.[75]

There has not been a formal liberal-legal TJ process in Bougainville. This is partly due to pragmatic decisions made during the peace process, as to achieve a permanent ceasefire, and later peace agreement, amnesty and pardons were granted to persons involved in offences related to the conflict.[76] This was seen as necessary to encourage them to participate in weapons disposal, particularly as the peace agreement left the political status of Bougainville open. Bougainvilleans were 'generally supportive' of the amnesty and pardons, but there was no consensus on how to deal with crimes that occurred during the conflict.[77] Several Bougainvillean CSOs called for the amnesties to be conditional on a truth and reconciliation process involving 'public recognition of wrongs done and forgiveness.'[78] Bougainvilleans more generally expressed mixed views; some called for a truth and reconciliation commission to tell 'the story of what happened,' others favoured customary reconciliation.[79] Ultimately, as several Bougainvillean constitution-makers claimed that a truth and reconciliation commission would be 'contrary to custom' and could inhibit weapons disposal,[80] the amnesty and pardons are reiterated in the Bougainville Constitution. The Constitution recognises that human rights 'issues' occurred during the conflict and requires the ABG to formulate a policy for dealing with them and for effecting reconciliation that utilises Bougainville 'customs and practices.'[81] Accordingly, in 2008 the ABG developed a taskforce to support local reconciliation. In 2009 it created a Ministry of Peace, Reconciliation and Weapons Disposal (later replaced by the Department of Bougainville Peace Agreement Implementation) and in 2012 it adopted a *Peace, Security and Weapons Disposal Strategy* which focuses on encouraging reconciliation guided by local practices.

A major challenge to TJ is that uncivil society groups remain outside the peace process. The most significant is the Me'ekamui, which occupies a large part of Bougainville Island near the Panguna mine. The Me'ekamui was founded by Francis Ona, who led the secessionist Bougainville Revolutionary Army (BRA) during the early years of the conflict. Ona had made a unilateral declaration of independence on behalf of the BRA and its Bougainville Interim Government during the early stages of the war, in May 1990.[82] When the

[75] Joanne Wallis, *Constitution making during State building* (New York: Cambridge University Press, 2014).

[76] *Bougainville Peace Agreement*, between the Papua New Guinea government, BPC, BIPG, BRA and BRF (30 August 2001), cl. 331 and 340(d); Papua New Guinea, *Constitution of the Independent State of Papua New Guinea* (16 September 1975), s. 344.

[77] Bougainville Constitutional Commission, *Report of the Bougainville Constitutional Commission: Report on the Third and Final Draft of the Bougainville Constitution* (Buka: Bougainville Constitutional Commission, 2004), 251.

[78] Sister Loraine Garasu quoted in Pat Howley, *Breaking Spears and Mending Hearts: Peacemakers and Restorative Justice in Bougainville* (London: Zed Books, 2002), 182.

[79] Bougainville Constitutional Commission, *Report of the Bougainville Constitutional Commission*, 252.

[80] Bougainville Constitutional Commission, *Discussion of Recommendations: Minutes of Full BCC Meetings, Friday 15 November to Monday 9 December* (Buka: Bougainville Constitutional Commission, 2002), 114–115.

[81] *The Constitution of the Autonomous Region of Bougainville* (2004), s. 187 and Sch. 6.1 and 6.2, s.187.

[82] Francis Ona, on behalf of the Interim government of the Republic of Bougainville, *REQUEST FOR RECOGNITION OF BOUGAINVILLE AS AN INDEPENDENT REPUBLIC*, letter to diplomatic missions in Port Moresby and foreign governments, enclosing the 'Declaration of Independence of the Republic of Bougainville', 16 May 1990. This declaration was later annulled by the *Honiara Declaration on Peace, Reconciliation and Rehabilitation on Bougainville*, between the government of Papua New Guinea and the BIG/BRA, 23 January 1991.

peace process gained momentum during the mid-1990s, Ona opposed it on the basis that his unilateral declaration stood. Consequently, he opposed the deployment of a multinational Truce Monitoring Group in 1997, and set-up armed roadblocks around a 'no-go zone' that included between five and ten percent of the Bougainville population. Ona later declared that this no-go zone was the independent 'Republic of Me'ekamui',[83] and the ten to fifteen percent of the BRA who remained loyal to him became known as the Me'ekamui Defence Force (MDF).

The Me'ekamui can be considered an uncivil society group because it engaged in unruly behaviour that challenged the peace process. Although Ona and his supporters did not actively try to derail the peace process, they maintained their roadblocks, the most important of which was at Morgan Junction on Bougainville Island, which constituted a serious limitation on freedom of movement, particularly for those in the south. After the ABG was formed in 2005, MDF members continued to man armed roadblocks, which meant the ABG did not exercise authority over the entire territory of Bougainville. However, the Me'ekamui were more than an armed group; the no-go zone was effectively running as a rival to the ABG, as it had its own institutions of government and dispute resolution, and security force. Although the ABG recognises and incorporates a significant number of local socio-political practices and institutions, the Me'ekamui claimed that its governance institutions were more firmly based in local tradition and custom.[84] This illustrates how, when state institutions are fragile, illegitimate or absent and liberal democracy is not consolidated, uncivil society groups are likely to emerge to challenge both the state and peace.

Ona's death in July 2005 created space for increasingly open discussion amongst the Me'ekamui people about the need to engage with the peace process, access ABG services and allow freedom of movement. Consequently, more Me'ekamui people joined in the peace process, including standing as candidates and voting in ABG elections. Two factions then emerged within the Me'ekamui leadership: the 'Original Me'ekamui Government' (OMG) led by Ona 'loyalist' Chris Uma; and the 'Me'ekamui Government of Unity' (MGU) led by 'dissidents' such as Philip Miriori. In 2006 the MGU opened a dialogue with the ABG. In August 2007 these talks culminated in the *Panguna Communiqué*, in which the MGU agreed that an administration would be established under the joint authority of the ABG and the MGU. This saw the MGU leadership, and much of the population of the no-go zone, 'effectively agree to join the peace process'.[85] A Panguna district administration office was then opened in late-2007. The MGU then formed a political party and fielded two candidates in the 2008 Presidential by-election. More people from the no-go zone were able to participate in the 2008 election, with the Morgan Junction roadblock opened to allow electoral officers to reach more of the area. As the capacity of the ABG developed, it became more attractive for Me'ekamui members to engage with it, rather than only with their rival 'government'.

As the legitimacy and effectiveness of the ABG increased, in late 2008 attempts to open the Me'ekamui no-go zone increased when the new ABG President James Tanis's reconciliation efforts culminated in the February 2009 *Panguna Meeting Resolution* between the ABG, MGU, Panguna landowners, chiefs, women's and youth leaders, and former

[83]'Me'ekamui' is similar to 'sacred land' in the Nasioi language of central Bougainville.
[84]Wallis, *Constitution Making During State Building.*
[85]Regan, *Light Intervention*, 115.

combatants. The Resolution recorded their agreement to advance reconciliation and to form new landowners' associations to negotiate re-opening the Panguna mine. MDF elements associated with the MGU and the OMG also began developing a weapons disposal program in late 2009.[86] In March 2010 detailed discussions occurred between the OMG, the MGU and the ABG, and culminated in a Memorandum of Understanding in which all three entities agreed to continue discussions regarding reopening the mine, establish local government in the no-go zone and advance reconciliation and weapons disposal. While the Memorandum involved 'little more than a commitment to continue talking' it was the first time that the three groups had met and, most significantly, the first time that Uma and the OMG 'effectively appeared to be entering into the peace process, even if only tentatively'.[87] Indeed, many followers of the OMG participated in the 2010 ABG election.

However, hard-line Ona loyalists continue to man the Morgan Junction roadblock, hampering the ABG's ability to penetrate some parts of the no-go zone. Despite these efforts, the return of ABG services has received such widespread support within the no-go zone that it has become untenable to entirely prevent ABG officers from entering. The men running the roadblock are also under increased pressure from MGU and OMG leaders, who held a customary reconciliation ceremony in April 2011 that was witnessed by ABG representatives, after which they pledged to work together to advance weapons disposal and the return of ABG services to the no-go zone. The OMG has since reiterated its agreement to work with the ABG and MGU in accordance with the ABG's 2011 *Panguna Peace Building Strategy*, which is intended to promote reconciliation guided by customary local socio-political practices and weapons disposal.

While elements of the Me'ekamui continue to maintain their autonomy from the ABG, significant parts of the Me'ekamui no-gone zone have gradually been incorporated into the ABG, or have at least come to acknowledge its legitimacy.[88] Therefore, while the Me'ekamui remains an uncivil society group, it is now less disruptive to the peace process and has engaged in informal TJ processes via an increasing number of customary reconciliation processes. This suggests that, while state illegitimacy or absence can create space for uncivil society groups to present themselves as alternatives to the state and disrupt peace and TJ processes, once state institutions become better established this can reduce the attractiveness of those groups.

The other prominent uncivil society group to challenge the peace process is led by Noah Musingku, who had operated a 'failed Ponzi scheme' in Papua New Guinea, and had fled to the no-go zone in 2003 to evade arrest.[89] He won Ona's support by promising that he had developed a 'new world economic system' that would provide financial support for the Me'ekamui government. Musingku also used Christianity to bolster his legitimacy, by drawing on Pentecostal 'prosperity theology' to support his claim that he could 'finance the end-time harvest' for his investors.[90]

---

[86]Personal communication from a village chief and prominent traditional peacemaker, 27 January 2011.

[87]Regan, *Light Intervention*, 117.

[88]Anthony J. Regan, 'Bougainville Update', paper presented at the State, Society and Governance in Melanesia Seminar Series, College of Asia and the Pacific, Australian National University, 27 November 2012.

[89]Regan, *Light Intervention*, 117. For Musingku's perspective see: *The Real Story of the Sovereign Nation of Bougainville Islands & the Twin Kingdoms of Papa'ala and Me'ekamui*, June 2012, http://www.ourbougainville.org/.

[90]John Cox, *Financing the End-Time Harvest: Pyramid Schemes and Prosperity Gospels in Papua New Guinea, State, Society and Governance in Melanesia Discussion Paper 2009/5* (Canberra: Australian National University, 2009), 7.

In May 2004 Musingku encouraged Ona to be crowned King of the 'Kingdom of Me'e-kamui', at which time Musingku declared himself 'Prince' of the associated 'Kingdom of Papala'. However, as it became increasingly clear that Musingku was unable to deliver his promised financial windfall, he fell out of Ona's favour in late 2004. Consequently, he retreated to an area near his home village in the south of Bougainville Island, accompanied by several MDF members who formed the basis of his 'Royal Guard'. He then used this guard to attempt to establish roadblocks, with the aim of creating a no-go zone around his 'Kingdom'. Therefore, like the Republic of Me'ekamui, the Kingdom of Papala constitutes an uncivil society group and has stayed largely outside the peace process. Like the Me'ekamui, the Papala is more than an armed group; it runs as a purported rival to the ABG and claims to have governance institutions and even its own 'currency'.

Musingku and his Papala supporters also engage in uncivil behaviour which has challenged the peace process and spurred the creation of other uncivil society groups. In 2006, local communities perceived that Musingku and his supporters were such a serious threat to peace and stability that a group of ex-combatants formed the Bougainville Freedom Fighters (BFF) to counterbalance them. Up to ten other armed groups also emerged for this purpose. There were several reported incidents of violence between the BFF and Musingku's guard. The presence of so many armed groups also led to local tensions, many of which arose from unresolved conflict, land disputes and the scarcity of economic opportunities.[91] These tensions were exacerbated by the fact that the ABG had a limited role in the south, largely as a result of the Me'ekamui Morgan Junction roadblock.[92] From 2005 to 2008 these tensions boiled over into other armed roadblocks and open conflict, resulting in up to 60 deaths.

The ABG attempted to reconcile with Musingku and held peace talks with him in September 2006, which resulted in a Memorandum of Understanding that provided for government services to be returned to the Papala no-go zone. As with the Me'ekamui, the increased legitimacy and effectiveness of the ABG made it harder for Musingku to offer the Papala as a comprehensive alternative. Enhanced efforts at promoting local reconciliation between the other armed groups then began in late 2007. As the capacity and legitimacy of the ABG increased, these efforts delivered results from mid-2008, and leaders of several armed groups began to exercise restraint and explore ways to end the conflict.[93] However, while the Me'ekamui have continued to expand their engagement with the ABG, Musingku has managed to preserve a significant amount of influence over the small area he claims to control. Although Musingku is generally regarded as a fraud by educated Bougainvilleans, his clever utilisation of modern technology, local custom and Christian principles has attracted support amongst some villagers, for whom the ABG and the liberal democratic governance it promises remain distant and difficult to understand. Therefore,

[91]Raymond Masono, Acting Chief Administrator, Bougainville Administration, speaking at 'Building Sustainable Peace in Bougainville Conference', Hutjena Secondary School, Buka, 13 June 2007; Rose Pihei, John Bosco and Jobson Misang, speaking at 'South Bougainville 2005–2008: Local Conflict, Reconciliation, Weapons Disposal and Peace-building', State, Society and Governance in Melanesia seminar, Australian National University, Canberra, 25 November 2008, http://asiapacific.anu.edu.au/news-events/podcasts/south-bougainville-2005-2008-conflict-reconciliation-disarmament-and-peace#.W2WXCtlzZEY.

[92]Regan, *Light Intervention*, 124.

[93]Interview with a former BRA commander and member of the ABG, 2 November 2010; personal communication from an international academic, 24 January 2011.

Musingku and his guard continue to operate as an uncivil society group, disrupting the peace process and remaining largely outside the ABG's attempt to foster TJ via customary reconciliations.

Uncivil society in Timor-Leste

As in Bougainville, uncivil society groups that have grown out of personal grievances and competing accounts of history have disrupted peacebuilding and TJ in Timor-Leste. After the Portuguese withdrew from Timor-Leste in 1974, a group of Timorese leaders declared independence in November 1975. In December 1975, Indonesia invaded the territory and occupied it for 24 years. Various Timorese groups opposed the occupation, which culminated in the Timorese people being given the opportunity to vote on their political future in a United Nations-run referendum in August 1999. An overwhelming majority opted for independence (78.5 percent), rather than autonomy within Indonesia (21.5 percent). Once the result of the vote was announced the Indonesian military and their supporting Timorese militias engaged in a scorched earth campaign. An Australian-led intervention force stabilised the territory, and the United Nations Transitional Administration in East Timor (UNTAET) built the new state. Although Timor-Leste (re)gained its independence in May 2002, for the first decade after independence state institutions struggled to establish either their legitimacy or effectiveness. This meant that the United Nations continued to maintain a sizeable presence and provide several public goods, as did local socio-political institutions at the village and hamlet levels.[94]

In Timor-Leste formal liberal-legal TJ mechanisms have included Special Panels for Serious Crimes[95] which were established under UNTAET and continued after independence.[96] The Panels had moderate success, primarily involving plea-bargained convictions against low-level Timorese militia members, before they were terminated in May 2005.[97] The accompanying Ad Hoc Human Rights Court for Timor-Leste in Indonesia was 'manifestly inadequate' and a Commission of Experts recommended (fruitlessly) that the UN Security Council create an international criminal tribunal.[98] While a Serious Crime Investigation Team was established under the UN mission in 2006,[99] it only had the power to investigate crimes and make recommendations to the Office of the Prosecutor General. It ceased operation without completing its investigations when the UN mission withdrew at the end of 2012. There have been some attempts to continue prosecutions within the Office of the Prosecutor General,[100] but as the Office is vulnerable to government

---

[94] Wallis, *Constitution Making.*

[95] 'Serious' crimes were defined as including: genocide; crimes against humanity; war crimes; and certain domestic crimes of torture, murder and sexual offences. These crimes must have occurred between 1 January and 25 October 1999. UNTAET Regulation No. 2000/15, *On the Establishment of Panels with Exclusive Jurisdiction over Serious Criminal Offences*, UN Doc. UNTAET/REG/2000/15, 6 June 2000.

[96] *Constitution of the Democratic Republic of Timor-Leste* (2002), s. 163(1).

[97] John Braithwaite, Hilary Charlesworth, and Aderito Soares, *Networked Governance of Freedom and Tyranny: Peace in Timor-Leste* (Canberra: ANU E-Press, 2012).

[98] UN, *Report to the Secretary-General of the Commission of Experts to review the Prosecution of Serious Violations of Human Rights in Timor-Leste (then East Timor) in 1999*, 26 May 2005, Annex II to *Letter dated 24 June 2005 from the Secretary-General addressed to the President of the Security Council*, UN Doc. S/2005/458, 15 July 2005.

[99] UN Security Council S/Res/1704, *On the Situation in Timor-Leste*, 25 August 2006.

[100] Independent Comprehensive Needs Assessment Team, *The Justice System of Timor-Leste: An Independent Comprehensive Needs Assessment* (Dili: Independent Comprehensive Needs Assessment Team, 2009); UN, *Report of the Security Council mission to Timor-Leste 3–6 November 2012*, UN Doc. S/2012/889, 28 November 2012.

influence this has affected its willingness to pursue them. Accordingly, an alliance of CSOs has called for UN support to continue the prosecution of serious crimes.[101]

Reconciliation efforts have focused on the *Comissão de Acolhimento, Verdade e Reconciliacao* (CAVR, Commission for Reception, Truth and Reconciliation), which was established in June 2001.[102] The CAVR was mandated to establish the truth about human rights violations that took place before, during and in the aftermath of the Indonesian occupation, and to facilitate reconciliation between victims and offenders at a community and national level. The CAVR is widely considered to have been a success, particularly because it took a non-partisan approach by finding that human rights abuses were committed by both pro-integration and pro-independence supporters.[103]

While there was widespread support amongst Timorese people for independence and the process of building the Timor-Leste state, there were (and remain) uncivil society groups who opposed the state-building process and who consequently stayed outside the TJ process and challenge the legitimacy of state institutions. These uncivil society groups include the *Conselho Popular de Defesa da República Democrática de Timor Leste* (CPD-RDTL, Council for the Popular Defense of the Democratic Republic of Timor-Leste), *Sagrada Familia* (Sacred Family), Colimau 2000 and martial arts clubs.

The most prominent example is CPD-RDTL, which was the 'best organised and structured' uncivil society group during the state-building process and first ten years of independence.[104] The membership of CPD-RDTL consisted of veterans of the military resistance to Indonesian occupation who thought that their contribution had been inadequately recognised, former Indonesian militia members and pro-integrationist activists,[105] and poor Timorese who felt marginalised during the state-building process and in independent Timor-Leste.[106] When it was founded in 1999, CPD-RDTL claimed 6,600 members and was led by Commander Olo Gari Aswain, a former resistance fighter who had led a failed coup attempt in 1984 to unseat independence hero Xanana Gusmao as the leader of the military resistance. CPD-RDTL refused to participate in the state-building process, based on its claim that certain Timorese leaders had already made a unilateral declaration of independence in 1975.[107]

After independence in 2002, CPD-RDTL continued to act as an uncivil society group by hardening its opposition to the Timor-Leste government, arguing that it was unrepresentative because it consisted of several leaders who had spent the Indonesian occupation in exile. CPD-RDTL was more than an armed group; as state institutions took several years to penetrate rural Timor-Leste, in the first few years after independence CPD-RDTL attempted

[101]Sisto do Santos, *Timor-Leste National Alliance for an International Tribunal Letter to UNSG*, 14 August 2012, http://easttimorlegal.blogspot.com.au/2012/08/timor-leste-national-alliance-for.html; Timor-Leste National Alliance for an International Tribunal, *An Open letter in response to the CTF report*, 18 July 2008, http://etan.org/news/2008/07anti.htm.

[102]UNTAET Regulation No. 2001/10, *On the Establishment of a Commission for Reception, Truth and Reconciliation in East Timor*, UN Doc. UNTAET/REG/2001/10, 13 July 2001, extended by *Law No. 13/2004* and *Law No. 11/2005.*

[103]CAVR, *Chega!*

[104]James Scambary, *A Survey of Gangs and Youth Groups in Dili, Timor-Leste*, report commissioned by Australia's Agency for International Development, AusAID, 15 September 2006, http://www.etan.org/etanpdf/2006/Report_Youth_Gangs_in_Dili.pdf.

[105]Damien Kingsbury, *East Timor: The Price of Liberty* (New York: Palgrave MacMillan, 2009), 57.

[106]Jill Jolliffe, 'Psychological Healing as a Prerequisite to Good Governance in East Timor', in *Democratic Governance in Timor-Leste: Reconciling the local and the national*, ed. David Mearns (Darwin: Charles Darwin University Press, 2008), 14.

[107]UN, *Progress Report of the Secretary-General on the United Nations Transitional Administration in East Timor*, UN Security Council, UN Doc. S/2001/719, 24 July 2001; Sara Niner, *Xanana: Leader of the Struggle for Independent Timor-Leste* (North Melbourne: Australian Scholarly Publishing Pty Ltd, 2009).

to act as a rival to the government, flying its own flag, collecting self-described 'taxes' and issuing its own 'identity cards'.[108] CPD-RDTL members also began to wear military uniforms, and are said to have engaged in unruly behaviour such as sometimes violent anti-government protests and criminal activity. Concerns about CPD-RDTL peaked in 2012, when about 800 of its members occupied an area in the southern Manufahi district.[109] These CPD-RDTL members are said to have slaughtered residents' animals and attempted to farm their lands. In response to criticism, CPD-RDTL claimed that it was setting-up a national farming cooperative to reduce Timor-Leste's dependence on food imports.[110]

As the Timor-Leste government improved its capacity and its reach into rural areas it attempted to engage and reconcile with CPD-RDTL. However, in 2013 it lost its patience with the group. Then Prime Minister Xanana Gusmao threatened to arrest CPD-RDTL members if they continued to wear military uniforms or fly an 'unconstitutional flag' and to dismiss any public servants found involved in the group.[111] Concerned about the destabilising effect of CPD-RDTL's presence, in March 2013 the strengthened government deployed police to disperse the group and return them to their home districts. As CPD-RDTL members continued to wear uniforms and to contest the legitimacy of the state, in March 2014 the government declared CPD-RDTL a proscribed organisation and banned its members from wearing military uniforms.[112] The government also authorised the police to act to quell its activities. CPD-RDTL leader Antonio Ai-Tahan was briefly put under house arrest after surrendering to police.[113]

Despite being declared illegal, CPD-RDTL is still said to function. More significantly, its uncivil activities have been continued, and expanded, by its affiliate, *Sagrada Familia*. *Sagrada Familia* was founded in 1989 during the resistance to Indonesian occupation, and once had up to 5,000 supporters.[114] *Sagrada Familia* draws on many of the same members as CPD-RDTL, but combines CPD-RDTL's rejection of the current Timor-Leste state with quasi-religious beliefs that syncretise the dominant organised religion, Catholicism, with local religious beliefs, *lulik*. *Sagrada Familia* is led by former resistance fighter Cornelio da Conceição Gama (known by his *nom de guerre,* L7) and its members are drawn from former resistance fighters and unemployed youths.[115]

Although *Sagrada Familia* nominally rejects the legitimacy of the government, as the government became more established and legitimate, it began to engage with it. In

---

[108]Jill Jolliffe, 'Timorese Police Mimic Violence of Ex-masters', *Asia Times*, January 8, 2004, cited in Andrea Katalin Molnar, *Timor Leste: Politics, history, and culture* (Abingdon: Routledge, 2009), 110.

[109]'CPD-RDTL continues to be a thorn in the side of the Timor-Leste Government', *East Timor Law & Justice Bulletin*, December 15, 2012, http://www.easttimorlawandjusticebulletin.com/2012/12/cpd-rdtl-continues-to-be-thorn-in-side.html.

[110]'CPD-RDTL accused of slaughterning the people's livestock in Fatuberliu, Defence Force Chief warns against protests against the State', *East Timor Law & Justice Bulletin*, November 23, 2012, http://www.easttimorlawandjusticebulletin.com/2012/11/cpd-rdtl-accused-of-slaughtering.html.

[111]'Prime Minister Gusmao threatens to wring the necks of CPD-RDTL dissidents like chickens and sack public servants involved in the group', *East Timor Law & Justice Bulletin*, April 18, 2013, http://www.easttimorlawandjusticebulletin.com/2013/04/prime-minister-gusmao-threatens-to.html.

[112]Fundasaun Mahein, 'Rule of Law or Rule of the Deal in Timor-Leste?', 7 March 2014, http://www.fundasaunmahein.org/2014/03/07/rule-of-law-or-rule-of-the-deal-in-timor-leste/; Democratic Republic of Timor-Leste, *Resolution of the National Parliament, Rejecting attempts at instability and threats to the rule of law*, 4 March 2014, http://www.jornal.gov.tl/public/docs/2014/serie_1/serie1_no9.pdf.

[113]'Ex-Guerillas Threaten Political Stability in East Timor', *Global Voices*, April 1, 2014, https://globalvoices.org/2014/04/01/ex-guerrillas-threaten-political-stability-in-east-timor/#.

[114]Geoffrey C. Gunn, *Historical Dictionary of East Timor* (Lanham: The Scarecrow Press, 2011).

[115]Scambary, *A Survey of Gangs and Youth Groups in Dili.*

2005 L7 created a political party, *Uniao Nacional Democratica de Resistencia Timorense* (UNDERTIM, Democratic National Union of the Timorese Resistance) and he was elected to parliament in 2007. L7 lost his seat at the 2012 elections and in 2015 he left UNDERTIM and joined the *Partidu Libertasaun Popular* (PLP, Popular Liberation Party). After he was returned to parliament in the 2017 elections, he was appointed to the Security Council of Timor-Leste. Following the 2018 elections, the PLP joined the ruling *Alianca para Mudanca e Progresso* (AMP, Alliance for Change and Progress) coalition government, with L7 as its leader.

Despite the fact that L7 has been incorporated into the Timor-Leste government, he retains strong uncivil society links. His brother, Paulino Gama (known by his *nom de guerre,* Mauk Moruk), returned to Timor-Leste from the Netherlands in 2013. Mauk Moruk had also participated in the failed 1984 coup against Gusmao, after which he had surrendered to Indonesian authorities and gone into exile. Upon his return he created another uncivil society group, the *Konselho Revolucionário Maubere* (KRM, Revolutionary Council of Maubere), which opposed the government, particularly the policies of then Prime Minister Gusmao.[116] Mauk Moruk and KRM gained supporters because they tapped into widespread frustration with the government's performance, particularly the slow and uneven rate of economic development in Timor-Leste.[117] Like CPD-RDTL, KRM members began to wear military uniforms and to instigate anti-government protests. Consequently, the same government resolution that proscribed CPD-RDTL proscribed KRM. In 2014, KRM began to conduct armed attacks on police. In response, the government mounted a joint police-military operation against KRM, during which Mauk Moruk was killed in August 2015. While Mauk Moruk's death effectively resolved the challenge posed by KRM, it had implications for the rule of law in Timor-Leste, with claims that the killing or Mauk Moruk (and others) was unlawful and that the operation against the KRM involved the excessive use of force and arbitrary arrests.[118]

Conclusion

The Bougainville and Timor-Leste cases demonstrate that conventional assumptions about the nature, function and ideology of CSOs and their role in peacebuilding and TJ provide only partial insights into 'actually existing' civil and uncivil society groups in conflict-affected societies.[119] While conventional accounts, which are predominantly western and based in liberalism, assume that CSOs will demonstrate civil behaviour and favour liberal democracy and international human rights norms, in conflict-affected societies uncivil society groups may challenge these assumptions. Indeed, in these contexts groups may broadly resemble typical CSOs when they first emerge, but gradually evolve into uncivil society groups. These uncivil society groups may also be armed, but

[116]'Former East Timor guerrilla leader and opposition figure Mauk Moruk killed in security operation, government says', *Sydney Morning Herald*, August 10, 2015, http://www.abc.net.au/news/2015-08-09/former-east-timor-guerrilla-leader-mauk-moruk-killed/6684058.

[117]Anna Powles and Jose KL Sousa Santos, 'Xanana Gusmao-Mauk Moruk: Timor struggles with its past and future', *The Interpreter*, December 5, 2013, https://www.lowyinstitute.org/the-interpreter/xanana-gusmao-mauk-moruk-timor-struggles-its-past-and-future?collcc=2682660872.

[118]US State Department, *Timor-Leste 2015 Human Rights Report*, https://www.state.gov/documents/organization/253017.pdf; Amnesty International, *Timor-Leste: Still No Justice for Past Human Rights Violations, Amnesty International Submission to the UN Universal Periodic Review*, 2016, https://www.amnesty.org/download/Documents/ASA5745132016ENGLISH.pdf.

[119]Mahmood Mamdani, *Citizen and Subject* (Kampala: Fountain Publishers, 1996), 1.

what distinguishes them from criminal or violent gangs is that they follow their own 'subversive ruliness' in pursuit of a political agenda, typically focused on socio-economic development rather than civil–political rights.[120] Moreover, while these uncivil society groups may be 'exclusive or discriminatory', they may also 'turn out to be more enduring and better organised than their more progressive counterparts' from civil society.[121] This reveals the 'fundamental ethnocentricity' of conventional accounts,[122] and has led some scholars to argue that the term 'civil society' is useless in non-western contexts.[123] However, others argue that it does have value, and that the solution is to analyse both civil and uncivil society in their specific contexts.[124] This suggests that understandings of what constitutes 'civil' society may differ across conflict-affected societies, and that what liberals describe as 'uncivil' society may, in context, be 'more authentic representatives of civil society'.[125] These so-called uncivil society groups would not necessarily be regarded as internationally legitimate, but they may nevertheless have strong local legitimacy. Consequently, to uncover more contextualised understandings of justice and to promote locally legitimate and effective TJ, and peace more broadly, it will be necessary to engage with both CSOs and uncivil society groups.[126] This engagement will need to challenge both assumptions about the universality of international human rights, particularly their emphasis on civil–political rights, and assumptions about its primacy in TJ practice.

A comparison of the Bougainville and Timor-Leste case studies offers specific lessons for the ways in which the peacebuilding and TJ literature conceives the role that uncivil society groups do, and should, play in peacebuilding and TJ. These lessons are most relevant to other cases from the Pacific Islands, and particularly the cultural area of Melanesia, which share strong similarities with Bougainville and Timor-Leste, but they are also suggestive for other conflict-affected societies where state institutions are weak and liberal democracy is not consolidated.

First, they demonstrate that, in conflict-affected societies in which state institutions are fragile, illegitimate or absent and liberal democracy is not consolidated, there is space for uncivil society groups to emerge to challenge both the state and peace by creating rival governance and security institutions. This illustrates the limitations of the statist nature of conventional understandings of liberal peacebuilding, which assumes the presence of a legitimate state, a separation between state institutions and society, and on a population that identifies as citizens. The Bougainville and Timor-Leste cases reveal that uncivil society groups may either reject entirely the legitimacy of state institutions or engage with them only in selective ways. Consequently, there is no distinction between civil

[120]Alex Shankland, 'OccupyLSX, unruly politics and subversive ruliness', *OpenDemocracyUK*, January 19, 2012, https://www.opendemocracy.net/ourkingdom/alex-shankland/occupylsx-unruly-politics-and-subversive-ruliness.
[121]Gready and Robins, 'Rethinking Civil Society', 970.
[122]Hann, 'Introduction', 1; John L. Comaroff and Jean Comaroff, *Civil Society and the Political Imagination in Africa: Critical Perspectives* (Chicago: The University of Chicago Press, 1999).
[123]Adam B. Seligman, *The Idea of Civil Society* (Princeton: Princeton University Press, 1992).
[124]David Lewis, *Civil Society in non-Western Contexts: Reflections on the 'Usefulness' of a Concept* (Civil Society Working Paper series 13, Centre for Civil Society, London School of Economics and Political Science, London, UK, 2001); Hann, 'Introduction'; Renee Jeffery, Lia Kent, and Joanne Wallis, 'Reconceiving the Roles of Religious Civil Society Organisations in Transitional Justice: Evidence from the Solomon Islands, Timor-Leste and Bougainville', *International Journal of Transitional Justice* 11, no. 3 (2017): 378–399.
[125]Kopecky, 'Civil Society, Uncivil Society', 4.
[126]Foley, 'Cautionary Tales'; Nicholas R. Micinski, 'NGO Frequent Flyers: Youth Organisations and the Undermining of Reconciliation in Bosnia and Herzegovina', *Journal of Peacebuilding & Development* 11, no. 1 (2016): 99–104.

society and the state, particularly as Me'ekamui and Papala groups deliver public goods typically expected to be provided by the state. This has challenged the ability of their members to participate in the formation of a social contract with broader society in the form understood by liberalism. This suggests that, while some of the TJ literature presents CSOs as an effective alternative to government in conflict-affected societies, this may have perverse consequences, as it may undermine the creation or strengthening of the liberal-legal state institutions on which many formal TJ processes rely. It also highlights the need for future research to clarify definitional boundaries, particularly to consider when an uncivil society group operating as a rival to the state effectively becomes a proto-state.

However, the cases also demonstrate that, when state institutions become better established and more legitimate it becomes increasingly difficult for uncivil society groups to present themselves as attractive alternatives to the state, which can encourage their engagement with the state and participation in peace and TJ processes. As the ABG has improved its legitimacy and effectiveness in Bougainville both the Me'ekamui and Papala have increasingly engaged with it and the peace process. In Timor-Leste, as the government became more entrenched CPD-RDTL similarly found it difficult to oppose it, and although *Sagrada Familia* purportedly opposes the government, its leader has formally engaged with it as a member of parliament.

Second, in both cases the uncivil society groups analysed have relied on several sources of legitimacy to generate support. The Me'ekamui and the CPD-RDTL have relied on partial interpretations of history (in these cases, previous unilateral declarations of independence) to challenge the legitimacy of the peace processes. The Papala and *Sagrada Familia* have relied on religious imagery to justify their claims to oppose state institutions and stay outside the peace and TJ processes. Religious imagery resonates strongly in both Bougainville and Timor-Leste, where rates of church attendance are high and the churches (particularly the Catholic Church) played a significant role in assisting their populations during their respective self-determination conflicts and in delivering public goods since. Similarly, for legitimacy all the uncivil society groups analysed have claimed to reflect local socio-political practices, which remain the most important source of everyday social and political ordering in Bougainville and Timor-Leste. They have also all relied for legitimacy on claims that they are advancing socio-economic development by providing public goods and, to differing extents, offering financial rewards to their followers, which is persuasive in the primarily subsistence barter economies of Bougainville and Timor-Leste. None of these sources of legitimacy reflect liberal peace values, including civil–political rights, which highlights the need during peacebuilding and TJ processes for nuanced and context-specific understandings of the way in which cultural, social and political power and legitimacy are understood and distributed in conflict-affected societies.

Third, the membership of the Me'ekamui and Papala in Bougainville, and CPD-RDTL and *Sagrada Familia* in Timor-Leste, consists in large part of ex-combatants. This highlights the importance of widespread disarmament, demobilisation and reintegration as a key component to peacebuilding and a pre-requisite to TJ processes, to reduce the likelihood that ex-combatants are attracted to such groups. It also highlights another definitional boundary that needs clarification, concerning when an armed uncivil society group gradually sheds its broader functions and operates primarily as a party to a conflict.

The membership of the uncivil society groups in question also consists of people who felt that they had been left out of the peace process or had gained few benefits from peace. This demonstrates the importance of trying to minimise the perception of exclusion from peace processes, particularly avoiding the perception that certain groups are 'second class' to others, depending on which side of the conflict they supported.[127] It also reiterates the emphasis placed on socio-economic development over civil–political rights in many conflict-affected societies and consequently highlights the importance of attempting to ensure that any peace dividend is equitably distributed amongst society.

Fourth, both cases demonstrate the influential role that individuals, their unresolved personal grievances and their competition for political power, can play in facilitating the emergence of uncivil society groups. In Bougainville tensions between Francis Ona and other Bougainvillean leaders regarding the conduct of the war and peace process encouraged Ona to retreat to the Me'ekamui no-go zone. Similarly, in Timor-Leste, tensions between on the one hand, Olo Gari Aswain, L7 and Mauk Moruk, and on the other hand, Xanana Gusmao and his supporters, stemming from the failed 1984 coup, as well as Gusmao's grip on political power since independence, have contributed to the formation of CPD-RDTL, *Sagrada Familia* and KRM. This highlights that more attention needs to be paid to the way in which history shapes the distribution and power in conflict-affected societies. It also suggests that efforts need to be put into encouraging power-sharing, or at least personal reconciliation between leaders, during peacebuilding and TJ processes.

Finally, the Bougainville and Timor-Leste cases underscore the need for more sensitivity to everyday socio-political practices and institutions and local historical, cultural, social and political contexts during peacebuilding and TJ.[128] While this may reveal uncivil society groups that subvert liberal peacebuilding and liberal-legal TJ processes, they may be legitimate according to local socio-political practices and norms. Engaging with these uncivil society groups may also necessitate utilising local justice mechanisms, such as customary reconciliation, as has occurred in Bougainville, which may violate international human rights norms, but be necessary to bring uncivil society groups into the peace process.[129] Ultimately, if peacebuilding and TJ processes are to achieve their aims of justice and enduring peace, they will need to reach an entire conflict-affected society whether civil or uncivil.

Acknowledgements

I thank the anonymous referees and the journal editorial team for their comments and suggestions. I also thank Alex Shankland for sharing the work of he and his colleagues on 'unruly politics'. This

[127]Interview with a Timorese intellectual, 12 May 2010.

[128]Lia Kent, 'Engaging with 'The Everyday': Towards a More Dynamic Conception of Hybrid Transitional Justice', in *Hybridity on the Ground in Peacebuilding and Development: Critical Conversations*, ed. Joanne Wallis, et al. (Canberra: ANU Press, 2018), pp. 145–161; Sally Engle Merry, *Human Rights and Gender Violence: Translating International Law into Local Justice* (Chicago: The University of Chicago Press, 2006).

[129]Joanne Wallis, Renee Jeffery, and Lia Kent, 'Political Reconciliation in Timor Leste, Solomon Islands and Bougainville: The Dark Side of Hybridity', *Australian Journal of International Affairs* 70, no. 2 (2016): 159–178.

article forms part of a broader project, Political Reconciliation in the Asia-Pacific, which was funded by ARC DP 140102388. As part of that project, some of the material in this article was presented at a workshop on 'Civil Society and Transitional Justice in Asia and the Pacific' that I co-organised with Lia Kent at the Australian National University on 29–30 September 2016.

Disclosure statement

No potential conflict of interest was reported by the author.

Funding

This work was supported by Australian Research Council [grant number DP140102388 The impact of political reconciliation].

Transitional justice and the spaces of memory activism in Timor-Leste and Aceh

Lia Kent

ABSTRACT
Taking Timor-Leste and Aceh, Indonesia, as case studies, this article examines the spaces that are imagined and created by activist-led commemorations of conflict-related violence. Focusing on recent commemorations of the Liquica Church Massacre in Timor-Leste and Simpang KKA in Aceh, it uncovers how these memory spaces are shaped and constrained by the interplay between the globally circulating discourse of transitional justice and the power dynamics resulting from the respective peace settlements. At the same time, it posits that these examples of memory activism contain creative possibilities for encouraging public debate and democratic participation, and for locally grounded forms of mourning. This is due to the multiple, dynamic, relational, spaces that emerge from the embodied encounters of those present at the commemorations.

Introduction

At a busy intersection in Lloksamewe, North Aceh, a small group gathers on 3 May each year to commemorate the killings that took place near the *Kertas Kraft Aceh* (KKA) pulp and paper mill in 1999. Victims' families, Acehnese human rights activists, and others, including students, congregate at a monument at the site of the killings. They hold handmade placards and signs that call for the investigation and prosecution of members of the Indonesian military (*Tentara Nasional Indonesia*/TNI) thought to be responsible for the killings.

In Liquica, a small town in Timor-Leste not far from the capital, Dili, people gather each year on 6 April to mark the anniversary of the 1999 Liquica church massacre. Victims' families and Dili-based human rights activists gather at the Liquica church for a Catholic mass. The mass is followed by a press conference, during which families and activists demand prosecutions of members of the TNI, Indonesian police and the pro-Indonesian *Besih Merah Putih* (Red and White Iron) militia group responsible for the massacre.

After almost 30 years of fighting between the TNI and Gerakan Aceh Merdeka (Free Aceh Movement/GAM), Aceh's conflict came to an end in 2005 with the signing of a Memorandum of Understanding (MoU) in Helsinki. The MoU granted the province an expanded form of autonomy within Indonesia. The 24-year Indonesian occupation of East Timor ended in 1999 with a UN-sponsored referendum on self-determination that ushered in the territory's transition to independent statehood. Despite the very different nature of the peace settlements in Timor-Leste and Aceh, the two commemorations described above appear, at first glance, to be strikingly similar. How might we account for this?

Globalisation has a powerful influence on memory cultures around the globe. The nation-state is no longer the 'natural container, curator and telos' of memory, but is just one among a number of actors and processes influencing memory construction.[1] Even local memorialisation practices appear to be shaped by the globally circulating discourse and practice of transitional justice. United Nations agencies and international NGOs produce a growing number of reports and provide expertise and financing for memory projects and sites in post-conflict societies. These activities are driven by assumptions not only about the importance of remembering for victims' families but also about the contribution that public remembrance can make to the consolidation and strengthening of the post-conflict state.

If globalisation is shaping local memory cultures, is this necessarily a bad thing? In a prominent argument, Daniel Levy and Natan Sznaider celebrate what they see as a 'transition from national to cosmopolitan memory cultures' that has taken place in the aftermath of the Holocaust.[2] Tracing global media representations of the Holocaust and the public remembrance of this event over the last fifty years in Germany, Israel and the USA, they suggest that the Holocaust has become a 'de-contextualized event'[3] that has allowed groups in diverse contexts to frame and articulate their own unique struggles for justice.[4] The transnational circulation of Holocaust narratives has, they argue, helped to unsettle heroic conceptions of national identity in ways that have the potential to challenge traditional understandings of sovereignty and become the 'cultural foundation for global human rights politics'.[5]

Others are more circumspect.[6] In a forceful critique of memorialisation's gradually move from the margins to the centre of the transitional justice framework, Lea David suggests that this has been accompanied by a shift from an 'awareness-oriented duty to remember' to a 'policy-oriented memorialization framework'.[7] This, she argues, is leading to the 'standardisation of memory' and to the problematic prescription of a 'proper' way to remember to societies emerging from conflict.[8] David argues that this has the potential to subsume

---

[1]Chiara De Cesari and Ann Rigney, 'Introduction: Beyond Methodological Nationalism', in *Transitional Justice: Circulation, Articulation, Scales*, ed. Chiara De Cesari and Ann Rigney (Berlin: De Gruyter, 2014), 1.

[2]D. Levy and N. Sznaider, 'Memory Unbound: The Holocaust and the Formation of Cosmopolitan Memory', *European Journal of Social Theory* 5, no. 1 (2002): 88.

[3]Ibid., 97.

[4]D. Levy and N. Sznaider, *The Holocaust and Memory in the Global Age* (Philadelphia, PA: Temple University Press, 2006), 4. See also Laila Amine and Caroline Beschea-Fache, 'Crossroads of Memory: Contexts, Agents, and Processes in a Global Age', *Culture, Theory and Critique* 53, no. 2 (2012): 102.

[5]D. Levy and N. Sznaider, 'Memory Unbound', 88.

[6]E.g. De Cesari and Rigney suggest the globalisation of memory practices has not necessarily displaced nation-state-centric understandings of identity and solidarity but may even have reinforced them. See De Cesari and Rigney, 'Introduction: Beyond Methodological Nationalism'; See also Amine and Beschea-Fache, 'Crossroads of Memory: Contexts, Agents, and Processes in a Global Age', 102; Lucy Bond, 'Intersections or Misdirections? Problematising Crossroads of Memory in the Commemoration of 9/11', *Culture, Theory and Critique* 53, no. 2 (2012): 111–28; Sharon Macdonald, 'Reassembling Nuremberg, Reassembling Heritage', *Journal of Cultural Economy* 2, no. 1–2 (2009): 117–34. Rosanne Kennedy, 'Reparative Transnationalism: The Friction and Fiction of Remembering in Sierra Leone', *Memory Studies* 11, no 3 (2018), 342–54.

[7]Lea David, 'Against Standardization of Memory', *Human Rights Quarterly* 39, no. 2 (2017): 304.

[8]Ibid., 307.

the 'specific histories, political and economic conditions and contexts' of those who have experienced harm.[9]

While acknowledging the value of these debates, the influence of globalisation on local memory cultures is more complex than they suggest. Close attention needs to be paid to the ways in which local actors are not only constrained by – but also navigate, adapt and transform – the power dynamics that result from the interplay between global and local discourses within specific contexts.[10] In this article, I focus on the possibilities and limitations of NGO activist-led commemorations of violence events that took place during the conflicts in Timor-Leste and Aceh. I describe these commemorations as forms of 'memory activism' because those who promote and organise them seek to encourage the public remembrance of a contested past to influence public debate and achieve specific outcomes.[11] A key goal of this article is to introduce a greater focus on space as an analytic category as a contribution to the growing body of literature on memory activism.

Specifically, this article is informed by the work of political geographers – including that of Doreen Massey – which, over the past few decades, has helped to open up thinking about political possibilities that are available when we think of space as *relational*, rather than as a flat surface or a 'container' in which action takes place.[12] Recognising that space is produced, in part, by bodies and the relations between them, opens the possibility that space is constantly being made and remade.[13] This enables an appreciation of the fact that, while space both reflects and reproduces unequal power relations, the potential to transform space, or create alternative spaces of memory, is always present, even if there are always discursive and material constraints upon these possibilities.

In the following sections I provide a brief background to the Timor-Leste and Aceh contexts, noting key similarities and differences, before situating the article within recent geographical scholarship on memory, space and power. I then provide an overview of the emergence of memorialisation as part of the transitional justice framework and consider some of the key, underpinning assumptions associated with this shift. The second part of the paper engages with observations and interview material gleaned during recent fieldwork in Timor-Leste and Aceh.[14] I first describe my observations of the 2017 Simpang KKA commemoration in North Aceh, and the 2018 commemoration of the Liquica Church massacre in Timor-Leste, paying particular attention to the spaces they imagine and create, before discussing key themes emerging from interviews with activists. By engaging both with my observations of the commemorations and the interview material I am able to work not only with activists' discursive accounts but also to interpret the visual, oral and affective and embodied spaces of the commemorations.[15] I conclude by reflecting on how activist-led commemorations in Timor-Leste and Aceh

---

[9]Ibid., 316.

[10]Kennedy, 'Reparative Transnationalism', 342.

[11]See Yifat Gutman, *Memory Activism: Reimagining the Past for the Future of Palestine* (Nashville, TN: Vanderbilt University Press, 2017); Jenny Wustenberg, *Civil Society and Memory in Postwar Germany*, (Cambridge: Cambridge University Press, 2017.)

[12]Doreen Massey, *For Space* (London: Sage, 2005).

[13]Ibid.

[14]This fieldwork was supported by the Australian Research Council under grant number DE:150100857.

[15]See Nicky Gregson and Gillian Rose, 'Taking Butler Elsewhere: Performativities, Spatialities and Subjectivities', *Environment and Planning D: Society and Space* 18, no. 4 (2000): 435. See also Sharon Macdonald, *Memorylands: Heritage and Identity in Europe Today* (Oxon: Routledge, 2013), 79.

are shaped – albeit differently – by transitional justice discourses and local power relations. At the same time, they hold creative possibilities for encouraging public debate and democratic participation, and for locally grounded forms of mourning, due to the multiple, dynamic, spaces that emerge from the embodied encounters of those present.

Timor-Leste and Aceh: similarities and differences

The article is part of a broader research project that examines the diverse ways in which 'non-state' actors, including NGOs, families of the dead, and veterans groups, are promoting the public remembrance of the conflicts that took place Timor-Leste and Aceh.[16] The project involves interviews, informal discussions, the observation of memory practices and an analysis of key documents. I have selected Timor-Leste and Aceh as case studies because, while they present some similarities as regions formerly or currently part of Indonesia, they also contain a number of differences relating to culture, conflict dynamics and socio-political factors, which allow for fruitful contrast. Shared experiences include a recent history of conflict involving armed struggles for national independence from Indonesia that began at roughly the same time. Indonesia invaded East Timor (as it was then known) in 1975, while the conflict in Aceh began in 1976/7.[17] In East Timor, the armed resistance was led by FALINTIL (the armed wing of the political party FRETILIN) and in Aceh, it was led by GAM.

A striking difference concerns the ways in which these conflicts ended and the nature of the ensuing peace agreements. The population of East Timor was given the opportunity to vote on whether to remain part of Indonesia in a UN-sponsored referendum in 1999, in which an overwhelming majority opted for separation. After a post-ballot period marred by a systematic campaign of violence conducted by pro-Indonesian East Timorese militias armed and trained by the TNI, and a two and half year period of United Nations transitional administration, Timor-Leste was recognised as an independent state in 2002.

By contrast, the Memorandum of Understanding (MoU) negotiated between the Government of Indonesia and GAM in Helsinki in 2005 granted an expanded form of autonomy to Aceh as a province within the state of Indonesia. The MoU allowed for the official recognition of Acehnese political parties and was predicated on a significant reduction in Indonesian troops and police, and the decommissioning of GAM weapons.[18] A key impetus for the peace agreement was the 2004 Boxing Day Tsunami, which killed approximately one hundred and sixty-five thousand people and devastated much of the capital, Banda Aceh. Peace talks resumed soon after the disaster and a massive international reconstruction effort was mounted.[19]

Another point of difference is the involvement of the international community in the respective peace processes and the degree to which transitional justice mechanisms were implemented. During the UN transitional administration of East Timor from 1999–2002, the UN assumed full sovereignty over the territory in what was one of the UN's most extensive state-building missions. It established two transitional justice mechanisms,

[16] I use the term 'non-state' in inverted commas because I question the sharp opposition between state and non-state.
[17] I use the term East Timor when referring to the pre-2002 period, and Timor-Leste when referring to the post-2002 period.
[18] Damian Kingsbury, 'A Mechanism to end conflict in Aceh', *Security Challenges* 1, no 1 (2005): 73.
[19] Edward Aspinall, 'Peace without Justice? The Helsinki Peace Process in Aceh', *Report for the Centre for Humanitarian Dialogue*, Geneva 2008.

a serious crimes investigations and prosecutions process and a truth commission (known by its Portuguese acronym CAVR). The Indonesian government established its own *Ad Hoc* human rights court to prosecute cases of serious crimes in its own jurisdiction. Following national independence, the governments of Indonesia and Timor-Leste signalled a new, reconciliatory, approach to addressing the past by establishing a bilateral Truth and Friendship Commission (CTF). Cumulatively these mechanisms have gone some way towards producing official documentation of the violence of the Indonesian occupation. There have, however, been no successful prosecutions of the TNI for East Timor-related violence and few of the recommendations of the CAVR and CTF have been implemented.

By contrast, while Aceh's peace process was monitored by the European Union-led Aceh Monitoring Mission, responsibility for its implementation rested with the Government of Indonesia and GAM. Although several transitional justice mechanisms including a human rights court, a truth commission, and compensation measures were included in the peace agreement, with the exception of the compensation measures, these have not yet been implemented. A key factor is that, despite the collapse of the authoritarian Suharto New Order regime in 1998 and the advent of the *reformasi* (reform) era, military interests continue to be represented in the state's power structures. It was only in 2016, that agreement for a provincially mandated Commission for Truth and Reconciliation (*Komisi Kebenaran dan Rekonsiliasi*, or KKR) in Aceh was reached after the Constitutional Court had declared the national TRC law unconstitutional in 2006. These contrasts raise interesting questions about whether the nature of the respective peace settlements in Timor-Leste and Aceh influences the shape, tenor and the stakes of NGO-led memory activism.

A final point of contrast concerns religious identification. The majority of Acehnese strongly identify as Islamic, while most East Timorese are self-identified Catholics. However, beyond formal religious identification, for both East Timorese and Acehnese, customary beliefs and practices (referred to as *adat*), and kinship relations, remain pivotal to the regulation of social life, and to understandings of identity, authority and the power of the dead.

Memory, space and power in Timor-Leste and Aceh

While space and place have always been central concepts in studies of social memory, in the past two decades there has been a profound shift in the ways these concepts are understood. Scholars increasingly view space not as a container or a static background but as socially constructed.[20] While not denying that there is a materiality to space, there is a growing recognition of its dynamic aspects and the extent to which it is brought into being by ideas, experiences, practices and performances.[21] For Doreen Massey, who has been a powerful influence in this field, space is constituted through the interactions and relations between bodies, and is always under construction.[22] This is the case not only for spaces that are relatively small-scale, but also for the space of

[20]Doreen Massey, 'Geographies of Responsibility', *Geografiska Annaler. Series B, Human Geography* 86, no. 1 (2004): 5–18; Phil Hubbard and Rob Kitchin, 'Introduction: Why Key Thinkers?', in *Key Thinkers on Space and Place*, ed. Phil Hubbard and Rob Kitchin (London: Sage, 2011), 1–17.

[21]Daniel Neep, 'State-space Beyond Territory: Wormholes, Gravitational Fields, and Entanglement', *Journal of Historical Sociology* 30, no. 3 (2017): 468; Doreen Massey, *For Space* (London: Sage, 2005), 9.

[22]Massey, *For Space*, 9.

the nation-state which is not viewed as a pre-existing territorial entity but as an 'idea' that needs to be continually reproduced through spatialised performances and practices of statehood.[23]

Just as space is being reconceptualised, so too is place. Place is increasingly thought of not *only* as a geographic location but as a 'fusion of social and material worlds'.[24] Hubbard and Kitchin describe place as 'a particular form of space, one that is created through acts of naming as well as the distinctive activities and imaginings associated with particular social spaces'.[25] In relation to social memory, then, we might think about space becoming transformed into a 'place of memory' through spatial practices that invest a particular space with meaning.[26] To create 'places of memory' or to 'emplace' memory, as Robinson puts it, is to make 'make memory socially visible'.[27] At the same time, physical sites of significance – for example locations where people were tortured or killed – can be transformed into 'social spaces' that 'resonate with political discourses' through acts of naming, performance and the placing of material artefacts (e.g. monuments).[28]

Because space is dynamic and relational, it is imbued with, and performative of, power dynamics. Not only are power relations enacted spatially but these relations influence the organisation of space itself.[29] Monuments, memorials and other spatial markers, such as military bases, deliver messages about 'how a space ought to be used' that seek to 'regulate its use or occupation'.[30] Moreover, not all actors have the same capacity 'to emplace memory into the social imaginary and the built environment'.[31] Political elites who possess superior access to resources have the capacity to establish museums, memorials, military cemeteries and national commemorative events. These practices and sites help to perform, both temporally and spatially, the power of the modern state; they project 'an illusion of permanence'[32] and territorial fixity and a state that 'both sits above and contains its localities, regions and communities'.[33]

At the same time, attempts to emplace memory are never all-encompassing. This is in part because, as Massey's work highlights, maintaining space requires *work*. In other words, it needs to be continually performed. It is also because space is *multiple*, as it is the space in which 'distinct trajectories coexist'.[34] Space is inscribed with various layers of meaning that are not necessarily visible to all and can be used and interpreted in multiple ways.[35] And while space is subject to ongoing boundary work by those who seek to

---

[23]James Ferguson and Akhil Gupta, 'Spatializing States: Toward an Ethnography of Neoliberal Governmentality', *Anthropologies of Modernity: Foucault, Governmentality, and Life Politics* 29, no. 4 (2008): 105–31; See also Alex Jeffrey, *The Improvised State: Sovereignty, Performance and Agency in Dayton Bosnia* (Malden, MA: John Wiley & Sons, 2012), 25.

[24]Annika Björkdahl and Stefanie Kappler, *Peacebuilding and Spatial Transformation: Peace, Space and Place* (London: Routledge, 2017), 18.

[25]Hubbard and Kitchin, 'Introduction: Why Key Thinkers?' 6.

[26]Annika Bjorkdahl and Susanne Buckley-Zistel, 'Spatialising Peace and Conflict: An Introduction', in *Spatialising Peace and Conflict: Mapping the Production of Place, Sites and Scales of Violence* (London: Palgrave Macmillan, 2016), 4.

[27]Joseph Robinson, *Transitional Justice and the Politics of Inscription: Memory, Space and Narrative in Northern Ireland* (London: Routledge, 2017), 122.

[28]Björkdahl and Kappler, *Peacebuilding and Spatial Transformation*, 81.

[29]Milena Komarova and Liam O'Dowd, 'Belfast, "The Shared City"? Spatial Narratives of Conflict and Transformation', in *Spatializing Peace and Conflict*, 281.

[30]Deirdre Conlon, 'Productive Bodies, Performative Spaces: Everyday Life in Christopher Park', *Sexualities* 7, no. 4 (2004): 464; 496.

[31]Robinson, *Transitional Justice and the Politics of Inscription*, 121.

[32]Barbara Misztal, *Theories of Social Remembering* (Berkshire: McGraw-Hill Professional Publishing, 2003), 52.

[33]Ferguson and Gupta, 'Spatializing States', 982.

[34]Massey, *For Space*, 9.

[35]Robinson, *Transitional Justice and the Politics of Inscription*, 113.

restrict the kinds of actors and activities that are permitted, others may seek to expand those boundaries or emplace their own version of events into space. These insights open up new ways of thinking about the political possibilities of space. Multiple spaces are at play in the context of social remembering, and these spaces are constantly being made and remade; they are never finished or closed.

At first glance, the intertwining of space, power and social memory is strikingly visible in both Timor-Leste and Aceh's memorial landscape. The dominant narrative of the conflict that is being spatially performed in Timor-Leste is a militarised, masculine, story of heroic liberation. This story, which celebrates the achievement of national independence as a culmination of 500 years of struggle against successive colonial occupiers, memorialises the 'heroes' and 'martyrs' of the resistance struggle. It is a narrative that is embodied in monuments like that of the statue of former FRETILIN founder Nicolau Lobato, and the Garden of Heroes' Cemetery, where the remains of former FALINTIL veterans are buried. The Nicolau Lobato statue, for instance, is located at the main intersection of the airport to the main road into Dili. It is one of the first images that visitors see and, as such, seems as directed to an international as much as a national audience. The Garden of Heroes Cemetery is also located in Dili district – not coincidently, right next to the newly established East Timorese military barracks – and the government is now attempting to construct heroes' cemeteries in an identical style across all Timor-Leste's 13 districts.

These state-sponsored memorial practices and sites might be viewed as performances of statehood. The Garden of Heroes cemeteries in particular perform the idea of a state that 'owns' those who died for the nation. The militarised, heroic, narrative responds to popular and political desires for a 'self-relying and externally acknowledged sovereign nation' that, given Timor-Leste recent emergence from colonial rule, Indonesian occupation and UN administration, are acutely evident.[36] At the same time, recent memorialising efforts do not, by and large, displace Indonesia's own efforts at memorialising. That the national Indonesian military cemetery remains in place and is well tended, and a shiny new Indonesian cultural centre now stands in a prominent position in Dili, speaks to the political and economic relationship with Indonesia that remains of profound political importance to Timor-Leste. These structures suggest that the post-conflict 'transition' has been less of a rupture than it seems, and that sovereignty as 'full autonomy' remains an unattainable ideal.[37]

It is perhaps not surprising that the dominant narrative of the past that is spatially performed in Aceh is more ambiguous, negotiated and at times contested than in Timor-Leste. Formal political authority is more dispersed here, and the transition from conflict to peace, and from authoritarianism to democracy, has been even more partial. Different sources of authority – namely Jakarta-based political leaders and the military, and GAM (many of whom are now in positions of power in the provincial government) – make different claims to legitimacy, in which they emphasise their central roles in delivering the peace and reconstructing the province. For instance, the TNIs ubiquitous slogans of 'Dame itu indah' (peace is beautiful) and 'Bersama Rakyat TNI Kuat' (Together with the community TNI is strong) are displayed on its regional, district and subdistrict

[36]Judith Bovensiepen and Maj Nygaard-Christensen, 'Petroleum Planning as State Building in Timor Leste', *Asia Pacific Journal of Anthropology* 19, no.5 (2018): 414.

[37]Ibid., 414. See also Danilyn Rutherford, *Laughing at Leviathan: Sovereignty and Audience in West Papua* (Chicago, IL: University of Chicago Press, 2012).

commands across the province. These claims not only seek to reinvent the military's role as peacemaker, but both spatially reflect and perform its ongoing presence and economic power of the military in everyday life. GAM has similarly sought to reinvent itself as peacemaker, promoting its role as the author of the Helsinki MoU that has delivered peace and prosperity to the population, and further cementing its claim to power through reference to its leadership of the Acehnese struggle for independence. Yet that there are limitations upon this claim is reflected in the absence of memorials to remember GAM resistance heroes and the fact that the remains of fallen GAM combatants are not gathered in centralised places but lie in discrete 'Makam Syharda' (martyrs graves), which are scattered in unmarked places throughout the landscape.

These spatialised and spatialising attempts to establish claims to legitimacy and authority should not however be viewed as all-encompassing. Space is dynamic and multiple and the space of lived experience can differ from abstract symbolic representations of it. Official spatial representations and performances can also be subverted or subtly reshaped by 'counter-performances'.[38] One important challenge to these official claims comes from the memory activism of NGOs in Timor-Leste and Aceh, which is infused with the globally circulating discourse of transitional justice. Before describing this activism let me first examine the assumptions about memorialisation that are contained within transitional justice discourse, and the expectations that are placed on civil society actors.

Transitional justice, memorialisation and civil society

In a recent article in Human Rights Quarterly, Lea David traces how memorialisation has gradually shifted from the margins to the centre of the transitional justice field. Initially appearing in the UN in the 1990s as a 'side-remark to the various forms of reparation for the victims of past abuses',[39] memorialisation came to be associated, in the late 1990s, with victims' 'right to know' (the truth about the past) and a state's concomitant 'Duty to Remember.' In a 1997 report by Louis Joinet, the former Special Rapporteur of the Sub-Commission on Prevention of Discrimination and Protection of Minorities, states are described as having a 'Duty to Remember' in order to guard against 'the development of revisionist and negationist arguments'.[40] In 2014, the UN Special Rapporteur in the field of cultural rights, Farida Shaheed, produced a special report on memorialisation processes that followed in the wake of several NGO reports on the topic.[41] As David suggests, these reports were meant to provide 'practical guidance' to societies emerging from state repression or violent conflict on memorialisation policies.[42]

The embrace of memorialisation by policy makers and practitioners has coincided with an emerging interest in 'locally resonant' and 'holistic' transitional justice responses.[43] While criminal prosecutions remain the core transitional justice mechanism, there are

[38]Reuben S. Rose-Redwood, 'Sixth Avenue is Now a Memory: Regimes of Spatial Inscription and the Performative Limits of the Official City Text', *Political Geography*, 27 (2008): 876.

[39]David, 'Against Standardization of Memory', 304.

[40]UN Economic and Social Council, 'Question of the Impunity of Perpetrators of Human Rights Violations (Civil and Political)', vol. 12912, 1997, 16.

[41]Farida Shaheed, 'Memorialization Processes' (United Nations General Assembly, 2014), doi:A/HRC/25/49.

[42]David, 'Against Standardization of Memory', 307.

[43]Rosalind Shaw and Lars Waldorf, 'Introduction: Localizing Transitional Justice', in *Localizing Transitional Justice*, ed. Rosalind Shaw, Lars Waldorf, and Pierre Hazan (Stanford, CA: Stanford University Press, 2010), 3–26.

increasing attempts to combine prosecutions with other mechanisms such as truth commissions, reparations programs, missing persons' commissions, local justice practices, history curriculum reform, and memorialisation, on the basis that this will allow transitional justice to become more responsive to particular local contexts. These shifts, while welcomed by some, have been greeted cautiously by others. Shaw and Waldorf argue for example that despite the putative interest in the 'local' there has been little sign that the field of transitional justice has been radically reshaped; it remains state-centric and oriented around a narrow vision of justice as criminal prosecutions.[44] Others suggest that transitional justice has become consolidated as a set of standardised practices, ideas and assumptions that now travels the globe as a kind of mobile transitional justice template.[45] Seen from this perspective, the rise of memorialisation within transitional justice discourse could be seen as heralding its mainstreaming within this template. Alongside trials and truth commissions, it has become another mechanism through which actors such as the UN, Western states and donors seek to bring pressure to bear on post-conflict states to meet their responsibilities to address the violent past.

Regardless of how we might characterise its effects, what is clear is that memorialisation is now linked to the pursuit of several transitional justice goals. The social expression of memory through commemorations, monuments and memorials is thought to contribute to the restoration of victims' dignity, by giving them or their family members a clear sign that their story is not forgotten but rather integrated into, and made visible as part of, a 'national' memory.[46] Memorialisation is also said to contribute to 'victims' right to truth'; it is viewed as a 'tool to call attention to past wrongdoing and pierce the silence engendered by repressive political authorities and institutions'.[47] Memorialisation is also assumed to contribute to broader societal goals such as criminal prosecutions of individuals who violated human rights, which are expected to act as a deterrent against future violence. The idea is that memorials, museums and commemorations can, by making victims and crimes visible to a wider public, 'awaken a conscience for their suffering, which might then lead to a change of opinion and greater public demand to put perpetrators of human rights violations to trial'.[48] A fourth and related assumption is that remembering will have a pedagogical power that will help prevent future abuses. The past is thought to offer 'lessons' which can be abstracted in order to prevent future injustices.[49] Only by remembering atrocities, it is argued, will the society in question learn not to repeat them. Finally, social remembering is thought to encourage forms of active citizenship, tolerance and democratic dialogue. The underlying idea 'is to create memorial institutions that enact the values and norms the new society is to be built

---

[44]Ibid., 4–5.

[45]Jelena Subotić, 'The Transformation of International Transitional Justice Advocacy', *International Journal of Transitional Justice* 6, no. 1 (2012): 106–25.

[46]Markus Weissert, *Memories of Violence, Dreams of Development: Memorialisation Initiatives in the Peruvian Andes* (Freien Universität Berlin, 2015), 94.

[47]Robinson, *Transitional Justice and the Politics of Inscription*, 37.

[48]Weissert, *Memories of Violence, Dreams of Development*, 92; Judy Barsalou and Victoria Baxter, 'The Urge to Remember. The Role of Memorials in Social Reconstruction and Transitional Justice', *Stabilization and Reconstruction Series*, no. 5 (2007): 9.

[49]Weissert, *Memories of Violence, Dreams of Development*, 10; L. Bickford and A. Sodaro, 'Remembering Yesterday to Protect Tomorrow: The Internationalization of a New Commemorative Paradigm', in *Memory and the Future: Transnational Politics, Ethics and Society*, ed. Y Gutman, A. Brown, and A. Sodaro (Hampshire: Palgrave Macmillan, 2010), 69.

upon and to educate the public – particularly the young – in empathy, tolerance and critical thinking'.[50]

As a reflection of the state-centric focus of transitional justice, the roles of civil society actors in memorialisation have, until recently, been neglected. The 'duty to remember' has largely been constructed as a duty of states.[51] This is beginning to change, and a range of reports have sought to highlight the dynamic and creative roles of civil society actors and organisations in memorialisation processes.[52] A 2007 report by the ICTJ suggests that 'in many contexts civil society has provided the most energy and innovation for memorialisation. NGOs generally have much more trust from a broader section of society. They are the only ones that can mobilize victims' groups'. They can also 'create more complicated, inclusive narratives that invite greater participation and debate'.[53] A report by the international NGO Impunity Watch suggests that 'civil society can challenge [the] status quo',[54] and their memory initiatives can 'sustain pressure for criminal prosecutions'.[55] The previously mentioned UN report on memorialisation by Farida Shaheed also emphasises the complementary roles played by civil society and the state in relation to memorialisation. It notes that:

> Authorities have a key role to play: they have the responsibility of managing the public space and the capacity to maintain monuments and museums and develop national strategies across territory and over the long term, taking into consideration a wide array of narratives. Civil society has the capacity to mobilise groups of the population, grant popular legitimacy, organise events and generate public debates.[56]

The suggestion underpinning these reports is that states will assume the key responsibility for memorialisation, and that civil society actors will play a complementary – and at times – counterbalancing role. Implicit is the idea that civil society can represent 'local' voices and will help to challenge and break the hegemonic memory culture imposed by national elites by promoting alternative narratives.[57] These reports also depict NGOs and civil society initiatives as 'microcosms of incipient liberal democracy' that create spaces in which 'rights-bearing individuals associate, participate and are empowered'.[58] They view civil society as an indispensable resource in fostering the successful 'local' ownership of transitional justice, which may be particularly needed in contexts where transitional justice mechanisms have been promoted as part of an externally led statebuilding intervention (as occurred in Timor-Leste), and where questions of legitimacy may surround such mechanisms.[59]

---

[50]Berber Bevernage, 'Narrating Pasts for Peace? A Critical Analysis of Some Recent Initiatives of Historical Reconciliation Through "Historical Dialogue" and "Shared History"', in *The Ethos of History: Time and Responsibility*, ed. Stefan Helgesson and Jayne Svenungsson (New York: Berhahn Books, 2018); See also Kris Brown, 'Commemoration as Symbolic Reparation: New Narratives or Spaces of Conflict?', *Human Rights Review* 14 (2013): 495.

[51]For example, see UN Economic and Social Council, 'Question of the Impunity of Perpetrators of Human Rights Violations (Civil and Political)'.

[52]For example, see Impunity Watch, '"Memory for Change": Memorialisation as a Tool for Transitional Justice Asia Exchange Report "Memory for Change" Memorialisation as a Tool for Transitional Justice', 2015; Brett et al., 'Memorialization and Democracy: State Policy and Civic Action'; Barsalou and Baxter, 'The Urge to Remember. The Role of Memorials in Social Reconstruction and Transitional Justice'.

[53]Brett et al., 'Memorialization and Democracy: State Policy and Civic Action', 28.

[54]Impunity Watch, '"Memory for Change": Memorialisation as a Tool for Transitional Justice', 31.

[55]Impunity Watch, 'Policy Brief: Guiding Principles of Memorialisation', no. January (2013): 9.

[56]Shaheed, 'Memorialization Processes', 19–20.

[57]Weissert, *Memories of Violence, Dreams of Development*, 97.

[58]Alexander Hinton, *The Justice Facade: Trials of Transition in Cambodia* (Oxford: Oxford University Press, 2018), 35.

[59]Vasuki Nesiah, 'Transitional Justice Practice: Looking Back, Moving Forward', *Report for Impunity Watch*, May 2016, 13.

When it comes to memorialisation, then, the transitional justice framework expects a great deal of civil society actors in contexts where political space may be highly circumscribed. Furthermore, there is a tension between the uncomplicated assumption that civil society stands outside of the state and holds the ability to challenge hegemonic narratives and the assumption that it will support and complement the state-building enterprise by fostering public participation and encouraging renewed forms of active citizenship. Reports about memorialisation and transitional justice also implicitly rely on a particular *kind* of civil society actor: a 'gentrified' civil society that is capable of negotiating with donors and state officials, writing project proposals in order to gain funding, and networking with international human rights organisations.[60] For human rights activists, navigating these expectations and competing pressures is not straightforward, as I will now discuss.

Memory activism in Timor-Leste and Aceh

Since the end of the conflicts in Timor-Leste and Aceh, human rights activists in both contexts have been seeking to promote the visibility of civilian experiences of violence in the public sphere. These activists are comprised of a relatively small group of educated, urban, elites who tend to be employed as staff of prominent local NGOs and are mostly of a younger generation compared to the current generation of political leaders. They are also connected to each other, having forged relationships through their mutual participation in study tours, international conferences, and their connections, as part of transnational advocacy networks, to international organisations such as ICTJ, International Coalition of Sites of Conscience, the Asian Federation against Involuntary Disappearances, and Indonesian-based donors and supporters such as Asia Justice and Rights.[61]

On 3 May 2017, as part of research fieldwork undertaken for this paper, I attended the commemoration of Simpang KKA, which was organised by the North Aceh Human Rights Victims Community (K2HAU), in Lloksamewe, with support from Kontras Aceh. Simpang KKA is thought to have been the worst killing that took place during the decades-long Aceh conflict. It took place in 1999, at a time when the period of *Reformasi* (reform) had just begun in Indonesia and when demands for a referendum for independence on Aceh – spurred on by developments in Timor-Leste – were at an all-time high.[62] Indonesian military forces fired on a crowd of citizens at a busy intersection (*simpang*) in retaliation for a soldier who had reportedly gone missing in the area a few days earlier, killing up to 39 people and wounding many others. At the time of the commemoration, none of the perpetrators had been arrested and tried for this incident and several different versions of the event (the military's, GAM's and victims' organisations) continued to circulate.

The first part of the commemoration took place at around 9am in the morning at the house of a Teunku (religious leader) whose son had been killed in the Simpang KKA incident. Together with a group of around 40–50 people, my research assistant and I sat on plastic mats outside the house under some plastic shade cloths, the men in a large circle, the women in another. The commemoration began with some rousing speeches

[60] Jeffrey, *The Improvised State: Sovereignty, Performance and Agency in Dayton Bosnia*, 110.

[61] In Timor-Leste some of the key organisations involved in memory activism are Asia Justice and Rights (AJAR), Yayasan Hak and Asosiasaun Chega! ba Ita (ACTBIT). In Aceh, it is KONTRAS ACEH and Koalisi NGO HAM.

[62] Anthony Smith, 'Aceh: Democratic Times, Authoritarian Solutions', *New Zealand Journal of Asian Studies* 4, no 2 (2002), 84.

from members of K2HAU, which called for the need for the state to bring the perpetrators of the killings to justice. There was then a long Islamic chant, in which the names of the dead were mentioned. Following the prayers there was a communal feast or kenduri. We then conducted a pilgrimage (*ziarah*) to the grave of the Teunku's son, walking slowly to small grave site nearby the house, hidden amongst the coconut trees. Some more prayers were conducted there, led by the Teunku.

Following the prayers, the group climbed into a bus and drove to the site of the Simpang KKA killings, where the main, public, commemorative event took place. A square and fairly non-descript monument now stands at the site of the killings, which was reportedly constructed by the Aceh Reintegration Agency (*Badan Reintegrasi Aceh*/BRA) during the post-conflict reconstruction period, with limited public consultation. Because it is located in the middle of a busy intersection, it is not a place where people might stop and reflect. Temporarily, on the morning of 3 May, some of the traffic was slowed. Students walked over to the centre of the intersection holding up homemade cardboard signs reading 'how can the people trust the law when the law enforcers are afraid of justice?' and a banner reading 'Remembering 18 years of the Tragedy Simpang KKA: Urging the Attorney General to accelerate the investigation of Simpang KKA.'

During this part of the commemoration, there seemed to be a celebratory mood in the air, but also a slight sense of tension. This can be explained, in part, by the presence of a man in plain clothes who, we later learned, was a member of the Military Intelligence, and the fact that, not far from Simpang KKA is one of the TNI's ubiquitous military posts that provides a stark reminder of the continuing presence of the military (TNI) in everyday life. During the event, the man associated with Military Intelligence questioned one activist about my presence (as the sole foreigner) at the event and tapped their answers into his mobile phone. Later that evening, we heard that the organiser of the event was called to the police station to answer questions about the commemoration. This demonstrates both the personal risks and potential exposure to state authorities that memory activists confront while undertaking memorialisation activities in contexts such as Aceh and of the complexity of any participation in local memorialisation events by international observers.

Like the Simpang KKA commemoration, the 2018 commemoration of Liquica church massacre in Timor-Leste had an activist agenda. A key element of this agenda involved a demand for prosecutions of those responsible within the Indonesian military. The Liquica church massacre took place on 6 April 1999, in the lead-up to Timor-Leste's referendum for self-determination, when up to 60 people were killed by the *Besih Merah Putih* militia group, with the active involvement of TNI and BRIMOB (Indonesian mobile police brigade). Most bodies have yet to be recovered after being taken away from the massacre site on trucks[63] and only one East Timorese militia member has been convicted for the events.[64] The Liquica Church commemoration was much larger than Simpang KKA, with over 100 people present at the church service. Its size was a reflection in part of the significant funding provided that year by the *Centro National Chega!* (CNC), a public institute established in 2017 to promote the implementation of the CAVR and CTF

[63]See Commission for Reception, Truth and Reconciliation (CAVR), *Chega!* Part 7.2, 1065–66.

[64]All the security officials tried in Indonesia's *Ad Hoc* Human Rights Court for their involvement in the massacre and other crimes were acquitted either at trial or on appeal. See East Timor and Indonesia Action Network (ETAN), 'East Timorese Deserve Justice: Statement by the East Timor and Indonesia Action Network on the Anniversary of the Liquica Church Massacre', https://etan.org/news/2009/04liquica.htm (accessed January 6, 2018).

recommendations. It also reflected the involvement of veterans' groups who, over the past few years, have played an increasingly prominent role in the commemoration. This, in turn, has propelled a shift in the spatial emphasis of the commemoration towards an increased focus on the Liquica Garden of Heroes cemetery.[65]

As at Simpang KKA, the first element of the Liquica church massacre commemoration involved prayers, in this case a Catholic mass. The congregation was packed to the brim at the early-morning service, and many people were standing outside. There were large numbers of school students present, dressed in their school uniforms. Families of victims had placed photos of the dead, flowers and candles at the front of the church. The emphasis of the sermon, which was given by two local priests, was on the dead as saviours. The sacrifices of the dead, which were equated with Christ's sacrifices, were also viewed as sacrifices for the nation. Holy communion took place, and the priests sprinkled holy water on the photos of the dead, the flowers and candles.

Following the church service, the next – arguably most dominant part – of the commemoration involved a 'mini seminar' and press conference, which took place in small covered outdoor area next to the church. The numbers present had dwindled by this point, as school children had headed off to school, and the audience seemed to be primarily composed of families of victims and some observers from Dili-based human rights organisations and the media. Also present were a local parliamentarian, the prosecutor general, the administrator of the district, representatives of the national victims' association, veterans' representatives, and the head of the CNC. Survivors of the massacre, including the former state secretary for youth and sport, spoke about their experiences of that day, and the events that occurred. The various dignitaries also spoke. As in the sermon at the Church, a key emphasis of the narrative delivered by state officials was that people had died for national independence and that it was therefore important for citizens to continue the struggle by participating in the nation's development. The message delivered by Eliza from the Liquica victims' group at the press conference had a slightly different tenor. She read a statement calling for, among other things, the state to place priority on justice and accountability, to preserve historical places in Liquica, to incorporate the truth commission report into the national curriculum, and to 'dignify victims' by making the Liquica massacre an official national public holiday.

Following a take-away lunch of rice and vegetables, the crowd gathered at a small angel monument, beside the church, for prayers, and a short reflection delivered by the priest. This monument had been built by the Liquica community, with the support of human rights activists, in 2006, and was inaugurated with a small ceremony involving the blessing of stone to put the souls of the dead to rest. Children of victims stood holding photographs of their deceased family members, which were then sprinkled with holy water by the priest. Finally, what was left of the crowd – around 30 or so people – walked, in the baking midday sun, through the streets of Liquica to the district Garden of Heroes Cemetery, recently built by the state. This is the site where the heroes of the resistance are buried (and where, I was told, the remains of some of those killed in the Liquica Church massacre were recently interred). The priest delivered another short reflection and then walked around the Cemetery sprinkling holy water. Families placed flowers on the graves of the dead and spent time talking to them and praying.

[65]This suggests that the dead are increasingly incorporated into the state-sanctioned heroic narrative.

Challenging dominant spaces of memory?

The commemorations just described deliberately seek to challenge dominant spaces of memory by emplacing alternative memories in the public imaginary. They aim to disrupt the public amnesia about the violence experienced by civilians and instead foster open discussion of these silenced narratives. Activists hope that, in the long-term this will lead to state acknowledgement which, in turn, will result in a political commitment to pursuing criminal prosecutions of those responsible for human rights violations. For this reason, a key aspect of activists' strategy involves attempting to ascribe a 'national' significance to events deemed 'local' in order to engender a response from political elites. While firmly directed at a national audience, activists seek to bring pressure to bear on the state by promoting the circulation of memories of civilian violence beyond it, including by leveraging their international connections with organisations such as ICTJ and Amnesty International, and the media. They also endeavour to foster new forms of solidarity amongst victims in order to generate a local demand for accountability of the Indonesian military.

Activists expressed these goals during interviews conducted during project fieldwork. In Timor-Leste, activists stressed that they sought to push the national government to implement the recommendations of the CAVR report which called for, among other things, the Indonesian government to take responsibility for the prosecution of members of its military responsible for human rights violations in 1999 (or, failing that, for the international community to establish an international criminal tribunal along the lines of the ICTY or ICTR). In Aceh, activists were directing their advocacy efforts both to their provincial government and the national government. In a context where there has been no state-sanctioned truth and reconciliation commission and little progress towards criminal prosecutions, they hoped to build greater public awareness of the human rights abuses committed during the conflict. They also hoped to push along the investigation of the Simpang KKA case (which, following an inquiry by the National Human Rights Commission, Komnas HAM, has been filed with the Attorney General's office). Activists also explained that they had stepped up their support for several commemorations in Aceh in order to support the work of the KKR – the newly established provincial-level truth commission – which they saw as an important step in the long road towards achieving prosecutions of the Indonesian military. As one interviewee explained, 'We want to show the government that there is support for the victims ... we also want to push the government to give the commissioners [of the new TRC] a chance.'[66]

Activists in both Timor-Leste and Aceh also articulated the view that social remembering would have a pedagogical power for individuals and for the nation. Commemorations were understood as a means of transmitting memories to the young generation so that they would become active, democratic, peaceful citizens. In both Liquica and Lloksamewe, young people were specifically enlisted to assist with the commemorations and were viewed as a key audience for them. The point, as one activist in Timor-Leste explained, 'is not just to tell stories and cry. We can learn from the past, to strengthen our independence'.[67] Another activist in Timor-Leste similarly explained that the goal is not just to

[66]Interview with human rights activist, Banda Aceh, May 4, 2017.
[67]Interview with human rights activist, Dili, Timor-Leste, April 4, 2018.

remember the event but the value of the event. 'Why did people die? Why did military kill? The lessons learned. We memorialise to learn.'[68]

These activist-led commemorations might be understood, then, as creative performances that seek to imagine and bring into being a different kind of state and an active citizenry that is capable of exercising and demanding their rights from that state. The state that is imagined is a protective, open, democratic and accountable state that acknowledges its 'duty to remember' the past in order to respond to victims' suffering and foster long term-peace, development and democracy. This hope was embodied in the desire expressed by both Timorese and Acehnese activists for the commemorations to become official, government-sanctioned and organised, events (even if they also conceded that governments had poor track records in terms of undertaking public consultation for these kinds of events). While in Timor-Leste, hopes were for national government support and in Aceh it was for provincial government support, activists in both contexts stressed that victims' groups should not have to organise commemorations themselves. Not only did this place too much of a burden upon them but government-organised commemorations would, they argued, provide an important form of recognition of victims' suffering by signalling that incidents such as Simpang KKA and the Liquica Church Massacre had been officially accorded a national significance.[69]

Yet, the attempts to ascribe a national significance to incidents of violence against civilians creates frustrations for activists. Key amongst these is that, by seeking to directly engage with the state, activist-organised commemorations are brought into dialogue with elite state and nation-building agendas. In Timor-Leste, where this agenda prioritises the remembrance of a heroic past and reconciliation with Indonesia, activists' demands tend to be ignored. In Aceh, where the transition has been more partial than in Timor-Leste, and where there has been no official documentation – or state acknowledgement – of the violence committed by the TNI, activists' claims engage with an antagonistic Indonesian government and military in a more proximate way, and the stakes of such activism and personal risks to activists are higher. This gives the spaces created by NGO activist-led commemorations in Aceh a more tenuous and fragile quality than those in Timor-Leste. The presence of the military intelligence representative at the gathering at the Simpang KKA monument in 2017, for instance, added an element of tension to the commemoration, delivering a message that these activities were being closely watched and were subtly violating moral codes regarding permissible actions in that space. This also means that at times memory activism can create further polarisation rather than bringing about the hoped – for recognition of victims. The perceived lack of official response to memory activism in Timor-Leste and Aceh also feeds into victims' groups expressions of weariness and disappointment about the fact that their expectations for prosecutions, public acknowledgement and reparations, having been repeatedly raised, remain unmet.

Another frustration relates to the fact that organising commemorations on an annual basis, and at a sufficient scale, requires activists to accumulate the requisite funding, social capital and legitimacy. Activists in both Timor-Leste and Aceh bemoaned the ongoing difficulties of sourcing funding for transport to bring families of victims based in disparate villages together, and food. They also lamented the difficulties of gaining

[68]Interview with human rights activist, Dili, Timor-Leste, March 28, 2018.
[69]Interview with human rights activist in Dili, Timor-Leste, March 28, 2017.

the participation of prominent officials and the media at these events. In Aceh, funding for local NGOs has dried up significantly since the post-tsunami humanitarian response, and donors now channel their (limited) Aceh funding through national NGOs. In Timor-Leste, there is a sense that, 15 years on from the end of the UN-sponsored state-building mission, donors are no longer interested in funding transitional justice activities. This temporally limited external support for and funding of memorialisation activities within transitional justice frameworks sits uncomfortably with timescales for communities dealing with legacies of past violence and injustice that often cross multiple generations over decades and centuries.

To expand their reach, and to facilitate the local ownership of commemorations, activists have supported the formation of local victims' groups, which are expected to liaise directly with local governments to secure support and funding and to evolve into a victim-led social movement demanding justice. But, in contexts of material deprivation, political sensitivity, poor roads, lack of transport, and competing priorities, members of local victims' groups do not appear to be emerging as the kind of self-reliant active citizens capable of demanding their rights from the state that activists would like them to be. Activists expressed their frustrations about the difficulties of building a rights consciousness amongst citizens. Coordinators of victims' groups spoke, in turn, of the problems of gaining funding for their activities and of the reluctance of their members – many of whom were subsistence farmers – to participate unless per diems were offered to cover their expenses.

The attempt to draw memories into the space of the nation-state and to influence state norms and practices also constrains the *kinds* of events that are selected for commemoration and the *ways* in which this remembering takes place. As people are invited to remember their experiences as human rights violations and express their demands for redress to the state, there is the potential to eclipse the plural and diverse ways in which people remember the past.[70] These forms of remembering may be grounded in very different spatial imaginaries, for instance the space of kinship networks, which is critical to the continuation of socio-political life for both Timorese and Acehnese. It also means that some events are prioritised above others. In Timor-Leste, activists have encouraged victims' groups in each district to choose one violent event in which ten or more people died together that can be representative of all the violent events in that district. In Aceh, activists are prioritising the commemoration of violent events that have been investigated by Komnas HAM and have been referred to the Attorney General's office for potential prosecution. In both contexts there is a focus on spaces that are likely to gain national visibility. Incidents that occurred close to a main road and not too far from major towns are chosen on the basis that it would be impossible to entice political leaders and the media to commemorations in remote, inaccessible, locations. As one activist in Aceh put it, 'how to get the media to come to Tapak Tuan? [the town that is in a relatively remote area near to the site of the Jambo Keupuk killings]. They will ask for money, per diems to attend'.[71]

Yet even if the aims of activists to draw these events into a national imaginary continue to be frustrated, my experience of the Liquica and Simpang KKA commemorations was

[70]See Peter Manning, *Transitional Justice and Memory in Cambodia: Beyond the Extraordinary Chambers* (London: Routledge, 2017), 133.
[71]Interview with human rights activist in Banda Aceh, Aceh, May 2, 2017.

that they succeeded, at least partially and perhaps inadvertently, in opening up other spaces of memory. These spaces enabled families, in some small way, to meet their obligations to the dead, and potentially opened up new spaces of public debate and democracy. To grasp these alternative spaces, it is necessary to look beyond the formal, articulated, goals of NGO activists and their discursive references to transitional justice goals to the embodied and relational aspects of the commemorations. Doreen Massey's observations about space as plural, relational, and always-in-flux are an important resource in making this shift.

Massey's insights remind us that we should be open to the possibility that activist-led commemorations create, through the very fact of bringing people together, and through the interrelations of those present, something more than that which is expressed in the public demands for formal justice. Put simply, Massey prompts us to be alert to the multiple, intersecting, spaces of memory that are brought into being during the course of activist-led commemorations, some of which exceed the formal goals and the national space imagined by NGO activism.

In Aceh, where the militarisation of social space continues to shape the 'affective climate of everyday life',[72] the annual commemorations at the site of the Simpang KKA massacre make an embodied claim to that place in a way that affectively transforms it, even if temporarily, from a space of surveillance into a space of political possibilities, democracy and public debate. In Timor-Leste, where there is not the same degree of military surveillance and policing of public space, the Liquica community has, to some extent, been able to reclaim the site of the massacre by constructing the small angel monument. Memories that complicate the official heroic narrative have thus been permanently 'emplaced' in the public sphere. Nonetheless, the annual Liquica commemorations play an ongoing role in re-sacralising a site that is, for the local population, remembered as a former site of terror and violence. This site is purified through the use of holy water and re-signified as part of everyday social space once more.

In my experience of the 2017 and 2018 commemorations, forms of community and sociality were also fostered through the interrelations of those present at these events that appeared have little relationship to peoples' identities as individual rights-holding members of a nation-state. During the public talks by survivors of the Liquica church massacre at the 'mini-seminar', the audience shared tears as well as laughter as they sat together and listened, as members of the Liquica community, to neighbours and friends recount the events leading up to that day, and of the ongoing everyday ramifications of losing family members. In Aceh, there was a festive atmosphere after the formal commemorative event was over, when the group reassembled at a local beach-side café to drink cold coconuts in the shade and chat informally.

The communal prayers and meal at the Teunku's house and the visit to the grave of the Teunku's son in North Aceh, and the gathering of victims' families at the small angel monument in Liquica further speak to how intimate spaces of memory and forms of sociality can coexist with, and infuse, formal commemorative events. In these spaces people seemed to come together – often in their identities as members of kinship groups – to create a space of mourning, to recognise and honour the dead, and fulfil their ongoing obligations to care

[72]Catherine Smith, 'A Stranger in One's Own Home: Surveillance, Space, Place, and Emotion During the GAM Conflict in Aceh', *Indonesia*, no. 100 (2015): 55.

for them. The creation of these intimate spaces serves as a reminder that social remembering is not only about imagining a nation state. It is also a form of care for the dead and of re-constituting sociality that takes on different socio-cultural forms, and is often an acute priority for families.

Conclusion

Spaces of memory activism in Timor-Leste and Aceh are shaped by the interplay between power relations resulting from the respective peace agreements and the globally circulating discourse and practice of transitional justice. That there are remarkable similarities amongst activists' strategies and goals speaks to the power of the discursive framework of transitional justice, which expects civil society to challenge hegemonic narratives and, at the same time, imagines the state as the natural container for social remembering and the delivery of prosecutorial justice. It also underscores how the continuing representation of elite military interests in the Indonesian state constrains both prosecutorial and memorialisation possibilities. While in neither context has there been an absolute rupture with the past, the more partial nature of the transition that has taken place in Aceh compared to Timor-Leste lends the spaces of memory activism created in the former a more fleeting, fragile and contested quality.

While remaining cognisant of the limitations of memory activism, by adopting a conception of space as multiple, produced by the relations between bodies, and always in-the making, I have been alert to its creative possibilities. This has enabled me to shift away from the dominant, imagined, space of the nation state to examine how multiple spaces of memory may be created. These spaces are shaped, in part, by the embodied interactions between those present at the commemorations, including relatives of the dead, who have customary, religious and familial obligations to the deceased, and personal needs for mourning. This means that there are moments when, during activist-organised commemorations, the space of the sacred can become more prominent than the space of secular human rights activism, when the space of mourning appears to take precedence over the space of protest and when the intimate space of extended kinship relations is more evident than the space of the nation-state.

These insights suggest that it is productive for scholars interested in the diverse effects of globalisation on memory cultures to adopt space as an analytic category. A recognition that space is multiple, dynamic, and relational complicates the assumption that globalisation is having an homogenising effect on local memory cultures. It enables an alertness to the dominant and unequal power relations that shape cultures of memory *and* to the creativity that memory activism may hold. Finally, there is a need for both activists and scholars to reflect on the spaces that are created through memory activism and whose interests these spaces serve. By seeking to accumulate the required social, economic and symbolic capital to influence state priorities, are activists inadvertently reproducing the state as an idealised space and overriding the need for the creation of other, more intimate, spaces of mourning? Given the global spread of transitional justice memorialisation frameworks, how might memory activism work – in a sustained and long-term way – with local priorities and local cultural resources for remembering? Such reflection might enable more attention to be paid to creating spaces of memory that resonate with everyday spatial imaginaries and locally grounded forms of caring for the dead.

Acknowledgements

Interviews and fieldwork undertaken referenced in this article were undertaken with ethics approval from the Australian National University's Human Research Ethics Committee (protocol 2015/339).

Disclosure statement

No potential conflict of interest was reported by the author.

Funding

Research for this article was supported by the Australian Research Council [grant number DE:150100857].

From transitional to performative justice: peace activism in the aftermath of communal violence

Birgit Bräuchler

ABSTRACT

Interventions such as courts and truth commissions are elements of an internationally established transitional justice (TJ) toolkit. Such measures are rarely sustainable or in place after the occurrence of mass violence. Those affected then have to themselves get active to restore social relationships. Civil society plays an important role in these transitions, but civil society also needs to be scrutinised to deconstruct reductionist conceptualisations in TJ discourses. Taking the Moluccan conflict and peace process as a case study, this paper looks into alternative ways that communities seek to transition from violence to peace and in the process ask for forms of justice not exclusively related to physical violence. Instead, communities focus on continuing social injustices that they believe underlie this violence. Analysis of the case study promotes an understanding of TJ not primarily as transitional, but as transformative and performative. In this way locally driven transitional justice mechanisms look not only into the past and legacies of violence, but also into legacies of harmony and peace and the emergence of integrative means in the future. The case study shows that forms of art in Maluku were turned into a force that aimed to reintegrate society divided by violence and unite society to resist exploitation and suppression by outside forces. Young people played important roles in this dynamic. The search for reconciliation in Maluku was in this way transformed into a broader struggle *against* structural violence and destructive outside interventions and *for* social justice and sustainable peace.

A big bird of paradise flies in panic across the street, a man lies on the ground, another rises threateningly with a spear above him. Ambon City provides the scene for this street theatre performed in 2013 by a group of artists and activists who fight an outside investor's plan to open up a huge sugar cane plantation in Indonesia's very East, Aru Islands, part of Maluku province. The project would destroy Aru's culture and environment that is home to the famous bird of paradise (*cendrawasih*). While the big bird stands for Aru's environment, the man on the ground symbolises the investor that threatens the Aruese habitat. The man with the spear represents Aru people who resist and fight back. At first sight, this well attended event is a typical case of performative resistance against corporate capitalism and environmental destruction and for local empowerment and indigenous rights. We find examples worldwide, from people performing in various cities joining the Occupy movement to the Native American protests against the Dakota Access Pipeline. What is different in Maluku is that the event is part of an extended transition and reconciliation process from violence to peace that was consecutively turned into a broader struggle *against* structural violence and destructive outside interventions and *for* social justice and sustainable peace.

All this is taking place after communal mass violence (1999–2004) that resulted in thousands of deaths, hundreds of thousands of displaced people and an ideologically and physically segregated society. The Indonesian government did not cater for the set-up of formal transitional justice mechanisms. No truth commissions and no courts were established to look into the masterminds behind the violence. Even if they had been established, the commissions and courts would have been limited in their capacity to deal with the structural violence that was crucial to the emergence of the conflict. Those affected by the violence had to get active themselves to develop mechanisms to restore social relationships and transition from violence to peace. The street theatre event is therefore part of a thriving peace culture in Maluku that includes efforts to revive and restrengthen local traditions that go beyond religious affiliation as bridge builders. It is also part of the emergence of an aspiring arts scene located primarily in Ambon and its surrounds. I have extensively discussed the development of a peace culture in Maluku in previous publications[1] and will here focus on the latter emergence of an arts scene and more recent developments. As some of the involved artists and activists told me, unlike in places like Yogyakarta or Bali, these new dynamics do not simply give expression to the youth's new hobbies, but rather are an emerging new force that aims to build bridges, restore and strengthen relationships in and between religious groups and develop established traditions further. They are conscious efforts to root and embody peace initiatives in daily life, restore social relations and work towards social justice. As an activist in Aru said, it is time for the youth to stand up and make up for the older generation's hesitance to protest in public.

In settings such as Maluku, the issue is not simply that classic transitional justice (TJ) mechanisms were not put in place. The underlying philosophy of such mechanisms does not speak to the local realities of a society that was torn by so-called communal violence and deeply damaged by the legacies of structural violence. Classic conceptions of transitional justice are limited because: (1) they focus on a stark division between victims and perpetrators that ignores the fluidity of these categories, (2) they are short-term, and (3) legalistic, (4) they focus on direct as opposed to structural violence and (5) they are based on the idea of a temporally limited transition from conflict to peace. We therefore need to get away from notions of TJ as 'formal institutions such as truth and reconciliation commissions (TRCs) and criminal trials', initiatives that directly 'respond to legacies of past violence'.[2] This does not imply that such mechanisms are not important, for instance, to track the masterminds behind the violence, but that they would fail to reconcile the affected people as they do not address

[1]See e.g. Birgit Bräuchler, *The Cultural Dimension of Peace. Decentralization and Reconciliation in Indonesia* (London: Palgrave Macmillan, 2015).

[2]Renee Jeffery, Lia Kent, and Joanne Wallis, 'Reconceiving the Roles of Religious Civil Society Organizations in Transitional Justice: Evidence from the Solomon Islands, Timor-Leste and Bougainville', *International Journal of Transitional Justice* 11 (2017): 380.

the complex legacies of structural violence and do not resonate with locally-grounded ways of peacebuilding. As this paper argues, we therefore need to add another perspective to dominant notions and come to an understanding of TJ, not primarily as transitional, but as transformative and performative, not only looking into the past and the legacies of violence, but also looking into past legacies of harmony and peace and into the emergence of new integrative means in the future. As Gready and Robins point out, we need to conceptualise TJ as 'a future-oriented approach to the past' that creates 'the conditions for a sustainable peace, and ... is an intrinsic part of peacebuilding'.[3] People in different cultural and political contexts deal differently with past violence, sometimes without explicitly addressing the violence, but always 'rooted in their own local histories and experiences'.[4] Nonetheless, that violent past is constantly present in projects striving for sustainable peace, social justice and a future that is open for dialogue.

This article first provides a brief outline of the Moluccan conflict, the structural issues leading to its escalation, and the peace process. The next sections develop the article's key concept, that of transformation through performative justice. As a first step it sketches initiatives that challenge dominant notions of TJ practice through reconceptualising TJ not primarily as transitional, but as transformative, thus moving away from a sole focus on past (physical) violence and complementing it through addressing continuing injustices. As a second step, it highlights the important role that civil society (CS) plays in these transitions meant to foster reconciliation, while also putting the concept of CS under scrutiny. The article hints both at the enormous potential of CS in the search of alternative means of delivering justice and highlights some shortcomings of conceptualisations of CS in TJ discourses. The next part focuses on the arts as a means to open up space for CS to engage in and promote such extended notions of TJ, thus pointing at important gaps in mainstream TJ practice. It focuses on the performative aspect of transformative justice[5] and on affective justice.[6] This is followed by an analysis of specific features of peacebuilding in Maluku and how this led to the emergence of a broader movement that aims to turn the search for peace into broader societal transformations towards social justice through performative justice, here exemplified with the SaveAru movement. This caters to the need to fill two gaps in the transformative justice project as identified by Gready and Robins, and that is the need for thick descriptions and assessments of transformative justice in specific social and regional contexts and the need for longitudinal studies.[7]

This research needs to be seen as part of my more than fifteen years of engagement with conflict and peacebuilding in Maluku, in the course of which I conducted extended stretches of participant observation and hundreds of (informal) interviews. In this particular paper I give voice to selected peace activists, artists and youths and the relationships

[3]Paul Gready and Simon Robins, 'From Transitional to Transformative Justice: A New Agenda for Practice', *The International Journal of Transitional Justice* 8 (2014): 350.

[4]Thomas Dick, 'Decolonising Labour Markets: The Australian South Sea Island Diaspora and the Role of Cultural Expression in Connecting Communities', in *Current Issues in Transitional Justice. Towards a More Holistic Approach*, eds. N. Szablewska and S.-D. Bachmann (Cham: Springer, 2015), 113.

[5]Gready and Robins, 'Transformative Justice'.

[6]Peter D. Rush, 'Preface. After Atrocity: Foreword to Transition', in *The Arts of Transitional Justice. Culture, Activism, and Memory after Atrocity*, eds. P.D. Rush and O. Simic (New York: Springer, 2014), vii.

[7]Gready and Robins, 'Transformative Justice', 359, 361.

they build in order to personalise experiences and better illustrate notions of 'an embodied everyday peace'.[8] Most of them had some kind of exposure to other cultural contexts, either by studying outside of Maluku or through travel related to their being emerging artists. These individuals and groups are thus not necessarily representative of Moluccan people, who have no such opportunities, but they open up and shape public spaces that many have access to and they act as facilitators, multipliers and trendsetters. Ambon City, Maluku's capital, provides the infrastructure and space for their engagement.

Conflict and peacebuilding in Maluku

With a population less than 1.5 million in 2009, Maluku Province in Eastern Indonesia covers several hundred islands. The archipelago became famous as the 'Spice Islands', the source of nutmeg and clove that attracted early traders and colonial powers, who also brought Islam and Christianity. Maluku provided the scene for one of the most protracted conflicts that broke out shortly after the step-down of Indonesia's authoritarian president Suharto. This conflict tore apart villages, families and other kin groups. The scale of violence that erupted in January 1999 and went on for almost four years took most observers by surprise, as Maluku and its roughly half Christian, half Muslim population used to be praised for interreligious harmony in a majority Muslim country. As it was mainly carried out between Muslims and Christians, the clashes were commonly called a communal or religious conflict. This explanation however, disregards the less visible structural violence that was crucial to the emergence of the conflict.

As conceptualised by Johan Galtung, structural violence involves abuse through system-inherent inequalities and injustices as opposed to more visible direct (physical) violence.[9] In the context of Maluku, there are several examples of structural violence. Ever since the arrival of the colonial powers in Maluku, religion has become a politicised subject. Although Moluccans had developed means to maintain harmony and keep their society integrated, developments such as the Islamisation of politics from Indonesia's centre from the late 1980s and 1990s challenged this. A demographic shift in Maluku through spontaneous (mainly Muslim) immigration, but also governmental transmigration programmes from the 1970s onwards further increased hidden tensions and competition in a precarious job market. The Indonesian security forces took sides in the violence, as a means to uphold their power that was supposed to be curtailed in the post-Suharto reformation era, but also giving expression to the central government's failure to control its security forces. Colonial powers and neo-colonial unification policies had also substantially manipulated and weakened traditional conflict resolution mechanisms and imposed on its regions a power hierarchy that grants very unequal access to power and decision-making, resulting in land grabbing and resource exploitation through outside forces. The central government, however, mainly blamed Moluccans themselves for the violence and refused to set up any formal TJ mechanisms. Its main strategy was to send increasing numbers of troops to Maluku. The report of an independent, national fact-finding commission that was sent to Maluku after the Malino peace agreement in 2002 was never published and masterminds behind the conflict were never named, let alone called to appear in a criminal trial. Moluccans thus had to find their own means of reconciling

[8]Helen Berents, 'An Embodied Everyday Peace in the Midst of Violence', *Peacebuilding* 3, no. 2 (2015): 186.
[9]Galtung, Johan, 'Violence, Peace and Peace Research', *Journal of Peace Research* 6, no. 1 (1969): 167–91.

and restoring peace, without formal judicial justice and 'truth'[10] that conventional TJ tools would focus on.

Right from the beginning, there were hundreds of initiatives to stop the violence by international organisations and NGOs, regional governments, academics, the media, local organisations and leaders, both religious and *adat* (a term for tradition and customary law), and common people on the ground – all of them for a long time without apparent success. Exhausted by the long-lasting violence, Moluccans had to develop a narrative that would allow for the reintegration of society and the restoration of social relationships with their neighbours, which is crucial for their livelihoods. As most of them were involved in the violence, one way or the other, it made no sense to look for culprits in their own ranks. This reiterates the point that classic TJ mechanisms, with their clear distinction between perpetrators and victims, would have failed. They knew they were all guilty, but they also knew that they had been living in harmony before. The unifying narrative that most Moluccans can identify with was that outside provocateurs triggered the unrests and used religion to turn Moluccans against each other. The many Moluccans I spoke to over the years were convinced that reconciliation and restoration of social relations occurred rather naturally, from the bottom-up, by drawing on local resources and institutions, cultural capital and social ties. From early on, religious leaders were also involved in peace efforts. The Moluccan reverend and peace activist Jacky Manuputty sees an urgent need to build a profound interreligious dialogue and empathy with the other's religion, not just mere coexistence.[11] After years of preparation, he established the Moluccan Interfaith Council or Lembaga Antar Imam Maluku (LAIM) together with other committed religious figures such as the Muslim scholar Abidin Wakano in 2004. Without neglecting the importance of the cultural dimension of reconciliation, LAIM aims to raise awareness about common positive values within religions, build up the capacity of religious communities to prevent and manage conflicts, advance interreligious coordination and cooperation, and study religion from a theological, relational and sociocultural point of view.[12] LAIM's efforts to involve the youth were part of a larger thriving youth culture developing in 'post-conflict' Maluku that used arts as creative means to engage with Moluccan traditions, restore, build or strengthen social relations and establish connections to a broader social justice discourse. Their commitment, I argue, took peacebuilding in Maluku to the next level, by not only addressing the visible recent violence, but also the more hidden structural violence that greatly contributed to the Moluccan conflict. It resulted in long-term engagement (as opposed to fixed-term interventions) that was responsive to the broader social and political context[13] and initiated transformation through performative justice. The following section outlines crucial recent approaches in the broader field of TJ practice and research that challenge dominant notions of transition and justice.

---

[10] John Braithwaite et al., *Anomie and Violence: Non-truth and Reconciliation in Indonesian Peacebuilding* (Canberra: ANU E Press, 2010); Bräuchler, *Cultural Dimension of Peace.*

[11] Jacky Manuputty, 'Membuka Pintu Dialog: Pembelajaran Dari Pengalaman ELAIEM (unpublished ms)', 2010; Jacky Manuputty, 'Titik-titik balik di jalan orang basudara', in *Carita Orang Basudara. Kesaksian dan Rekaman Sejarah atas Tragedi Kemanusiaan di Maluku (pre-print version)*, ed. J. Manuputty (Ambon: Lembaga Antar Iman Maluku, 2014).

[12] Jacky Manuputty, 'Lembaga Antar Iman Maluku / Maluku Interfaith Institution (PowerPoint Presentation)', 2006; Manuputty, 'Membuka Pintu Dialog'; Manuputty, 'Titik-titik balik'.

[13] Laura McLeod, Jovana Dimitrijevic, and Biliana Rakocevic, 'Artistic Activism, Public Debate and Temporal Complexities: Fighting for Transitional Justice in Serbia', in *The Arts of Transitional Justice. Culture, Activism, and Memory after Atrocity*, eds. P.D. Rush and O. Simic (New York: Springer, 2014), 37.

Transitional justice, civil society and transformation

Transitional justice is generally understood as the efforts to cope with the aftermath of (in most cases intra-state) mass violence, authoritarian regimes or despotisms, and thus foster the transition to security and peace in divided societies.[14] Today, after various paradigm shifts,[15] TJ implies transition to a democratic and peaceful society and long-term reconciliation. Next to forgiveness and amnesty, the enforcement of human rights and law and the search for truth are considered the main instruments of TJ within an international peace discourse that is oriented towards Western ideas of human nature and society, democracy and peace.[16] A focus on institutions and top-down interventions has triggered critique of the TJ field for being andocentric, state-focused, Eurocentric or West-oriented, and anthropocentric, which is the main reason for major shortcomings of classic TJ models as briefly noted in the introduction.[17] It is argued that, by promoting the idea of a successful alliance between democracy and a liberal market economy producing peace, TJ 'has become part of a hegemonic discourse that links development and peacebuilding to a liberal statebuilding project that sees liberal democracy as its endpoint'.[18]

Such critiques have led to an awareness amongst critical TJ scholars and practitioners that TJ needs to be localised,[19] with a focus on what people at the local level perceive to be justice and the integration of so-called 'traditional justice' mechanisms into formal TJ processes.[20] It has also led to the awareness that, in order to generate sustainable peace and reduce the chances of a resurgence of conflict, TJ needs to strive for broader social justice. It needs to look into structural inequalities and tensions that underpin poverty and conflict,[21] and into the legacies of colonial (and neo-colonial) violence and its long-term effects. This requires a different time frame that goes beyond fixed-term TJ mechanisms and allows for the empowerment of conflict-affected people.[22] As van der Merwe put it, the 'most recent outbreak of war or phase of authoritarian rule is just one historical layer that requires contextualisation within a longer history of conflict'.[23]

The local contextualisation of TJ has led to the promotion of civil society organisations, usually as important intermediaries between outside interveners and conflict-affected people. However, civil society (CS) is rarely defined, or the definitions are vague and non-uniform and do not reflect the 'accumulated freight of centuries of European

[14] Susanne Buckley-Zistel, 'Transitional Justice als Weg zu Frieden und Sicherheit: Möglichkeiten und Grenzen' (SFB-Governance Working Paper Series Nr. 15, 2008), 3.

[15] Ruti G. Teitel, *Transitional Justice* (New York: Oxford University Press, 2000).

[16] Bräuchler, *Cultural Dimension of Peace*, 2–4.

[17] Paul Gready and Simon Robins, 'Rethinking Civil Society and Transitional Justice: Lessons from Social Movements and 'New' Civil Society', *The International Journal of Human Rights* 21, no. 7 (2017): 956; Natalia Szablewska and Sascha-Dominik Bachmann, 'Current Issues and Future Challenges in Transitional Justice', in *Current Issues in Transitional Justice. Towards a More Holistic Approach*, eds. N. Szablewska and S.-D. Bachmann (Cham: Springer, 2015), 355.

[18] Gready and Robins, 'Transformative Justice', 341.

[19] See e.g. Kieran McEvoy and Lorna McGregor, eds., *Transitional Justice from Below: Grassroots Activism and the Struggle for Change* (Oxford/Portland, Oregon: Hart, 2008); Rosalind Shaw and Lars Waldorf, eds., *Localizing Transitional Justice: Interventions and Priorities After Mass Violence* (Stanford, CA: Stanford University Press, 2010).

[20] Bräuchler, *Cultural Dimension of Peace*, 11–24.

[21] Gready and Robins, 'Transitional to Transformative', 346; Natalia Szablewska and Clara Bradley, 'Social Justice within Transitional Justice: The Case of Human Trafficking and Sex-Work in Cambodia and Myanmar', in *Current Issues in Transitional Justice. Towards a More Holistic Approach*, eds. N. Szablewska and S.-D. Bachmann (Cham: Springer, 2015), 265.

[22] McLeod et al., 'Artistic Activism'; Szablewska and Bachmann, 'Current Issues', 348.

[23] Hugo van der Merwe, 'Conclusion: The Role of Local Civil Society in Shaping Transitional Justice in Africa', in *Advocating Transitional Justice in Africa. The Role of Civil Society*, eds. J. Brankovic and H.V.D. Merwe (Cham: Springer, 2018), 214.

intellectual debate' that might not be generalisable to other parts of the world.[24] In the TJ literature, CS is often conceived as a unified and homogeneous entity 'that is simultaneously distinct from and complementary to the state'; as such, CS organisations 'are typically portrayed as supporting a TJ agenda that promotes liberal–legal justice strategies and global accountability norms'.[25] For Backer, CS contributions are vital to any TJ process as they contribute to data collection on human rights abuse and monitoring, representation and advocacy in policy debates, facilitating collaboration with communities and consultation, service delivery (e.g. counselling for victims), the promotion of restorative justice and compensation, further investigations, research and education.[26] He adds that in any TJ approach, we need to make sure 'that civil society is consulted, deployed and remains an asset even after the formal process.'[27] This gives expression to a rather instrumentalist and disempowering view, in which the state (or outside interveners) is always the reference point and CS is meant to fill certain gaps in a preconceived process, thus contributing to a rather superficial implementation of the local contextualisation of TJ.[28]

A broad conceptualisation of CS includes diverse collective actors such as special interest groups, faith-based organisations, traditional and community groups, researchers and research institutions, non-governmental organisations (NGOs), women and youth groups, social and political movements, activists and artists, (non-profit) business associations or some combination thereof.[29] What is rarely problematised is the varying degree to which such groups are organised or institutionalised. However, the extent to which they are organised (often in a hierarchical manner) or have spokespersons is crucial to their involvement in official peacebuilding. Outside donors and state interveners predominantly focus on NGOs as they are easy to find and usually experienced in communicating with outside actors. They cater for the interveners' need for institutionalised and organised legal partners and alleged representatives of local communities' interests. However, these organisations are often not representative of heterogeneous populations and a diverse CS.[30] In that sense, the notion of CS as it is represented in TJ discourse is rather reductionist; CS is an artificial entity that is disconnected from local everyday life and can easily lose its counter-hegemonic force.[31]

A clear example of how CS is treated in a simplistic or reductionist way in TJ discourse and practice can be seen in the case of youth. Youth are particularly important in post-conflict settings as the carriers of a society's future. However, often they are left out of classic TJ mechanisms or they are depicted as victims. This is one of the reasons why they are increasingly targeted by an international aid industry that wants to 'rescue'

---

[24] Chris Hann, 'Civil Society', in *Encyclopedia of Social and Cultural Anthropology*, eds. A. Barnard and J. Spencer (London/New York: Routledge, 2010), 122.

[25] Jeffery et al., 'Reconceiving Civil Society', 379–80.

[26] David Backer, 'Civil Society and Transitional Justice: Possibilities, Patterns and Prospects', *Journal of Human Rights* 2, no. 3 (2003).

[27] Ibid., 311.

[28] Gready and Robins, 'Rethinking Civil Society', 957, 960–1.

[29] Drawing on and expanding examples provided by Thania Paffenholz, 'Civil society', in *Routledge Handbook of Peacebuilding*, ed. R. Mac Ginty (London/New York: Routledge, 2013), 352.

[30] Thania Paffenholz, 'Civil Society and Peacebuilding (Summary of Results for a Comparative Research Project)' (CCDP Working Paper 4, 2009), 14.

[31] Roger Mac Ginty, 'Indigenous Peace-Making Versus the Liberal Peace', *Cooperation and Conflict* 43, no. 2 (2008): 144; Oliver P. Richmond, 'Becoming Liberal, Unbecoming Liberalism: Liberal-Local Hybridity via the Everyday as a Response to the Paradoxes of Liberal Peacebuilding', *Journal of Intervention and Statebuilding* 3, no. 3 (2009): 325.

and empower them.[32] Such a reductionist view, again, involves the risk to reduce them to be 'a resource to be mined in order to extract knowledge about peace'[33] and it overlooks the multiple roles that youth can play as victims, perpetrators, revolutionaries and agents of positive change.[34] Looking at youth as peacebuilders,[35] it is important to also acknowledge their political agency and possible leadership in these processes, with youth having agendas and responsibilities in both conflict and peace. Often, youth not only come first in peacebuilding, but they also fight on the front lines during conflict. The victim-perpetrator dichotomy that is reflected in classic TJ mechanisms ignores such fluidity in transitional contexts.[36]

Such reductionist notions of CS become particularly problematic in cases where there is not a powerful regime fighting its people, but rather people fighting people, neighbours fighting neighbours, as in the Maluku case. In such settings we need to look at the 'micro-politics of reconciliation at the communal and intercommunal levels'.[37] This requires an understanding of local forms and logics of social relations and their transformations, the cultural expressions of grief, anguish, loss, but also harmony and peace.[38] It requires peace researchers and workers to distance themselves from the instrumentalisation of CS as partners in one-off peace or reconciliation events, with limited time frames, a selective nature, and with scope and content shaped by outsiders. Looking into emerging, non-institutionalised and performative forms of activism, CS needs to be reconceptualised as a constantly changing and diverse field that is able to challenge inter/national policy makers, adapt TJ processes to local needs and priorities, speak to broader social inequalities and re/claim public spaces for increased active citizenship and deliberation.[39]

Such reconceptualisation of CS, Gready and Robin argue, requires a shift from the narrow legalism of transitional justice to a focus on 'justice in transition' or 'transformative justice' that is defined more broadly and highly contextualised.[40] They describe transformative justice as a social project that is continuously in the making, prioritises local agency and relates to both acts of past violence and continuing injustices and structural violence.[41] It shifts focus 'from the legal to the social and political, and from the state and institutions to communities and everyday concerns' and emphasises 'the need for a future marked not just by unity and reconciliation but also by disagreement and ongoing activism for change'.[42] Often it is social movements and other forms of collective action that drive change, contest hegemonic and 'mainstream social, political and transitional paradigms, and model alternatives to them', which is largely ignored in the TJ

---

[32]Alpaslan Oezerdem and Sukanya Podder, *Youth in Conflict and Peacebuilding: Mobilization, Reintegration and Reconciliation* (New York: Palgrave Macmillan, 2015), 7.

[33]Siobhan McEvoy-Levy, 'Youth', in *Routledge Handbook of Peacebuilding*, ed. R. Mac Ginty (London/New York: Routledge, 2013), 297–9, 166.

[34]McEvoy-Levy, 'Youth'; Oezerdem and Podder, Youth, 209; Pruitt, *Youth Peacebuilding*, 1–9.

[35]Heather Elliot, *Children and Peacebuilding: Experiences and Perspectives* (Melbourne: World Vision Australia, 2002).

[36]Caitlin Mollica, 'The Diversity of Identity: Youth Participation at the Solomon Islands Truth and Reconciliation Commission', *Australian Journal of International Affairs* 71, no. 4 (2017): 381.

[37]Kimberly Theidon, 'Intimate Enemies: Reconciling the Present in Post-War Communities in Ayacucho, Peru', in *After Mass Crime: Rebuilding States and Communities*, eds. B. Pouligny, S. Chesterman, and A. Schnabel (Tokyo/New York: United Nations University Press, 2007), 97.

[38]Bräuchler, *Cultural Dimension of Peace*, 32.

[39]Jasmina Brankovic and Hugo van der Merwe, 'Editors' Preface', in *Advocating Transitional Justice in Africa. The Role of Civil Society*, eds. J. Brankovic and H.V.D. Merwe (Cham: Springer, 2018), ix; Merwe, 'Conclusion', 221–2.

[40]Gready and Robins, 'Transformative Justice'.

[41]Gready and Robins, 'Rethinking Civil Society', 957, 972.

[42]Gready and Robins, 'Transformative Justice', 340, 356.

discourse.[43] Whereas NGOs are mostly results-based, social movements are sources of collective identity, which gives them 'the potential to create as well as mobilise constituencies [that are marginal to governance and TJ] and reveals social movements as potential tools of personal transformation through conscientisation'.[44] Social movements are out to confront, provide critical perspectives and create alternative social and public spaces to engage with the legacies of past violence and continuing social injustices and thus have 'the potential to provide a locally informed, broad-based and more democratic justice in transition'.[45]

Local choices as to how to deal with a violent past in divided societies, restore social relations and foster reconciliation often include performative approaches and arts.[46] Peter Rush argues that TJ 'can only be mediated by history and by visceral notions of personal and collective responsibility', what he calls 'affective justice'. For Rush, affective justice is not so much an emotion, as a bodily feeling, a corporeal sonority, a rhythm that places bodies on the line, an obligation that haunts and unsettles the narratives of transitional justice'.[47] As he continues to explain, 'if the form of justice is cultural, then its force is not so much normative as affective'.[48] Arts can be used as critical intervention to open up alternative spaces for TJ that can trigger debates about how to best reconcile a society and foster social change.[49]

Arts, performance and civil society

An increasing consideration of music and art in conflict transformation and peacebuilding started to emerge in the 1990s, which is closely tied to the arts' role in providing and strengthening a sense of identity.[50] During conflict, the negation of 'the other' often becomes an inherent part of one's own collective identity.[51] According to Kelman, reconciliation processes have to aim towards removing such negation and accepting the other group's identity, with both sides ideally moving towards a more shared identity (without replacing each group's core identity), expressed through shared symbols or rituals. Artistic engagement can facilitate such changes by providing a way of expressing people's lived experiences, including personal conflict trauma.[52] Arts-based peacebuilding can be an effective tool to engage CS groups and 'to bring together identity groups through sharing common cultural experiences, raising awareness about past suffering, and engaging communities in creative projects'.[53] Studying the nexus of art and peacebuilding, Premaratna and Bleiker highlight three key contributions artistic engagements can make to

[43]Gready and Robins, 'Rethinking Civil Society', 956.
[44]Ibid., 958.
[45]Ibid., 963, 965.
[46]Szablewska and Bachmann, 'Current Issues', 349.
[47]Rush, 'After Atrocity', vii.
[48]Ibid., viii.
[49]McLeod et al., 'Artistic Activism', 26–7.
[50]Arild Bergh and John Sloboda, 'Music and Art in Conflict Transformation: A Review', *Music and Arts in Action* 2, no. 2 (2010): 6.
[51]Herbert C. Kelman, 'Reconciliation as Identity Change: A Social-Psychological Perspective', in *From Conflict Resolution to Reconciliation*, ed. Y. Bar-Siman-Tov (Oxford: Oxford University Press, 2004).
[52]Nilanjana Premaratna and Roland Bleiker, 'Arts and Theatre for Peacebuilding', in *The Palgrave Handbook of Disciplinary and Regional Approaches to Peace*, eds. O.P. Richmond, S. Pogodda, and J. Ramovic (London: Palgrave Macmillan, 2016), 84–5.
[53]Craig Zelizer, 'The Role of Artistic Processes in Peace-Building in Bosnia-Herzegovina', *Peace and Conflict Studies* 10, no. 2 (2003): 62, 67.

peacebuilding: (1) the potential broadening of peacebuilding beyond more formal institutional approaches, e.g. by addressing the emotional legacies of war; (2) the provision of context-specific solutions that can possibly gain more legitimacy on the ground than outside TJ interventions; and (3) the highlighting of voices alternative to those heard in more formal peacebuilding models, voices that emerge from within CS.[54] Zelizer has identified four types of arts-based approaches to peacebuilding for Bosnia–Herzegovina: arts as a training tool, a product, a process, and as social protest, something I will come back to in my concluding reflections.[55] Premaratna and Bleiker emphasise that arts are inherently political, but 'they engage the political in very different and more creative ways than conventional approaches do'.[56] Arts draw from society but simultaneously change the perception and values of this society and thus make political transformation accessible for a variety of CS groups. An arts approach that is embedded in local practice and involves both producers and audience, acknowledges the agency of the grassroots and potentially empowers them (not only local elites); it can give expression to the complexity of sociocultural realities and enable the co-creation of inclusive narratives, which liberal peacebuilding commonly neglects.[57] Such increased concern with artistic practice has also begun to emerge in the critical TJ scholarship.

The scene described at the beginning resembles what the critical TJ scholar Simic (based on Robin Soans) calls 'documentary theatre' that is a play that the audience expects 'to be political, where the format is unconventional, while the material is contentious and challenges their opinions'.[58] It is not the re-enactmend of the experienced physical violence, but of some of its structural causes. Hobson conceptualises such performative enactments of locally situated concerns as contextual and embodied expressions of justice that reveal existing power relations and the underlying structural violence.[59] What Hobson has coined 'performative justice'[60] comes into being through its enactment and by (re)claiming public spaces that are turned into performative sites of local struggles, resistance, the resignification of meaning and the expression of collective feelings.[61] Artistic performances offer a stage for voices and experiences of marginalised people, allows the audience to 'witness' human rights violations and suffering, engage in dialogue about past violence and related social inequalities, and thus offers an artistic engagement with the future.[62] Such performances are at the same time strategies for intervention and resistance.[63]

[54]Premaratna and Bleiker, 'Arts and Theatre', 82–3.
[55]Zelizer, 'Artistic Processes', 67.
[56]Ibid., 83.
[57]Ibid.
[58]Olivera Simic, 'Stories We Tell: Documentary Theater, Performance, and Justice in Transition', in *Post-Communist Transitional Justice. Lessons from Twenty-Five Years of Experience*, eds. L. Stan and N. Nedelsky (Cambridge, UK: Cambridge University Press, 2015), 253.
[59]Kersty Hobson, 'Enacting Environmental Justice in Singapore: Performative Justice and the Green Volunteer Network', *Geoforum* 37 (2006): 673.
[60]Ibid., 674.
[61]Tazim Jamal and Rob Hales, 'Performative Justice: New Directions in Environmental and Social Justice', *Geoforum* 76 (2016): 178; Nadia Siddique, Hadi Marifat, and Sari Kouvo, 'Culture, Theatre and Justice: Examples from Afghanistan', in *The Arts of Transitional Justice. Culture, Activism, and Memory after Atrocity*, eds. P.D. Rush and O. Simic (New York: Springer, 2014), 130.
[62]McLeod et al., 'Artistic Activism', 40; Simic, 'Documentary Theater', 253.
[63]Simic, 'Documentary Theater', 255.

Arts and music can open up alternative, transformative and inclusive spaces for CS to 'envision different understandings of themselves and others' and to engage with peacebuilding, without explicitly talking about peace, by applying existing skills in new ways.[64] Increasing numbers of arts projects for peacebuilding such as music therapy for children, joint folk arts exhibitions or multicultural art workshops need to be carefully analysed to prevent the arts becoming yet another investment strategy of outside interveners.[65] This is not to say that short-term projects do not have positive effects, but they are less likely to produce sustainable outcomes. As Bergh and Sloboda emphasise 'relying on short term, strong emotional reactions to aesthetic experiences is counter productive'; long-term personal and social change only happens when people actively participate on all levels in musical engagement that is embedded in their everyday lives.[66]

In Maluku, such political agency for peace was something growing from within, be it a group of peace provocateurs, artists or youth promoting tourism to change the region's negative image and foster economic development. However, this did not happen in isolation, but in specific social, political and cultural settings, in which established peace activists and youth inspired each other. In Maluku, music and arts gave youngsters in particular the opportunity to see others not primarily as Muslims or Christians, but as someone to hang out with, to help and to envisage a joined future that offers space to live their lives the way they like. Artistic expressions turned out to be extremely effective as bridge builders and tools of resistance. They facilitated a change in communication and the development of a joint identity that draws on established Moluccan traditions, but, at the same time, creatively develops them further through youth culture and according to the needs of a 'post-conflict' society. Arts proved to be an important means to engage the young and the old in long-term peacebuilding and a broader struggle for social justice. Artistic engagement allowed Moluccans to simultaneously develop 'context-specific solutions' (see below) and draw on a broader national and international arts scene. It thus goes beyond an integrative space imagined through arts,[67] but makes the co-creation of a shared identity part of lived reality, which has snowball effects on the wider society. Such engagement enabled the complementation of traditional and new art forms and the integration of younger and older generations. The crucial point was that those initiatives were born out of the communities themselves, which contrasts cases where the reconciliatory potential of artistic engagement is hijacked by the peace industry through one-off events, as 'outside interventions' that select its participants and thus create further inequalities.

The Moluccan case thus exemplifies the need for and the implications of a transformative approach to justice. Moluccan peace activists and CS groups looked not only at the aftermath of violence, but into structural issues underlying it, thus not only aiming to transition from violence to non-violence and peace (often in a mere negative sense) but paving the way for broader social transformations and change. By engaging in what I call performative justice Moluccan peace activists can enact such struggles in daily life and in public space. Performative justice provides the means to make 'justice' accessible

---

[64]Lesley J. Pruitt, 'Music, Youth, and Peacebuilding in Northern Ireland', *Global Change, Peace and Security* 23, no. 2 (2011): 215; Lesley J. Pruitt, *Youth Peacebuilding: Music, Gender, and Change* (Albany: SUNY Press, 2013), 9.

[65]Bergh and Sloboda, 'Music and Art', 6; Siddique et al., 'Culture, Theatre, Justice', 127; Zelizer, 'Artistic Processes', 10.

[66]Bergh and Sloboda, 'Music and Art', 11–2.

[67]Premaratna and Bleiker, 'Arts and Theatre', 90.

for the public, to make them engage with it, thus raising awareness (locally, but also nationally and internationally through strategic media use and networks), exerting pressure on the government and other influential groups and individuals and envisioning another shared future. The following sections will further concretise that transformative potential.

Performative justice and resistance in Maluku

Over the last decade, the regional government aimed to change Maluku's image from a trouble spot to *The Wonderful Islands Maluku*,[68] by promoting the province's beauty and richness. With few exceptions, the government prefers to put the conflict aside as a dark spot in history and strive for good governance and economic development, something direly needed given the tremendous setbacks during the financial crisis in 1997 and the conflict. With promotional coffee table books and flyers the government reaches out for tourists and investors.[69] However, books printed in Ambon do not always travel easily when compared, for instance, with social media. Youth were equally fed up with Ambon's image as a trouble spot and decided to support the government's endeavours,[70] with their own creative means, with greater reach and potential to actively reintegrate society. Pierre, an Ambonese youth activist said, many of today's young people in Maluku were born during or after the violence. They have no memory of it and no memory of what it was like before the conflict when Muslim and Christian kids played together and shared experiences beyond religious affiliations. They inherited stories of conflict and war and grew up in segregated environments, some of them only getting to know children of 'the other side' in school or even university. That's why he sees an urgent need to open up space and opportunities for young people to get together, intermingle with the older generation and engage in the restoration of the Moluccan tradition of *basudara*, that is brother- and sisterhood, and a struggle for broader social justice. Pierre and friends do so through provoking Moluccans to peace through creativity. This requires a range of skills, including media skills and literacy in both local tradition and a global human rights discourse, and a variety of local, national and international networks.

Peace provocateurs

In September 2011, a Muslim motorcycle driver died in a Christian area – according to some, an accident, according to others, murder. The incident immediately caused the circulation of rumours and the arson of dozens of Christian and Muslim houses thus triggering fears that violence might escalate again.[71] Speedy intervention was needed and LAIM members like Jacky and Abidin and some youth got active.[72] They set up an information

[68]Yoyok Widoyoko, ed. *The Wonderful Islands Maluku: Membangun Kembali Maluku Dengan Nilai-Nilai dan Khazanah Lokal, serta Prinsip Entrepreneurial Government, Beragam Potensi dan Peluang Investasi* (Jakarta/Ambon: Gibon Books/Pemprov Maluku, 2008).

[69]See e.g. R.Z. Leirissa et al., *Ambonku: doeloe, kini, esok* (Ambon: Pemerintah Kota Ambon, 2004); Lembaga Kebudayaan Daerah Maluku, *The Magnificant Underwater World of Ambon Island, Maluku – Indonesia* (Ambon: LKDM, 2010); M. Noer Muis et al., *Amazing Ambon – Above, Under and Beyond* (Jakarta: NMbooks, 2010); Karel Albert Ralahalu, *Otonomi Daerah Di Tengah Konflik: Merencang Success Story Implementasi Otonomi Daerah di Provinsi Maluku* (Ambon: Media Otda, 2006).

[70]See also Admin, 'Paparisa Ambon Bergerak, Rumah Bersama Komunitas Kreatif', *Ambon Ekspres*, October 30, 2015.

[71]International Crisis Group, 'Indonesia: Trouble Again in Ambon', Asia Briefing No. 128, 2011.

[72]Bräuchler, *Cultural Dimension of Peace*, 96–8.

filter team, checked rumours through social media, telephone and SMS (that were also used to spread the rumours) and pressured the national media through journalist networks to stick to the facts and not provoke further unrest. As a result, the situation was quelled and no more incidents of extraordinary violence followed. These people called themselves *provokator damai* or peace provocateurs – an idea that soon attracted national and international attention. It is meant to give expression to their proactive support and facilitation of grassroots reconciliation and peacebuilding in everyday life, where peace does not come about naturally, but everyone is asked to contribute whatever s/he can to foster societal transformation and change.

Two young Moluccan film makers, Rifky Husain and Ali Madi Salay, produced an award winning film in 2012 entitled *Provokator Damai* (Peace Provocateurs) that was screened in Indonesian TV and invited to international film festivals. The documentary tells the story of people's experiences and feelings during the interfaith sleepovers organised by LAIM and how insecurity and fear turned into tears and the expression of a deep longing to return to a peaceful life. Another film reaching out way beyond Maluku is *Cahaya Dari Timur: Beta Maluku* (Lights From the East: I am Moluccan, 2014, directed and produced by Angga Dwimas Sasongko and Glenn Fredly). Based on a true story, the film is about Sani Tawainella from Tulehu village (Ambon Island), who failed to become a professional footballer and then decided to train Muslim and Christian kids in football during the conflict to prevent them from joining the fighting. The film tells about the various difficulties he faced in organising and training an interreligious football team of youngsters, some of them traumatised by the violence, and how he finally managed to motivate them to unite and win the Indonesia under-15 football cup in Jakarta.

The Peace Provocateur Movement utilises social media and a website that provides information about peacebuilding, reconciliation and interfaith dialogue and how others can learn from the Moluccan experience (http://ambon.provokatordamai.org/). Another tangible and influential outcome of their efforts is a collection of *Basudara Stories of Peace from Maluku.*[73] Due to the traumatic nature of their experiences, it took contributors a long while to overcome their inhibitions and share rather than suppress and forget their stories; the book took years to realise. Once it was out, an English version followed to reach out to the wider community with lessons learned in Maluku. It tells the stories of people who were deeply entrenched in the conflict and how the violence interrupted, shaped and transformed their life histories and relationships. It tells stories of people who dared to cross boundaries and work for the restoration of social relationships in the midst of violence, believing in *basudara* tradition, and thus provides an alternative reading to the various academic studies on the conflict. For all involved, it was a transformative experience that not only engaged with the past, but laid the ground for a shared future. This is an important endeavour in an environment, where an official and public engagement with the past has not taken place. As Gerry van Klinken put it in the book's foreword: 'The silence has come to an end today!'[74] Moluccan peace campaigners also received

[73]Jacky Manuputty et al., eds. *Carita Orang Basudara. Kisah-kisah Perdamaian dari Maluku* (Ambon: Lembaga Antar Iman Maluku, 2014); Jacky Manuputty et al., eds., *Basudara Stories of Peace from Maluku. Working Together for Reconciliation* (Clayton, VIC: Monash University Publishing, 2017).

[74]Gerry van Klinken, 'PREFACE. Ale Rasa Beta Rasa – What You Feel, I Feel: Compiling History Together in Ambon', in *Basudara Stories of Peace from Maluku. Working Together for Reconciliation*, eds. J. Manuputty et al., (Clayton, VIC: Monash University Publishing, 2017), xv.

national awards for their efforts. Jacky was awarded the Maarif Award in 2007, Rudi Fofid in 2016. Rudi is a journalist, poet and key in promoting peace journalism in Maluku. The award is given to people with local leadership that promotes tolerance, pluralism and social justice at the grassroots (http://maarifinstitute.org/). Youth and arts groups that share the enthusiasm for peace and the strong belief in Moluccan tradition are part of the Peace Provocateur Movement. *Ambon Bergerak* or Ambon in Motion is one of the constituting networks that consists of a number of arts groups – all social-media-savvy youth that come together to be creative, have fun and take responsibility for social integration in public space.

Ambon Bergerak

> The social conflict in Maluku inflicted wounds,
> ripped the memories of the life of brothers and sisters …
> but …
> the conflict also made young people talk again about the true values of Maluku.
> Talk again about how to restore intact brother- and sisterhood,
> being a creative and caring young person … [75]

These words are faded in at the start of the video *INSPIRATOR Maluku Hiphop & Ambon Bergerak* who were invited to contribute to and perform for a programme called 'Inspiration from Indonesia's East', part of a broader initiative funded by multiple donors to develop Eastern Indonesia (Forum Kawasan Timur Indonesia, Bakti Foundation). As I had variously heard during and after the conflict, it was the decline and the degradation of such cultural values that enabled the outbreak of violence. This woke Moluccan society up to save what is left.[76] Ambonese youngsters like Pierre, an architect and lover of IT and arts, Yuli, a member and researcher of the National Human Rights Commission in Maluku, and Burhanuddin, a graduate of the Australian National University, were key to get 'Ambon moving' and better network artists and youth. In early 2015, they opened up Paparisa Ambon Bergerak to give their movement a home – *paparisa* being a Moluccan term for a shared house or hut where family and friends can meet. As one of the activists emphasised, the place became both symbol and space for the interaction of youths in Ambon. The place is open 24/7 for people and artists who want to exchange ideas, paint, make music, read or organise workshops and provides an alternative for meeting places such as cafés and streets.

Several independent creative communities have emerged in Ambon and surroundings over the last decade and then joined into Ambon Bergerak, including blogging, IT, film, hip-hop, literature, theatre, tourism and environment, photography and painting, with various overlaps between the groups. Most of them formed between 2008 and 2010 with an increasing socio-political engagement after the September 2011 incident – many inspired by leading peace figures such as Rudi and Jacky. Social media such as Facebook, Instagram, Twitter, Path and YouTube play important roles in the youth's promotion of their work and social engagement and in their struggle to change the negative image of Ambon and Maluku. That's why funding initially came from ICT Watch, but will remain a challenge in the future. The initiators' mission is to connect creative communities for

[75] Yayasan Bakti, INSPIRATOR Maluku Hiphop & Ambon (produced 2012, published in YouTube 2016), Forum Kawasan Timur Indonesia, 2012/2016, https://www.youtube.com/watch?v=FG4o_zspgeY (accessed November 13 2016), author translation.

[76] Jacky Manuputty, 'The Turning Point on the Road of Basudara Relationships', in *Basudara Stories of Peace from Maluku. Working Together for Reconciliation*, eds. J. Manuputty et al., (Clayton, VIC: Monash University Publishing, 2017), 116.

synergy effects, to foster development and encourage a creative industry and alternative incomes for youth, thus overcoming some of the structural challenges they face. They see themselves as a social movement reaching out for a broader public through activities such as trotoart (sidewalk art), street theatre, concerts, poetry readings, live painting and photography. And this is where their activities as continuing efforts diverge from fixed-term peace interventions and classic TJ efforts that focus on a specific period of violence rather than the long-term social injustices underlying it. They strive, in this article's terminology, for transformation through performative justice.

To contribute to Maluku's image change, the blogger community got together with nature lovers and environmental activists and started to engage in a campaign called *Maluku Baronda* to promote the islands' beauty. 'If you google "Maluku" or "Ambon", you get pictures of conflict, destruction and violence. With such a negative image, Maluku cannot move forward.' As one of the initiators explained, they wanted to fight the Moluccan unrests in Google and rebrand Maluku. The main thrust was to post positive images in a variety of media to reach as many potential travellers as possible (see e.g. MalukuBaronda or the AyoKeMaluku campaign in Instagram, Twitter, Facebook). The photographer community helps with pictures from beautiful spots and traditional ceremonies that illustrate that Maluku is a safe place.

The Moluccan Hip-Hop Community (MHC) consists of groups and independent rappers. It started to take shape in 2004 and was founded in 2008.[77] Through their music, they wanted to express Moluccan voices, feelings and realities. Morika, an Ambonese youngster who had studied in Ambon, Jakarta and overseas is one founding member. As a poet, he is also active in the literature community and takes great effort to include Moluccan tradition and ancient mantra that he collects from villages into his art. MHC was invited to the Ambon Jazz Festival twice (2009 and 2010) and Glenn Fredly, a prominent Indonesian musician who hails from Maluku and shares the vision to build Maluku through music, has produced several albums with them, among others 'Beta Maluku' (I am Maluku) that has been presented in Jakarta and abroad in 2011. Both Morika and Mark, another MHC member, are convinced that music has responsibility and has to have a message and positive power. For Revellino, Rap and MHC are places to share peace, critique and the power of tradition. Mark was one of two rapping the introduction to the video mentioned earlier called 'Lawamena resurrection'. The song asks youth to keep moving forward, to not break the pledge of the ancestors and raise awareness about Moluccan culture and values. Hip-hop was something readily available after the conflict: it is easy, cheap and only needs simple equipment. Moreover, as we learn from these youths, hip-hop philosophy very much matches the idea of ancient kapata, traditional rhymes telling Moluccan village myths and history from which these musicians take inspiration. They use hip-hop in its original sense, as nonviolent 'rhythmic repetition of resistance',[78] and as a means for self-expression and protest that is recognisable to many young people.[79] The video closes with another song produced by MHC, the SaveAru song (see below).

Poetry is another powerful tool to give voice to the unheard. Rudi and others take great efforts in opening up spaces for youths to engage in critical arts and share their work in

[77]Molukka Hiphop Community, 'Profile', Ambon, 2008.

[78]Jan Jagodzinski, *Music in Youth Culture. A Lacanian Approach* (New York: Palgrave Macmillan, 2005), 64.

[79]Kathrin Lock, 'Who is Listening? Hip Hop in Sierra Leone, Liberia and Senegal', in *Resounding International Relations: On Music, Culture and Politics*, ed. M.I. Franklin (New York: Palgrave Macmillan, 2005), 142; Pruitt, *Youth Peacebuilding*, 54.

public, in some of the cafés mushrooming in post-conflict Maluku, on various events from workshops to street performances, and in a variety of media. Rudi and other Moluccan poets have edited several poetry volumes relating and reflecting on the Moluccan way to make war and peace, involving people from across the region, across generations, and from various educational backgrounds, using Indonesian, Ambonese Malay or other local languages. In one of them, commissioned by the governmental Language Office of Maluku Province, we find the poem *Biarkan Katong Bakalae*, composed by Jacky,[80] that has been quoted and read on various occasions, for instance on the anniversary event of the September 2011 incident. It reminds people that if they have to fight, they need to quickly reconcile again as has always been the case in Maluku before the outbreak of mass violence (see also *Biarkan Kami Bakalae*, https://www.youtube.com/watch?v=kocPeU4D2gA, 12 February 2018). Weslly, a poet and future reverend who had studied in Ambon, also contributed to the volume. Himself a refugee from Buru, he liked the spirit of togetherness in Ambon Bergerak activities; for him, writing has a cathartic effect. Others experienced the same kind of catharsis with other art forms such as photography or painting. Weslly is convinced that it is small things, done on a regular basis, that will bring peace and prepare Maluku for the future. Writing poetry from within one's heart, talking and sharing with and inspiring others is one way of helping to transform feelings of resentment and disappointment into feelings of hope and brotherhood.[81]

Painters use their art to build bridges. Tessart, one of Ambon's emerging young artists, is part of the painter community and Ambon Bergerak. He puts his art into the service of movement actions such as street theatre or concerts, which, in turn, helps to make his art increasingly popular. Himself a Christian, Tessart went to Muslim villages in 2012 to learn how to paint Arabic characters. He and his family had to flee during the conflict and his mother was worried about him spending so much time in Muslim villages. For Tessart, his artistic engagement is a peace tool that not only brings Christian and Muslims together, but also the young and the old. Ambon Bergerak members are very sensitive to conflict and social issues more generally, he states. For instance, they used their networks and media skills to help those affected by heavy flooding in Ambon, collected funds for victims of (impending) volcano eruptions in East Nusa Tenggara and Northern Maluku, or shared a meal with orphans when breaking the fast during Ramadham. The most elaborate 'relief campaign' was the SaveAru movement.

#SaveAru

hypocritical rulers and greedy middlemen
secretly agreed to sell themselves
and pawn adat land
then thousands of ursia and urlima took to the streets
as anger of the arafura (our ancestors) rises from the islands and the mangroves
(Excerpt from SaveAru song, MHC & friends, author translation)

To close the circle, let us revisit the big bird flying across the street in Ambon City in 2013. The performance was part of a larger movement to counter continuing social injustices in Maluku and save Aru from social, cultural and environmental destruction that emerged

[80]Rudi Fofid, *Biarkan Katong Bakalae: antologi puisi penyair Maluku* (Ambon: Kantor Bahasa Maluku, 2013).
[81]Weslly Johannes, Beta Sayang Kenangan (27.8.2015) Molucca Project, 27.8.2015, 2015, http://www.moluccaproject.com/2015/08/weslly-johannes-beta-sayang-kenangan.html (accessed February 7 2018).

from peacebuilding initiatives previously described. It brings the concept of performative justice to fruition, for which the rising awareness of the close connection between the recent violence and social inequalities caused by historical and recent Indonesian power politics had laid the foundation. The investor, a strategic alliance of 28 businesses, wanted to open up 500.000 ha out of roughly 630.000 ha covered by the Aru Islands which would leave no space for any traditional livelihoods and settlement patterns. Whereas the government had encouraged the investor to conduct feasibility studies, neither had sought prior informed consent of the affected population and the feasibility studies were highly flawed, thus violating national law and international conventions. The issue was taken up in 2011/2012 by a few individuals in Aru and an environmental NGO in Ambon, and then developed into a strong movement within a couple of months. Protest emerged in various forms and on various levels. Villagers in Aru were mobilised on a broad scale by Aru activists. They joined hands with market women, journalists, NGO activists, academics, religious figures and civil servants – across the generations, traditional affiliations and religions. According to the movement's coordinator in Aru, an unprecedented case of anarchism on Aru. They personally delivered their statements and signatures to the House of Regional Representatives and ministries in Jakarta. Local, national and international mainstream media critically covered the case and sympathisers worldwide posted their photos with the #SaveAruIslands slogan in social media. Embong, an Ambonese photographer, assembled these photos on a giant poster that was put up in Ambon during the trotoart event and in Aru to let the locals know that they were not alone. Influential figures like Jacky and Glenn put up a petition on change.org and even the Moluccan Protestant Church supported the movement. Jacky as head of its Research and Development Body has been working hard over the last couple of years to raise an environmental consciousness in the church. Given that Aru is majority Protestant, the church's support was important. The combination of resistance in Aru, skilled intermediaries, social media and arts made the movement go viral and, in the end, stop the project.

The SaveAru movement provided established peace figures and youth the opportunity to utilise their skills, energy, networks and vision to fight the plantation project that threatens one of the poorest Moluccan districts and one of the main sources of Moluccan identity, *adat* land. It gave them an opportunity to seek a kind of justice that goes beyond addressing the direct violence committed during the narrow confines of the Moluccan conflict. When students and *adat* elders from Aru approached Jacky for help, he had no difficulties reaching out to the peace provocateurs and Ambon Bergerak. Aiming at a broader social justice they were ready to take action and coordinate with environmental and human rights activists in Ambon, Aru and Jakarta. All activities were shared in social and other media, with the powerholders in Ambon, Jakarta and the world at large. Academics talked in front of the parliament. Bloggers and IT-savvy people set up media accounts and made the news go viral. Burhanuddin designed the movement logo – a bird of paradise and hashtag SaveAruIslands, black on white – and an infographic visualising the extent of the planned intrusion. Arts communities organised events such as concerts and street performances, distributed flyers and created movement T-Shirts. Various artists contributed to the 2013 event in Ambon City, in front of popular Ambon Plaza, where the capitalist threat and the local people's resistance were re-enacted in the theatre performance described in the introduction. Tessart, for instance, was engaged in live painting, there was live music, a photo booth to take pictures of passers-by with the #SaveAruIslands, poetry reading, etc. Dance and theatre groups also put up an installation on the car-free-day in Ambon for SaveAru. Regular music and poetry events paid tribute to the Aru case, including a huge jazz concert at Independence Square, hosting Boi Akih from the Netherlands with their Moluccan singer Monica Akihari and local bands from MHC, funded by the provincial government and various sponsors. Monica dedicated one of her songs to the Aru case, Rudi read some poems and Tessart contributed with drawing the four band members in bird-of-paradise shapes. Rudi and Morika edited and contributed to volumes such as *Revolusi Cendrawasih*, a poetry collection against deforestation, or *Mata Aru* (Aru's Eyes), a poetry anthology for the defence of Aru.[82] Their illustrator friends enriched the books with sketches.

The lyrics of the SaveAru song are a mix of Indonesian, Aruese and English, thus making it accessible for many. It is sang by artists and laymen on various occasions, but also circulated online, via social media, and included in videos and films in which local, national and international activists such as Forest Watch Indonesia document the Aru case. The song denounces greedy and corrupt power holders who grab indigenous people's land, which made Urlima and Ursia, Aru's large societal groups, go to the streets and defend their heritage and livelihoods, the forests, mangroves, fishing and hunting grounds and rare species such as the black cockatoo or the bird of paradise. The song ends with a verse about the ancestors calling, asking Aru people to take up their bows and arrows and not give up their land. Poetry, music, songs, paintings, etc. are all shared online thus increasing both the artists' fame and awareness about Aru, well beyond Maluku. As one of the musicians emphasised, the combination of youth, music and social media is extremely powerful and easily goes viral; it is an ideal means to make the movement grow.

Concluding reflections

The dynamics and complexities of the Moluccan peace process require an understanding of TJ that moves away from the idea of a temporally limited transition from one status to another, from conflict or war towards peace that is facilitated by outside intervenors and formal legal procedures. Moluccans had to develop their own means of reintegrating society and bringing about transformation and change in ways that addressed the structural violence underlying the recent conflict. The continuing engagement of peace activists in Maluku is proof of the success of performative justice. Their analysis allows this article to fill gaps in the transformative justice project through thick descriptions and assessments of transformative justice in specific social and regional contexts. The article contributes to the further exploration of the performative justice concept elaborated by Hobson and Jamal and Hales,[83] here conceptualised as a form of social activism that can affect change and transformation and thus counter classic notions of TJ through performativity.[84] The article has also made a case for a CS concept that not only looks at the institutionalised efforts for peace such as NGO work, but that also accommodates the

[82]Revelino Berry, Rudi Fofid, and Weslly Johannes, eds., *Revolusi Cendrawasih. Kumpulan puisi perlawanan terhadap upaya pembabatan hutan Aru* (Ambon: www.savearuisland.com, 2013); Revelino Berry, Rudi Fofid, and Weslly Johannes, eds., *Mata Aru. Antologi Puisi Pembelaan Untuk Aru* (Ambon: www.savearuisland.com, 2013).
[83]Hobson, 'Environmental Justice'; Jamal and Hales, 'Performative Justice'.
[84]Compare Judith Butler, 'Performative Agency', *Journal of Cultural Economy* 3, no. 2 (2010): 147.

various (partly very unorganised and spontaneous) actors and actions engaged in broader struggles against social injustices that are crucial triggers of violent conflict.

In Maluku, all four types of arts-based approaches to peacebuilding identified by Zelizer above are in place: arts as a training tool (i.e. training youths as artists and creative bridge builders), a product (i.e. something youths can ideally live from and something with a message), a process (i.e. an opportunity to change communication patterns and develop joint narratives), and as social protest (i.e. as a means to counter conflict, injustice and raise awareness), with lots of overlaps.[85] These four aspects help to emphasise the multi-dimensionality of performative justice in Maluku that can give youth future perspectives, education (difficult during the years of conflict), jobs and chances to explore alternative livelihoods. It requires multiple approaches in a struggle for broader social justice, which is crucial for in-depth, locally rooted and sustainable peacebuilding and reconciliation efforts. As one of the coordinators of Ambon Bergerak put it, their long term goal is a youth movement that builds and maintains peace in creative and nonviolent ways, through continuous activities and regular meetings. It makes them stay in touch and alert so that they can react quickly in case issues of conflict or social injustice emerge such as the September 2011 incident or the Aru case. Smaller groupings have started to adopt the 'Save' hashtag strategy. Most of them do not get very far though without the necessary base, networks and engagement behind it. As the SaveAru case shows, grassroots movements for peace and social justice cannot simply be copied or introduced or imposed from the outside but need to grow from within (of course often inspired and helped by outside actors or more established figures) and over a long period of time.

In the long run, however, as Jacky has pointed out in relation to setting up LAIM and as I have emphasised in my own work,[86] Moluccans not only need to engage in celebrating their shared traditions and joint (peaceful) identities, but also in understanding differences (that were instrumentalised to mobilise for violence). The strategy should not be 'forgive and forget', but 'remember and change'.[87] The peace movement in Maluku is definitely engaged in remembering and changing and, on top of that, I want to suggest, can prepare the ground for further peaceful engagement with difference. Both the celebration of a shared identity and the respectful acknowledgment and understanding of specific group identities (be they religion, youth culture or specific cultural groups) need to be layers in a more comprehensive process, which many more actors need to get involved in. Ambon Bergerak is one important element in a complex peacebuilding landscape and broader efforts to address issues of structural violence such as injustices in the access to education, jobs, land and other resources. One might argue that most of the actions take place on Ambon Island or in Ambon City. But one also needs to remember that Maluku's capital is a multicultural hotspot; it is from here that conflict and violence were carried into the villages (and the other way around) and it is here where people from all islands and villages come together and carry the (re)emerging spirit of brother- and sisterhood back into their villages. As Embong put it, Ambon has become a laboratory

---

[85]Zelizer, 'Artistic Processes', 67.

[86]See e.g. Birgit Bräuchler, 'Christian-Muslim Relations in Post-Conflict Ambon, Moluccas: Adat, Religion and Beyond', in *Religious Diversity in Muslim-majority Southeast Asia: Areas of Toleration and Conflict*, eds. B. Platzdasch and J. Saravanamuttu (Singapore: ISEAS, 2014); Birgit Bräuchler, 'Modes of Interreligious Coexistence and Civility in Maluku', in *Dynamics of Religion in Southeast Asia*, ed. V. Gottowik (Amsterdam: Amsterdam University Press, 2014); Bräuchler, *Cultural Dimension of Peace*.

[87]Oezerdem and Podder, Youth, 216.

for peace. Results so far have been mostly positive. Taken together with other initiatives such as the revival of traditional leadership and the restrengthening of traditional alliance systems,[88] Maluku has turned into a role model for grassroots peace building, nationally and internationally. Moluccan peace activists have been awarded prestigious Indonesian prizes and are consulted by the Indonesian government and invited to become involved in nationwide processes of peacebuilding and interfaith dialogue – a call to learn from the country's east. In the future, continuous research on Maluku's struggle for social justice needs to firmly position these developments in broader investigations into Moluccan CS and youth culture. It also needs to look into whether such movements manage to survive without state support and how they deal with the potential commercialisation and ensuing de-politicisation of their art.[89]

Acknowledgements

I would like to thank the peace provocateurs, Ambon Bergerak and members of the SaveAru movement for sharing their insights and ideas on peacebuilding and a more just future for Maluku and Indonesia.

Disclosure statement

No potential conflict of interest was reported by the author.

Funding

This work was supported by the German Foundation for Peace Research (Deutsche Stiftung Friedensforschung, DSF) [grant number FP 04/15 – SP 03/12-2014].

ORCID

Birgit Bräuchler http://orcid.org/0000-0002-4599-3582

88. For a critical evaluation see Bräuchler, *Cultural Dimension of Peace.*

89. Robin L. Turner, 'Youth, "Tradition" and Peace Building: Mobilising for Just Governance in Rural South Africa', *Peacebuilding* 3, no. 2 (2015): 138–9; Jagodzinski, *Music in Youth Culture.*

Exploring the link between mine action and transitional justice in Cambodia

Dahlia Simangan and Rebecca Gidley

ABSTRACT

This paper examines mine action in Cambodia and its implications for common conceptions of civil society and transitional justice. The complexities of past Cambodian conflicts and the strained state-civil society relationship at present have led to a complicated legacy of landmines. The collective harm Cambodian people have experienced also blurs the line between victimhood and perpetration of crime, further complicating transitional justice in the Cambodian context. Exploring the link between mine action and transitional justice in Cambodia reveals that civil society organisations involved in mine action are not separate from the state contrary to the common conceptualisation of civil society as autonomous. It also demonstrates that mine action is responding to more complex elements of Cambodian conflicts than the retributive model of transitional justice. The participatory approaches to mine action highlight local agency and active involvement, which are crucial in creating a civil society that encourages an empowered citizenry.

Introduction

The current transitional justice mechanisms in Cambodia do not reflect the complexities of past conflicts. Cambodia's modern history does not lend itself to an easy discussion of two sides of a single conflict. It was embroiled in the Vietnam War, with Prince Norodom Sihanouk attempting to maintain neutrality between the communist and capitalist forces in the 1960s, before being overthrown in a coup by the pro-US General Lon Nol in 1970. During the late 1960s and early 1970s Cambodia was extensively bombed by the US, much of it in secret missions. The Lon Nol government came under increasing pressure from the communist Khmer Rouge, which took control of Phnom Penh on 17 April 1975. In the subsequent 3 years, 8 months, and 20 days their regime resulted in the deaths of 1.7–2.2 million Cambodians from overwork, disease, and executions.[1] A Vietnamese-backed army supported by Khmer Rouge defectors overthrew the regime in January 1979. The new government renamed Cambodia the People's Republic of Kampuchea (PRK), and then as the State of Cambodia (SoC) in 1989. Many of the same people have

[1] ECCC, 'Demographic Expert Report: Khmer Rouge Victims in Cambodia, April 1975-January 1979, A Critical Assessment of Major Estimates', D140/1/1, September 30, 2009.

been leading Cambodia since 1979, now as Cambodia's ruling party, the Cambodian People's Party (CPP). Despite controlling most of the country the PRK was denied international recognition in the 1980s, with the UN continuing to recognise the Khmer Rouge's representation. The Khmer Rouge and other non-communist resistance groups continued to wage guerrilla warfare from Thai border camps. In response the Phnom Penh government launched the K5 plan to create a barrier along the Thai-Cambodia border using landmines.

The decades of immense political instability and internal conflict have left a deadly legacy confronting the Cambodian people today. Cambodia has one of the highest contaminations of landmines and explosive remnants of war (ERW)[2] in the world. The parties to the wars and conflicts dropped bombs and laid mines all around the country, with the highest concentration in the borderlands. Cambodia's western part has landmines, the eastern provinces sit on unexploded ordnances, while the central part is affected by both.[3] Accurate records of the locations of landmines are virtually non-existent, including those around civilian communities, and Cambodia's wet seasons have moved and further buried some of the landmines.[4] The conflicts in Cambodia have left an estimated four to six million landmines and other unexploded ordnances (UXOs).[5] The US State Department has a record of 2.75 million tons of US bombs being dropped in Cambodia from 1965 to 1973, including 27.9 million pieces of cluster munitions.[6] The Cambodian government has recorded a total of 64,720 casualties of landmines and other ERW from 1979 to 2017. Of these casualties 19,758 (31%) were killed, 35,941 (55%) were injured, and 9021 (14%) were amputated.[7] A survey conducted from 2000 to 2002 revealed that at the time 46% of Cambodian villages, or 6416 villages, may have had mine-contaminated lands.[8] In 1991 the competing factions signed the Agreements on a Comprehensive Political Settlement of the Cambodia Conflict and, a year later, the United Nations Transitional Authority in Cambodia (UNTAC) was deployed to administer the country and conduct the first national elections. The post-election arrangement was a coalition government led by the co-premiership of Hun Sen from the CPP and Prince Norodom Ranariddh of the royalist FUNCINPEC party, until Hun Sen staged a coup to dislodge Ranariddh in 1997.[9] The complexities of Cambodia's conflicts naturally led to a complicated legacy of landmines. However, these complexities are not reflected in the transitional justice mechanisms, which currently only address the Khmer Rouge-era crimes.

This paper investigates the link between mine action and transitional justice against the backdrop of state-civil society relations in Cambodia. The purpose of this investigation is to

[2]ERW consist of unexploded ordnance (UXO) and abandoned explosive ordnance (AXO). Landmines are not within the legal definition of ERW. UN, 'Protocol V of the 1980 UN Convention on Certain Conventional Weapons', Article 2.

[3]UN Mine Action Service, 'Cambodia: 2018 Summary Graphs', *Portfolio of Mine Action Projects*, https://www.mineaction.org/en/portfolio-of-mine-action-projects (accessed March 2018).

[4]Ibid.

[5]Royal Government of Cambodia (RGC), 'Request for an Extension of the Deadline for Completing the Destruction of Anti-personnel Mines in Mined Areas in Accordance with Article 5', April 30, 2009, apminebanconvention.org/fileadmin/APMBC/clearing-mined-areas/art5_extensions/countries/Cambodia-ExtRequest-Received-11May2009.pdf.

[6]RGC, *National Mine Action Strategy (NMAS) 2018–2025* (Phnom Penh: CMAA, 2017), 1.

[7]CMAA, 'Cambodia Mine/ERW Victim Information System: Monthly Report for December 2017', cmaa.gov.kh/en/report/cmvis-report-december-2017 (accessed July 2018).

[8]RGC, *NMAS*, 1.

[9]Sihanouk founded FUNCINPEC, the French acronym for the National United Front for an Independent, Neutral, Peaceful and Cooperative Cambodia. Despite FUNCINPEC obtaining the greatest number of votes, Sihanouk negotiated the post-election power-sharing arrangement after Hun Sen's threat to destabilise the country. UNTAC endorsed the arrangement and completed its mission in September 1993.

explore potential venues for civil society to engage with transitional justice amidst shrinking democratic spaces, such as in Cambodia. Mine action is one of a number of domains where transitional justice and civil society organisations (CSOs) overlap. Cambodia officially started mine action with the establishment of the Cambodian Mine Action Centre (CMAC) in June 1992 during UNTAC's mission.[10] Since then, mine action in Cambodia has evolved into a structured and coordinated strategy, and has managed to clear approximately half of lands contaminated with landmines/ERW,[11] reduce the number of casualties each year, provide assistance to victims and their families, and conduct mine risk education programmes. It has also become intertwined with the other domains of Cambodian society: politics, civil society, economic development, and post-conflict reconciliation. While numerous reports prove that the presence of landmines stunts economic development,[12] few studies situate mine action in the context of state-civil society relations and in the implementation of transitional justice. This paper, therefore, seeks to answer the question: What is the impact of mine action on transitional justice in Cambodia?

Mine action refers to humanitarian mine clearance, education, victim assistance, global advocacy, and stockpile destruction.[13] Mine action became a key component of humanitarian aid in the early 1990s and gained international backing with the adoption of the Ottawa Treaty (formally the Convention on the Prohibition of the Use, Stockpiling, Production and Transfer of Anti-Personnel Mines and on their Destruction).[14] It started with a technical focus and later included the social and economic dimensions of mine clearance and victim assistance.[15] Civil society is a key player in promoting mine action at the global and national/local levels. The International Campaign to Ban Landmines (ICBL) is a global network of non-governmental organisations (NGOs) working to free the world of anti-personnel landmines and support the victims of landmines, and campaigned for the adoption of the Ottawa Treaty. The Ottawa Treaty incorporates social justice for the victims by stipulating each State Party's obligation in 'provid[ing] assistance for the care and rehabilitation, and social and economic reintegration, of mine victims'.[16] With the participation of civil society and the incorporation of victim assistance schemes, mine action is also now considered a crucial component of post-conflict peacebuilding[17] but its possible integration with transitional justice mechanisms remains largely unexplored despite the distributive justice potential of its welfare-based activities. To contribute to this sparse scholarship we explore the potential contribution of mine action to transitional justice

[10]Prior to the establishment of CMAC, the UN Advance Mission in Cambodia (UNAMIC), a precursor of UNTAC, started mine awareness programmes and mine clearance operations. Isolated and unregulated demining efforts started as early as 1979 along the Cambodian-Vietnamese border. RGC, 'Request for an Extension'.

[11]Land contamination was first estimated at 4544 square kilometres in 2002. The Cambodian government reported in May 2018 that 1691 square kilometres of land have been cleared since 1992. The section entitled 'Clearing a Deadly Legacy' provides more details.

[12]GICHD, *Linking Mine Action and Development: States Affected by Mines/ERW* (Geneva: GICHD, November 2009); Ian Bannon, 'Landmine Contamination: A Development Imperative', *World Bank: Social Development Notes* 20 (October 2004).

[13]GICHD, 'Introduction to Mine Action', gichd.org/what-is-mine-action/introduction-to-mine-action/#.WyB7ujMzbMI (accessed August 2018).

[14]UN, 'Convention on the Prohibition of the Use, Stockpiling, Production and Transfer of Anti-personnel Mines and on their Destruction', September 18, 1997.

[15]Kristian Berg Harpviken, Ananda S. Millard, Kjell Erling Kjellman, and Bernt A. Skåra, 'Measures for Mines: Approaches to Impact Assessment in Humanitarian Mine Action', *Third World Quarterly* 24, no. 5 (2003): 889–908.

[16]UN, 'Convention on the Prohibition', Article 6.3.

[17]Kristian Berg Harpviken and Bernt A. Skåra, 'Humanitarian Mine Action and Peace Building: Exploring the Relationship', *Third World Quarterly* 24, no. 5 (2003): 809–22.

in Cambodia as well as analyse the relationship between mine action-related CSOs and the Cambodian government.

We draw our data for analysis from existing literature on transitional justice and mine action, and interviews with relevant government officials and key staff of demining operators.[18] We asked the interview participants about the achievements of and challenges to mine action, particularly the engagement of demining operators with the Cambodian government and local communities. We also attended the National Mine Action Conference in Phnom Penh in May 2018 and observed a demining unit working on a minefield south west of Siem Reap.[19] The data from field observation, elite interviews, and existing literature inform a qualitative case study analysis of Cambodia's mine action in relation to transitional justice and within the Cambodian context of state-civil society relations. The discussion of this paper starts with the role of civil society in transitional justice and the existing mechanisms for Cambodian CSOs' working on transitional justice, especially within the judicial processes of the Extraordinary Chambers in the Courts of Cambodia (ECCC or the Khmer Rouge Tribunal). This exploration requires a brief discussion of state-civil society relations in Cambodia in order to explore the potential of mine action in serving as an additional venue for CSOs to engage with the government and contribute to transitional justice. The discussion proceeds to the ongoing mine clearance efforts in Cambodia and how the state and civil society contribute to these efforts. We then explore the prospective impact of mine action on transitional justice and the conundrums of integrating mine action to transitional justice in Cambodian context. The connections between mine action, transitional justice, and CSOs are particularly pertinent in Cambodia where state influence and control are pervasive.

Civil society and transitional justice in Cambodia

Civil society is an expression of the public's ability to organise and coordinate its actions through free associations in view of influencing state policy.[20] In this sense, 'civil society is not so much a sphere outside political power; rather it penetrates deeply into this power, fragments and decentralizes it'.[21] A civil society is, therefore, inclined to adopt and promote liberal norms because it needs the freedom to organise and regulate itself. With a state that significantly reduces democratic spaces, options available for civil society to penetrate, fragment, and decentralise the dominant political power are limited. On the other hand, civil society can also exist in partial independence or even as an integrated part of the state.[22] In a state with authoritarian tendencies, such as in Cambodia, civil society endures by employing alternative and creative means of influencing policy, sometimes in support or in partnership with the state. Civil society's work, therefore, may include not just the traditional political critique of the state's power but also a public service orientation. The political, economic, and socio-cultural perspectives

[18]We were not granted interviews by the HALO Trust and MAG Cambodia despite several attempts in May 2018.
[19]We were not able to join a CMAC demining unit due to interrupted communication amidst then upcoming July 2018 elections.
[20]Charles Taylor, 'Modes of Civil Society', *Public Culture* 3, no. 1 (1990): 95–118.
[21]Ibid., 117.
[22]Ibid.

of civil society speak to its pluralist composition, activities, and goals.[23] This conceptualisation explains the work of civil society on wide-ranging issues, including mine action and transitional justice.

Transitional justice is a term that emerged in the early 1990s, particularly in a three-volume work edited by Neil Kritz, in the context of the end of the Cold War and transitions to democracy.[24] There is no single agreed upon definition but prominent transitional justice scholar Ruti Teitel defines it as the 'conception of justice associated with periods of political change, characterized by legal responses to confront wrongdoings of repressive predecessor regimes', and transitional justice is generally taken to include mechanisms such as trials, truth commissions, reparations, and institutional reform.[25] Over the last two decades transitional justice has come to be seen as a necessary element of post-conflict settlements, although it has not always been followed through to fruition.[26] Early transitional justice scholarship focused mostly on the mechanisms themselves, and particularly prosecutorial mechanisms from a legalist perspective.[27] But there is much more to transitional justice.

More recent transitional justice scholarship increasingly recognises the link between civil society and transitional justice mechanisms.[28] From the community reconciliation process in Timor-Leste[29] to grassroots initiatives in some parts of Eastern Europe,[30] civil society plays an important role in supporting transitional justice mechanisms both at the global and local levels.[31] However, the primary focus of this scholarship has been on politically active and human rights-focused CSOs. The types of roles associated with civil society, and which have been analysed so far, are related to documenting abuses, advocating for the creation of transitional justice mechanisms, encouraging public engagement with these mechanisms, and disseminating their findings and reports.[32] The focus leans towards forms of direct engagement with transitional justice mechanisms, such as discussing the ways civil society could 'participate in transitional justice processes', rather than broader connections between civil society and transitional justice.[33] CSOs can be more flexible than transitional justice mechanisms, and well-established organisations

---

[23]For the different conceptions of state-civil society relations, see Simone Chambers and Jeffrey Kopstein, 'Civil Society and the State', in *The Oxford Handbook of Political Theory*, eds. John S. Dryzek, Bonnie Honig, and Anne Phillips (New York: Oxford University Press, 2006), 363–81.

[24]Neil Kritz, ed., *Transitional Justice: How Emerging Democracies Reckon with Former Regimes*, 3 vols. (Washington, DC: United States Institute of Peace Press, 1995).

[25]Ruti G. Teitel, 'Transitional Justice Genealogy', *Harvard Human Rights Journal* 16 (2003): 69; International Center for Transitional Justice, 'What is Transitional Justice?', ictj.org/about/transitional-justice (accessed November 2018).

[26]See, for example, Meenakshi Gunguly, 'Transitional Justice Efforts in Sri Lanka Fall Short', *Human Rights Watch*, September 20, 2018, hrw.org/news/2018/09/20/transitional-justice-efforts-sri-lanka-fall-short.

[27]Judith N. Shklar, *Legalism* (Cambridge, MA: Harvard University Press, 1964); Gary Jonathan Bass, *Stay the Hand of Vengeance: The Politics of War Crimes Tribunals* (Princeton: Princeton University Press, 2000).

[28]David Backer, 'Civil Society and Transitional Justice: Possibilities, Patterns and Prospects', *Journal of Human Rights* 2, no. 3 (2003): 301.

[29]The Timor-Leste Commission for Reception, Truth and Reconciliation (CAVR), *Chega! The Final Report of the Timor-Leste Commission for Reception, Truth and Reconciliation (CAVR)* (Jakarta: KPG in cooperation with STP-CAVR, 2013).

[30]Olivera Simić and Zala Volčič, eds., *Transitional Justice and Civil Society in the Balkans* (New York: Springer, 2013).

[31]See also, Teitel, 'Transitional Justice Genealogy', 69–94; Marlies Glasius, ed., *The International Criminal Court: A Global Civil Society Achievement* (London: Routledge, 2005); Paul Gready and Simon Robins, 'Rethinking Civil Society and Transitional Justice: Lessons from Social Movement and "New" Civil Society', *The International Journal of Human Rights* 21, no. 7 (2017): 956–75.

[32]Eric Brahm, 'Transitional Justice, Civil Society, and the Development of the Rule of Law in Post-conflict Societies', *International Journal of Not-for-Profit Law* 9, no. 4 (2007): 62–3.

[33]Backer, 'Civil Society', 301.

already have the local credibility and networks necessary to help connect a new transitional justice mechanism with the population it is supposed to serve.[34] This role of civil society in connecting to the local can be particularly relevant when people are suspicious of the government that has established the transitional justice mechanism or where it has been established in whole or in part by international actors. A mutually strengthening relationship has also been identified between transitional justice and civil society, with both being seen as part of the means of building liberal democracy in post-conflict societies. One key aspect of rebuilding society after mass violence that both can contribute to is to restore, or create, a strong civil society to facilitate people's self-perception as active citizens with agency.[35]

From more narrow beginnings there have also been attempts to add nuance to earlier discussions of civil society and transitional justice relationships. In 2002 Naomi Roht-Arriaza wrote about the 'misleading' ways that civil society 'is often discussed as a monolithic grouping'.[36] In contrast to this portrayal there can be competing agendas amongst CSOs, and the distinction between state and civil society is not always clear, with movement of key personnel between the two spheres or with close connections across the divide.[37] Similarly, the role that religious organisations play in interacting with transitional justice mechanisms and conceptions adds nuance to ideas about civil society's role in these processes. Religious organisations do not always support the imported secular human rights approach, and studying their involvement shows the ways that local conditions impact on norms.[38]

Nonetheless, the emphasis has remained on certain types of engagement at the expense of others. Both transitional justice mechanisms more broadly, and the scholarship about their relationships with civil society, pay little attention to economic factors, focusing instead on political and civil rights. As Zinaida Miller notes, transitional justice 'has historically excluded issues of economic inequality, structural violence, redistribution and development'.[39] This exclusion is particularly significant as transitional justice mechanisms create a narrative and, sometimes, a structure of legal accountability which delineates what is acceptable and what is not. Leaving out the social and economic consequences and implications of a conflict from transitional justice discourse denotes that they are not important, that they do not need restitution, and that they were not crimes in the first place. Work on religious civil society by Renée Jeffery, Lia Kent, and Joanne Wallis has brought forward some examples of unclear boundaries around these issues, such as churches in the Solomon Islands that took on responsibilities that normally belong to the state and so straddled the gap between state and society. They also describe how in Timor-Leste justice had a broader meaning than the dominant liberal legal

---

[34]Martina Fischer, 'Civil Society in Conflict Transformation: Strengths and Limitations', in *Advancing Conflict Transformation*, eds. Beatrix Austin, Martina Fischer, and Hans J. Giessman (Opladen/Framington Hills: Barbara Budrich Publishers, 2011), 294; Brahm, 'Transitional Justice', 65.

[35]Fischer, 'Civil Society', 305.

[36]Naomi Roht-Arriaza, 'Civil Society in Processes of Accountability', in *Post-Conflict Justice*, ed. M. Cherif Bassiouni (New York: Transnational Publishers, 2002), 98.

[37]Ibid.

[38]Renée Jeffery, Lia Kent, and Joanne Wallis, 'Reconceiving the Roles of Religious Civil Society Organizations in Transitional Justice: Evidence from the Solomon Islands, Timor-Leste and Bougainville', *International Journal of Transitional Justice* 11, no. 3 (2017): 380, 384.

[39]Zinaida Miller, 'Effects of Invisibility: In Search of the "Economic" in Transitional Justice', *International Journal of Transitional Justice* 2, no. 3 (2008): 266.

understanding, so more practical measures were included under the label of justice.[40] There has so far been much less consideration of the possible transitional justice connections to service delivery CSOs.

When service delivery CSOs are considered, it is primarily related to direct contributions to transitional justice. For example, there is an emphasis on the work done by legal clinics or counselling services, with examples from South Africa and Latin America being particularly common.[41] Even these services are considered far less frequently than the involvement of civil society that is more focused on political and civil rights, in part because ideas of civil society come primarily from Western European contexts and focus on a clearer state-civil society divide.[42] Service delivery focused CSOs do not fit easily into this division from the state but often operate in spaces where the state is 'simply absent'; they are not necessarily working against the state or in competition with it.[43] However, in this model civil society is fulfilling roles that could be considered as belonging to the state and therefore begins to resemble the state, blurring the lines of division between the two. A predominance of this type of civil society can result in what Geoff Wood labelled a 'franchise state': rather than CSOs contributing to an engaged citizenship they can facilitate a model of citizenship that only relates to passively receiving services.[44] Sabeel Rahman has explored this phenomenon in Bangladesh, where a combination of domestic pressures against politically focused CSOs and international donor preferences for funnelling money for services through civil society rather than the government has led to a shift away from civil society focused on 'promoting political mobilization and accountable government, to the apolitical delivery of basic services'.[45]

Cambodian civil society expanded significantly during and after UNTAC's mission. However, in recent years it has come under increasing restrictions. In particular, in 2015 the government passed the Law on Associations and Non-governmental Organisations (LANGO), which introduced new requirements for the registration of NGOs and financial disclosure, and an obligation of political neutrality. Melissa Curley has identified this law as part of 'the recent trend of the government's use of legislation as a political tool to control and manipulate political opponents and government critics'.[46] The role of donors is also a contentious element of Cambodian civil society. The extent of aid dependency among Cambodian NGOs means that the interests and priorities of donors are one of the driving factors in the direction of civil society.[47] The high level of corruption in the Cambodian government also means that foreign donors are more willing to give money to CSOs than to the government, again contributing to the push towards a more service delivery model.[48] The situation in Cambodia is similar to that in Rwanda. As Paul Gready

[40]Jeffrey, Kent, and Wallis, 'Reconceiving the Roles', 389, 392.
[41]Backer, 'Civil Society', 304.
[42]Simone Chambers and Jeffrey Kopstein, 'Civil Society and the State', in *The Oxford Handbook of Political Theory*, eds. John S. Dryzek, Bonnie Honig, and Anne Phillips (Oxford: Oxford University Press, 2006), 366.
[43]Ibid., 374.
[44]Geoff Wood, 'States without Citizens: The Problem of the Franchise State', in *NGOs, States, and Donors: Too Close for Comfort?* eds. David Hulme and Michael Edwards (London: Macmillan Press, 1997), 79–83.
[45]Sabeel Rahman, 'Development, Democracy and the NGO Sector: Theory and Evidence from Bangladesh', *Journal of Developing Societies* 22, no. 4 (2006): 451.
[46]Melissa Curley, 'Governing Civil Society in Cambodia: Implications of the NGO Law for the "Rule of Law"', *Asian Studies Review* 42, no. 2 (2018): 262.
[47]Jörn Dosch, 'The Role of Civil Society in Cambodia's Peace-Building Process', *Asian Survey* 52, no. 6 (2012): 1070.
[48]Ibid., 1068.

identifies, there is a strong guilt complex amongst international donors about failure to act during the genocide which contributes to a situation where foreign donors contribute significantly financially but do not have a lot of legitimacy to push for particular changes or policies in the government. As in Cambodia, Rwandan government's 'preferred *modus operandi* for civil society remains service delivery and gap filling'.[49] Ultimately, as Jörn Dosch characterises it, Cambodian civil society is 'best understood as a state-tolerated, and, in some limited cases, state-coopted, loosely organized, collective actor that comes into play wherever and whenever the government does not, or cannot, get involved'.[50]

Given this definition, what then is the relationship between civil society and transitional justice in Cambodia? Referring to transitional justice in Cambodia is most commonly considered to mean the Extraordinary Chambers in the Courts of Cambodia (ECCC). The ECCC is a hybrid domestic/international tribunal that is currently operating on the outskirts of Phnom Penh to put on trial the senior leaders and those most responsible for crimes during the Khmer Rouge regime. The ECCC is not the first transitional justice mechanism in Cambodia (amongst others there was a trial in 1979 and a process resembling a truth commission in 1983), but it is the first to be recognised and labelled as transitional justice and is the focus of this paper. The ECCC has attracted significant scholarly attention with accounts of the long negotiations that created the ECCC,[51] considerations of the legal processes and outcomes,[52] analysis of the extent to which the ECCC represents a period of transition for Cambodia,[53] assessments of the limits put on the ECCC by domestic politics,[54] and work specifically addressing the role of civil society that is discussed below. The role and perspective of victims have also been a prominent element of scholarship around the ECCC.[55]

As a court the ECCC is a retributive mechanism, which focuses on punishing the perpetrators. Despite the court's improved outreach, reparation, and victim participation programmes over time, as discussed later, these are still only tied to the trials rather than to the broader Khmer Rouge period. Hence, these programmes are derived first and foremost from the ECCC's retributive forms. The ECCC has been criticised for the small number of people it has convicted; only three so far, and probably ever. This means that very few Cambodians will see punishment or accountability for the direct perpetrators of crimes against them and their families. There is broad support for the ECCC according to a 2008 survey, with 87% saying it should be involved in responding to the Khmer Rouge regime.[56] However, in the very same survey, more than half of respondents said the

[49]Paul Gready, '"You're Either With Us or Against Us": Civil Society and Policy Making in Post-Genocide Rwanda', *African Affairs* 109, no. 437 (2010): 641.

[50]Dosch, 'The Role of Civil Society', 1072.

[51]Tom Fawthrop and Helen Jarvis, *Getting Away with Genocide? Elusive Justice and the Khmer Rouge Tribunal* (Sydney: University of New South Wales Press, 2005).

[52]John D. Ciorciari and Anne Heindel, *Hybrid Justice: The Extraordinary Chambers in the Courts of Cambodia* (Ann Arbor: University of Michigan Press, 2014).

[53]Alexander Hinton, *The Justice Façade: Trials of Transition in Cambodia* (Oxford: Oxford University Press, 2018); Alexander Hinton, 'Uncle San, Aunty Yan, and Outreach at the Khmer Rouge Tribunal', in *Genocide and Mass Atrocities in Asia: Legacies and Prevention*, eds. Annie Pohlman and Deborah Mayersen (New York: Routledge, 2013), 86–98.

[54]Kirsten Ainley, 'Transitional Justice in Cambodia: The Coincidence of Power and Principle', in *Transitional Justice in the Asia-Pacific*, eds. Renée Jeffery and Hun Joon Kim (New York: Cambridge University Press, 2014), 125–56.

[55]Rachel Killean, *Victims, Atrocity and International Criminal Justice: Lessons from Cambodia* (London: Routledge, 2018); Maria Elander, *Figuring Victims in International Criminal Justice: The Case of the Khmer Rouge Tribunal* (New York: Routledge, 2018).

[56]Phuong Pham et al., *So We Will Never Forget: A Population-based Survey on Attitudes About Social Reconstruction and the Extraordinary Chambers in the Courts of Cambodia* (Human Rights Center, University of California, Berkeley, 2009), 34.

money would be better spent on other issues, and 76% of those surveyed 'said it was more important to focus on problems Cambodians face in their daily lives than to address crimes committed during the Khmer Rouge regime'.[57] This percentage increased to 83% in a 2010 follow-up survey after the first trial. The same survey also showed an increased preference (from 53% in 2008 to 63% in 2010) for spending on something other than the ECCC.[58] In both surveys respondents ranked justice low in terms of individual and government priorities and placed economic issues as a top priority.[59] These figures suggest that Cambodians' attitudes toward the ECCC are not simple. The Cambodians value retribution through the ECCC, but they also want their basic needs as a community addressed. This desire for victim-centred and forward-looking service provision is considered a distributive type of justice, which is 'directed, not at the requiting of a past deed, but at the creation of a society whose members shall be provided with the goods of life'.[60] Despite their teleological differences, retributive and distributive justice can be simultaneously pursued. In Cambodia, the Victim Support Section of the ECCC and the work of local NGOs aim to complement the court-based retributive process of the ECCC with victim-centred and needs-based reparations.

The retributive model has significant flaws and shortcomings, which the ECCC and civil society have later worked to address. One important innovation at the ECCC has been the participation of civil parties although, initially, there was little planning or resources to support their inclusion. In this system victims can apply to be parties to the proceedings as civil parties. The lack of planning within the ECCC meant that much of the initial work of recruiting civil parties, documenting their stories, applying for status before the court, and provisions for legal representation was done by CSOs. Ninety-three civil parties participated in the ECCC's first case and close to four thousand in its second, when the ECCC and its Victim Support Section took on a more dominant role after the strong presence of civil society in the organisation of civil parties for the first case.[61] The court's outreach capacity was also limited at first, and this was another space that CSOs occupied in relation to transitional justice in Cambodia. However, the relationship between the ECCC and civil society has not been straightforward. Many CSOs, some of whom had also been involved in supporting the court's work, have been critical of aspects of its operation. As Christoph Sperfeldt notes, 'the ECCC has not engaged in strategic coordination with civil society', and it has also been impacted by 'existing frictions from the domestic public policy setting'.[62] Nonetheless, both the initially limited funding for victim-centred elements of the ECCC and the existing connections between CSOs and communities have already made civil society an important part of transitional justice.

Civil society has also played a key role in projects that have operated around the ECCC but separately from it. The existence of the ECCC has encouraged more research and advocacy concerning experiences during the Khmer Rouge regime that had not previously

---

[57]Ibid., 35.

[58]Phuong Pham et al., *After the First Trial: A Population-based Survey on Knowledge and Perception of Justice and the Extraordinary Chambers in the Courts of Cambodia* (Human Rights Center: University of California Berkeley, 2011), 19.

[59]Ibid.

[60]Lucius Garvin, 'Retributive and Distributive Justice', *The Journal of Philosophy* 42, no. 10 (1945): 270–7.

[61]Christoph Sperfeldt, 'From the Margins of Internationalized Criminal Justice: Lessons Learned at the Extraordinary Chambers in the Courts of Cambodia', *Journal of International Criminal Justice* 11, no. 5 (2013): 1120.

[62]Christoph Sperfeldt, 'Cambodian Civil Society and the Khmer Rouge Tribunal', *International Journal of Transitional Justice* 6, no. 1 (2012): 153, 154.

received significant attention. For example, forced marriage and sexual violence have become prominent issues about which there had long been silence but which emerged because of civil party applicants at the ECCC, and the first study of the experiences of LGBT Cambodians during the Khmer Rouge regime was published in 2015.[63] A range of organisations run small-scale reconciliation and mental health projects, including testimonial therapy conducted by the Transcultural Psychosocial Organization and a theatre project launched by Youth For Peace.[64] The Khmer Rouge period had also disappeared from the school curriculum in the early 1990s. In 2007 the Documentation Center of Cambodia (DC-Cam) published *A History of Democratic Kampuchea (1975–1979)*.[65] It has gained an increasingly central and officially backed place in Cambodia's history curriculum.[66] Although the Khmer Rouge period was taught in schools during the 1980s it was a highly politicised version of history. This DC-Cam book is the first time the Khmer Rouge has been included in a more detailed, descriptive, and less political manner.[67]

These civil society projects have operated largely outside of the ECCC but there are also projects which have been explicitly recognised as a form of reparation. For example, the judgement in the second case included the ECCC's endorsements of a National Remembrance Day, provision of therapy for victims, historical exhibitions, public memorials, and publications on the case, and civil party participation.[68] These endorsements imply the ECCC's recognition of these projects, which are externally-funded and thus could have been run entirely separately from the ECCC, as official reparations. Given this background the following sections will explore state-civil society relations in the context of mine action and the potential for mine action to contribute to transitional justice.

Clearing a deadly legacy

The Cambodian government has entered into international agreements on the clearance of landmines/ERW.[69] It became a party to the Ottawa Treaty in 1999, and chaired and hosted the 11th Conference on States Parties to the Mine Ban Treaty in 2011. In 2008 Cambodia reported the complete destruction of all stockpiled anti-personnel mines.[70] Cambodia is also a state party to the UN Convention on the Rights of Persons with Disabilities (CRPD), which ensures the protection of the rights of landmine survivors with disabilities.

---

[63]Emily Wight, 'Gender-based Violence: Khmer Rouge Survivors Given a Platform', *Phnom Penh Post*, January 24, 2014; George Wright and Sek Odom, 'Study Details KR Abuse of Transgender People', *Cambodia Daily*, March 3, 2015; Kasumi Nakagawa, *Gender-based Violence Against Sexual Minorities During the Khmer Rouge Regime* (Cambodian Defenders Project, 2015).

[64]Mom Kunthear and Cassandra Yeap, 'Words Help KR Survivors Heal', *Phnom Penh Post*, May 4, 2012; Prak Thida and Tharum Bun, 'Bright Idea: Peace Theatre', *Phnom Penh Post*, May 19, 2010.

[65]Dy Khamboly, *A History of Democratic Kampuchea (1975–1979)* (Phnom Penh: Documentation Center of Cambodia, 2007).

[66]Dy Khamboly, personal interview, 25 February 2014, Phnom Penh.

[67]Previous attempts to include Cambodia's modern history had stumbled over how to represent the post-Khmer Rouge period. Pin Sisovann and Matt Reed, 'Textbook Delay Reflects Sensitivity of Cambodia's Recent History', *Cambodia Daily*, March 23, 2002; Pin Sisovann, 'Prime Minister Orders Recall of Textbooks', *Cambodia Daily*, April 29, 2002.

[68]Trial Chamber, ECCC, 'Case 002/01 Judgement', August 7, 2014, 597–622.

[69]It is important to note at this point the Cambodian government's tendency to sign international agreements without clear plans for implementing them. On countries with weak domestic institutions signing international agreements see, Oona Hathaway, 'Why Do Countries Commit to Human Rights Treaties?' *The Journal of Conflict Resolution* 51, no. 4 (2007): 588–621.

[70]As of 2018 Cambodia retains 1429 anti-personnel mines for research development and training purposes. UN, 'Cambodia', apminebanconvention.org/states-parties-to-the-convention/cambodia/ (accessed August 2018).

Previous reports of inadequate support for victims[71] prompted the government to prioritise the provision of support to survivors and victims of landmines/ERW. The Cambodian government has also acceded to the 1980 UN Convention on Certain Conventional Weapons (CCW), and all its related protocols, except Protocol V relating to ERW. The government is currently reviewing its compliance capabilities vis-à-vis Protocol V and the Convention on Cluster Munitions, and aims to accede to them by 2020.[72] Regionally, in May 2016 Cambodia initiated the establishment of the ASEAN Mine Action Center (ARMAC), headquartered in Phnom Penh. ARMAC aims to enhance awareness programmes, promote victim assistance, and share research and development with the region.[73]

Cambodia's 25 years of experience in demining has brought key achievements. In 2016 the numbers of victims of landmines and unexploded ordnances dropped below 100 for the first time. In 2017 the number of casualties was at a record low of 57. By the end of the same year Cambodia had released 1691 square kilometres of contaminated land for productive use, and found and destroyed 1,049,130 anti-personnel mines, 24,644 anti-tank mines, and 2,719,177 ERW articles.[74] Cambodian deminers are skilled and have gone overseas under the UN peacekeeping operations framework to conduct training programmes and workshops for deminers in other mine-affected countries. Cambodian deminers are also motivated, having lived close to landmines/ERW and witnessed their destructive effects. One of the reasons why they choose to work as deminers is that they want to see a safer Cambodia for their children and for all Cambodians.[75]

Mine action in Cambodia is also highly coordinated, with streamlined guidelines and sophisticated protocols for demining operators, national strategic plans for all stakeholders, and constant post-clearance monitoring of operators' activities. The demining operators in Cambodia are the Cambodian Mine Action Centre (CMAC), the Royal Cambodian Forces (RCAF), the HALO Trust, the Mine Action Group (MAG), Norwegian People's Aid (NPA), APOPO, and the Cambodian Self-Help Demining (CSHD). To streamline all mine-related activities the government established the Cambodian Mine Action and Victim Assistance Authority (CMAA) in 2001. The CMAA regulates, monitors, and coordinates entities belonging to the mine action sector in Cambodia. These coordinated efforts have increased the efficiency of demining operations, sustained mine risk education programmes, and improved victim assistance programmes.[76]

The task of clearing Cambodia's deadly legacy is far from over. Unable to meet the original 2010 deadline, the government requested another ten years to complete the clearance of all anti-personnel landmines under the stipulations of the Ottawa Treaty. The extension, however, has proven to be too short to clear the magnitude of the contamination. In May 2018 the National Mine Action Conference was held in Phnom Penh to bring together international and national stakeholders in improving the efficiency and

[71]Landmine and Cluster Munition Monitor, 'Victim Assistance', *Landmine Monitor 2009*, the-monitor.org/en-gb/reports/2009/landmine-monitor-2009/victim-assistance.aspx (accessed August 2018).
[72]RGC, *NMAS*, 6.
[73]For details, see aseanmineaction.org/.
[74]These statistics were reported at the 2018 National Mine Action Conference.
[75]CSHD deminers in Kampong Kdei village located around 60 kilometres south east of Siem Reap, personal interviews, May 2018.
[76]As of 2018, 69,125 mine awareness sessions for 5.87 million Cambodians and surveys in 2485 villages with 23,500 persons with disabilities, including 5800 landmine/ERW victims, have been conducted since 1992. These data were presented at the 2018 National Mine Action Conference.

re-aligning the priorities of Cambodian mine action. At the conference the government released the National Mine Action Strategy (NMAS) 2018–2025, setting a new target 'to release all known landmines and prioritized cluster munitions contaminated areas, and to minimize the residual risks caused by [ERW] in Cambodia' by 2025.[77] To reach this target Cambodia needs $406 million to clear the remaining 1970 square kilometres of contaminated lands. The government expects to source this amount from its national budget and development partners.[78] Some commentators believe that this target is unrealistic considering the slow pace of demining in Cambodia[79] and the foreseeable reductions in funding from donors that have started channelling financial resources to other mine-affected countries.[80] For example, the US government, which has contributed a total of $120 million to mine clearance in Cambodia since 1993, plans to prioritise funding to countries in the Middle East in view of Cambodia's successes in mine action and rising national income.[81]

If the current pacing and funding circumstances do not improve Cambodia will have to extend its target beyond 2025. The country has sufficient technical expertise and coordinated management in mine action, but funding remains the main obstacle given the expected reductions in international funding and minimal national budget allocation.[82] Another obstacle is the slow pace of innovation in demining technologies in Cambodia. Leonard Kaminski, an operations manager for the HALO Trust in Cambodia from 1992 until 2013, has observed that demining operators in Cambodia have been using the same technology because of insufficient funding for more efficient technologies.[83] He further explained how local operators swear by the thoroughness of and low deminer casualties from manual demining. However, a slower process means longer exposure to the dangers of landmines and UXOs for civilians. Demining operators implied an acknowledgment of this shortcoming during the National Mine Action Conference when they showed interest in shifting towards more efficient and effective demining practices. Given this context, what then are the relationships between mine action, civil society and the state in Cambodia?

Mine action as a link between state and civil society?

Hun Sen and the CPP continue to have a political stronghold over Cambodia, and this includes mine action. The Cambodian mine action structure, with the exception of independent demining operators, is attached to the CPP. The CMAA is a government

[77]RGC, *NMAS*, 5. Ly Thuch, senior minister and vice-president of CMAA, clarified during the 2018 National Mine Action Conference that a mine-free Cambodia means a Cambodia clear of anti-tank and anti-personnel mines. For the country to be free of all UXOs by 2025, $190 million is needed and deminers have to clear 1000 square kilometres per year. The target aligns with the goal of the Maputo +15 declaration of completing the obligations under the Ottawa Treaty by 2025.

[78]CMAA will develop a resource mobilisation strategy to source financial and in-kind support from the national budget, development partners, and philanthropic donations, but pledges from these sources remain unclear as of May 2018. RGC, *NMAS*, 27.

[79]Staff of demining operators, personal interviews, May 2018, Phnom Penh.

[80]Zsombor Peter and Aun Pheap, 'Follow the Money', *Cambodia Daily*, June 25, 2016.

[81]Niem Chheng and Martin de Bourmont, 'Less US Funding for UXO Clearing', *Phnom Penh Post*, March 17, 2017.

[82]The Cambodian government has spent a total of $160 million, and international donors have contributed $473 million to Cambodian mine action since 1992. This amount excludes equipment and vehicles, based on a presentation at the 2018 National Mine Action Conference.

[83]Personal interview, 24 May 2018, Phnom Penh.

agency with Hun Sen as its president. CPP members are embedded in mine action planning agencies from national level to community level. They also fill the leadership structure of the CMAC, the largest demining operator in Cambodia. Corruption scandals permeated the CMAC in the past,[84] prompting the creation of the CMAA as a check-and-balance mechanism and to revitalise mine action in Cambodia. However, CPP members sitting in planning and operational agencies could raise potential conflicts of interest and undermine this mechanism. Given that the decision-makers in the CMAA and CMAC are CPP members it is hard to counter-argue that the CPP's politics are not enmeshed in the administration of mine action in Cambodia.

The state exercises power over mine action agencies in Cambodia by regulating their demining operations and streamlining their funding and activities. In this case CSOs involved in mine action in Cambodia are not separate from the state. As the overseer of all mine action activities the CMAA has the authority to accredit demining operators and suspend their operations. It is false to claim that this strategy is operationally detrimental but there have been speculations of politicisation in the accreditation of demining operators. For example, a 2005 report raised the possibility of the CMAC suppressing informal deminers not because of safety concerns but because of the benefits it gets from the 'lucrative demining franchise'.[85] Informal deminers work on private and individuals lands, which are not on the priority list of large demining operators, and have cleared as many lands as formal organisations.[86] The CMAC and CMAA maintained that their decisions were based on safety standards and not due to political or commercial interests of the CPP or its members.

As CPP members CMAA and CMAC officials carry with them the politics of the CPP. In April 2017, for example, CMAC director-general Heng Ratana drew a comparison between Cambodia's single-party rule and how the single party leadership in Japan, Singapore, and Malaysia has ensured 'sustainability, security, and orderly development' and 'developed their democratic system based on their own values, cultures and social principles'.[87] In the CMAC's museum in Siem Reap the CPP's victory over the Khmer Rouge is displayed in imposing framed pictures emphasising a key element of the CPP's political platform about saving the country from the Khmer Rouge. Moreover, sending Cambodian deminers for UN peacekeeping is a national strategy to bolster the international image and prestige of the Cambodian government amidst criticisms of its human rights violations.[88] These cases exemplify how the CPP uses demining to enhance its legitimacy.

During the first half of the 1990s demining became a political tool for the CPP to win the hearts of the Cambodian people. At a time when the Khmer Rouge threat was still present in Cambodia the coalition government seemed to prioritise the demining of areas where the CPP's political clout was relatively weak. Kaminski has observed this politics-based, instead of needs-based, prioritisation during the early years of the CMAC.[89] This prioritisation was also aligned with Hun Sen's Win-Win policy of encouraging Khmer Rouge cadres to defect to the government by ensuring their safety and protection, thereby hastening

[84]Phelim Kyne, 'CMAC Scandals Prompt Management Purge', *Phnom Penh Post*, August 6, 1999.
[85]Michael L. Fleisher, *Informal Village Demining in Cambodia: An Operational Study* (Handicap International, 2005).
[86]Elena Lesley, 'Village Landmine Hunters Trigger Controversy', *Phnom Penh Post*, May 20, 2005.
[87]Andrew Nachemson, 'Official's Parallels Ignorant: Analysts', *Phnom Penh Post*, April 20, 2017.
[88]Vannarith Chheang, 'Peacekeeping Contributor Profile: Cambodia', *Providing for Peacekeeping*, last updated January 2014, providingforpeacekeeping.org/2014/04/03/contributor-profile-cambodia/.
[89]Personal interview, 24 May 2018, Phnom Penh.

the end of the civil war. Hun Sen's Win-Win policy is a proud legacy of the Cambodian government, such that even the RCAF booth at the 2018 National Mine Action Conference's exhibition showcased the successes of this policy. Eventually, the defeat of the Khmer Rouge allowed easier access to areas they formerly controlled for mine clearance, and some of the former cadres even became deminers.[90] Like the Win-Win policy, mine action helps the Cambodian government create a responsible and accountable image in the eyes of its people and the international community. Also, like the ECCC, mine action helps the CPP reinforce its saviour narrative in Cambodian history and society.

The responses of key officials of mine action agencies varied when asked whether demining in Cambodia is politicised. According to Aksel Steen-Nilsen, the country director of NPA Cambodia, politics does not influence mine action because demining is generally a technical activity and the Cambodian government has a good working relationship with mine action agencies. Michael Heiman of APOPO also spoke of the technical nature of demining work, which makes political issues irrelevant. CMAA officials also claim that election cycles do not have an impact on the activities of mine action agencies. On the other hand, some interview participants were more reluctant to agree that mine action is not politicised. They implied that Cambodian politics has some influence on demining activities, especially in terms of funding. For example, in 2017 the US government suspended its funding towards mine action after the Cambodian government purged its opposition with a crackdown on independent media and organisations critical of the government, and the arrest of Kem Sokha, president of the opposition Cambodia National Rescue Party (CNRP), which was dissolved by the Cambodian Supreme Court. The US government later resumed its funding with a $1.8 million grant towards mine clearance in the eastern provinces of Cambodia.[91]

Political imperatives may influence the motives, means, and implications of mine action. At the same time, the technical nature of demining can also complement the interests of political actors. The work of mine action CSOs in Cambodia, despite being regulated by CPP-led government agencies, coincides with the government's development priorities, contrary to human rights CSOs, for example, that are critical of the government's authoritarian practices. It is not to the strategic and operational advantage of mine action agencies to get involved in debates on democratic governance in Cambodia. After all, demining operators have to cooperate with the regulating government in order to continue their demining activities but their cooperation may not necessarily imply endorsement of such authoritarian practices. For CSOs criticisms of the government may invoke criminal charges against them or even forced closure. The government has been prosecuting and shutting down human rights organisations and independent critical media based on LANGO, which restricts Cambodia's already threatened freedom of expression and association.[92] Within a repressive environment mine action CSOs wishing to continue their work in Cambodia have to set political differences aside and focus on mine clearance to create a working relationship with the government. They need to maintain a level of tolerance towards the government's authoritarian tendencies

[90]Seng Kimseang and Reuters, 'Former KR Help in Mine Clearing', *Phnom Penh Post*, October 20, 1995.
[91]Meas Sokchea, 'United States Donates $1.6 Million to CMAC', *Phnom Penh Post*, June 1, 2018.
[92]Human Rights Watch, 'Cambodia: Onslaught on Media, Rights Groups', August 25, 2017, hrw.org/news/2017/08/25/cambodia-onslaught-media-rights-groups.

and find issues of mutual concern. The technical aspect of demining and the significant restrictions on freedom of expression and association explain the cooperative but apolitical relationship between mine action agencies and the Cambodian government.

Cambodia's shrinking freedom of expression and association leaves few venues for citizen participation. The Cambodian mine action has the potential to fill this gap by providing opportunities for grassroots participation. First, the deminers we talked to expressed their pride in being a part of mine clearance as a national endeavour. Other than being deminers some Cambodians also work as educators in mine awareness programmes. Cambodian deminers and educators are often based in and around their villages where they can connect easily with their communities in emphasising the relevance of mine action. This type of involvement encourages participatory approaches[93] and potentially increases local capacity for future community-based engagements to serve as venues for democratic deliberation. In turn this increased capacity enhances local agency to demand civil rights and social empowerment. Second, mine action agencies consult with village chiefs and villagers in identifying their needs. The CMAA identifies priority areas[94] for demining based on inputs and reports from villagers. They also receive reports of identified landmines from local police, which receives information from the villagers. The Mine Action Planning Units serve as bridges between bottom-up and top-down approaches in planning and prioritisation. Third, the CMAA is proud of its participatory approaches from planning stage to land release.[95] For example, the hand-over process for cleared lands involves landowners, villagers, local authorities, demining operators, quality managers, and other relevant stakeholders.

While independent mine action agencies are not necessarily enmeshed in Cambodian politics they can potentially encourage civil society promotion. Mine action has shown the potential to support local involvement and local empowerment through its participatory approaches, to promote socio-economic development, and to sponsor needs-based and victim-centred assistance programmes. NPA, for example, aligns its humanitarian demining activities with the promotion of civil society and community development, and increasingly supports local organisations advocating for increased democratic participation. NPA encourages political deliberations on the issue of human rights protection by ensuring that the releasing of cleared lands coincides with the protection of land rights.[96] In the past the CMAC has supported local empowerment through its Community-Based Mine Risk Reduction (CBMRR) network of volunteers. The volunteers work at the community level in

> supporting communities to play a greater role in determining the mine-action priorities in their villages; providing ongoing risk education at a local level to civilians at high risk; and ensuring greater integration with victim assistance services and community-development

[93]Working with village deminers might be the start of community participation in Cambodian mine action. Chris Dammers, 'Participatory Monitoring and Evaluation of Humanitarian Mine Action in Cambodia', in *Participatory Monitoring of Mine Action: Giving Voices to Citizens of Nicaragua, Mozambique and Cambodia*, ed. Susan Willett (Geneva: UN Institute for Disarmament Research, 2003), 82.

[94]Priority areas are productive land meant for farming and construction sites for education and health centres. Low priority areas are those with smaller residential populations.

[95]Mol Roeup Seyha, Deputy Secretary General, CMAA, personal interview, 29 May 2018, Phnom Penh. Land release is the removal of threats from landmines/ERW through appropriate measures, such as technical and non-technical surveys, and clearance activities. GICHD, 'Land Release', gichd.org/topics/land-release/#.Wxysj1OFPeQ.

[96]Aksel Steen-Nilsen, country director of NPA Cambodia, personal interview, 22 May 2018, Phnom Penh. For details, see npaid.org/Our-Work/Countries-we-work-in/Asia/Cambodia.

projects that could assist with providing alternative income-generation activities for groups at risk.[97]

CBMRR activities have contributed to mobilising and empowering individuals and communities in exercising their rights and role in identifying local solutions for their local priorities, at least within the mine action sector.[98] In this light the participatory mechanisms of mine action contribute to capacity-building that could influence Cambodian politics. They therefore have the potential, as discussed below, to contribute to broader processes of transitional justice.

Mine action as an instrument of transitional justice?

Mine action, like transitional justice, is susceptible to politicisation especially in a post-conflict setting where democratic institutions are weak and civil society participation is undermined. Mine action and transitional justice, as components of peacebuilding, both deal with past atrocities and promote accountability for the activities committed during the war, but they have practical and ideational differences that can also be complementary. They operate in different spaces for different issues, and yet they are linked. Transitional justice in Cambodia is retrospective while mine action is prospective. Retrospective justice is backward-looking and focuses on retribution, like the ECCC, while prospective justice is forward-looking and encourages social restoration.[99] The ECCC identifies the perpetrators and demands corrective action for their wrongdoings. Although the recognition of victimhood and assistance to the victims of the Khmer Rouge is available in the ECCC through the Victim Support Section, they are only secondary to the assignment of perpetrator's guilt and accountability. Mine action, on the other hand, deals more with the victims of landmines than the perpetrators or those who laid the landmines. The activities of mine action, particularly the economic and social assistance to victims, can be considered as a form of local justice, a concept Jon Elster developed as the appropriate allocation or distribution of benefits and burdens by institutions.[100] Mine action's calls for economic and social assistance to victims encourage the participation of service delivery CSOs in distributing the economic benefits of cleared lands to the groups most disadvantaged by the presence of landmines.[101] Mine action, therefore, is a local or distributive form of justice because it values the need for safety of the Cambodian people and provides welfare to individual victims of landmines, income and jobs to former combatants, and opportunities to segments of society – from government agencies to farming communities, for example.[102]

---

[97]Ruth Bottomley and Chan Sambath, 'Community Empowerment and Leadership in Cambodia', *Journal of Conventional Weapons Destructions* 14, no. 2 (July 2010): 12.

[98]Ibid., 11–16. According to a CMAC official (e-mail communication, July 2018) projects similar to CBMRR are still ongoing but we were not able to receive additional information.

[99]Jeremy Webber, 'Forms of Transitional Justice', *Nomos* 51 (2012): 98–128.

[100]Jon Elster, *Local Justice: How Institutions Allocate Scarce Goods and Necessary Burdens* (New York: Russel Sage Foundation, 1992).

[101]Actors of distributive justice may act optimally on behalf of disadvantaged groups. Ibid. See also, Jon Elster, 'The Empirical Study of Justice', in *Pluralism, Justice, and Equality*, eds. David Miller and Michael Walzer (Oxford: Oxford University Press, 1995). Oxford Scholarship Online, 2003.

[102]See Morton Deutsch, 'Equity, Equality, and Need: What Determines Which Value Will Be Used as the Basis of Distributive Justice', *International Journal of Psychology* 31, no. 3 (1975): 137–49.

Mine action provides individual/collective and material/symbolic reparation to the victims of landmines. Victim assistance is a key component of Cambodian mine action strategy and is a useful starting point in linking mine action to transitional justice. The CMAA has a Victim Assistance Department working closely with the Ministry of Social Affairs, Veterans and Youth Rehabilitation and other international organisations in providing physical rehabilitation and socio-integration services assistance to victims and survivors of landmines/ERW. Services, such as the provision of prosthetics, group counselling, physical therapy, and vocational training, are available to victims and their families. For its 2025 target the CMAA aims to improve assistance to survivors and affected communities through risk education, care and support to survivors and indirect victims, and increasing of livelihood capacity.[103]

Victim assistance under the CMAA has short-term and long-term programmes. For example, in cases of accidents, the CMAA provides emergency assistance in the forms of hospitalisation and immediate medical care. Eleven physical rehabilitation centres across the country produce assistive products and provide physical rehabilitation services to persons with disabilities, including landmine/ERW victims. The services provided include the production and repair of prosthetics and orthotics, provision of wheelchairs and other devices, physiotherapy treatment, and outreach services. The CMAA also envisions long-term and sustainable victim assistance. Vocational training programmes allow landmine/ERW victims to engage in income-generating activities that are appropriate to their disabilities. Vocational training is in line with the CMAA's objectives of improving the livelihood capacity of victims and ensuring their socio-economic participation after their accidents. The CMAA is also supporting more than a thousand self-help groups in the country. Self-help groups are venues for direct and indirect victims to come together to discuss their issues and offer social support. The CMAA emphasises regular and proper data collection from volunteer survivor networks and stakeholders to provide an integrated approach to victim assistance. It trains local officials in data collection, data management, and local consultation, and conducts capacity-building of local authorities in relation to victim assistance. The Victim Assistance Department aims to complete the collection and disaggregation of data on landmines/ERW victims who have received the services from relevant stakeholders in order to improve its programmes.[104]

More than the acknowledgment of victimhood and assistance to victims, mine action also promotes social and economic empowerment of individuals and communities. Mine action agencies in Cambodia acknowledge the negative impact of landmine/ERW threats on the socio-economic development of mine-affected communities. One of the goals the CMAA lists in its NMAS 2018–2025 is to contribute to economic growth and poverty reduction by supporting national, sub-national, and local development priorities. The Cambodian government encourages mine action agencies to align their demining activities with the socio-economic needs of local communities. For instance, the CMAA, with the support of the Japanese government, has constructed 28.3 kilometres of rural and farm roads, five community ponds, a concrete bridge,

---

[103] RGC, *NMAS*, 6.

[104] The discussion of CMAA's victim assistance programmes is based on a presentation by Mao Bunnhath, Advisor and Director of Victim Assistance Department of CMAA, personal interview, 25 May 2018, Phnom Penh.

and two water gates, prepared 494 hectares of agricultural land, and trained 661 farmers.[105]

The CMAA streamlines policies and mechanisms of victim assistance for national, sub-national, and local stakeholders. It conducts public forums for persons with disabilities, local officials, and stakeholders three times a year to identify the issues and needs concerning the victims of landmines/ERW and their families. Such public forums help the CMAA to identify the needs of victims (for example, victims have requested more vocational training, small grants for businesses, and agricultural land). A lack of funding, however, prevents full coverage of said forms of victim assistance. According to Mao Bunnhath, advisor and director of the CMAA's Victim Assistance Department, they will increase their efforts to better communicate the availability of vocational training to victims and their families.[106] To broaden the coverage of victims eligible for assistance the Ministry of Social Affairs, Veterans and Youth Rehabilitation plans to provide identification cards to persons with disabilities for easier access to medical benefits and certain discounts.

Landmines/ERW continue to victimise the Cambodian people decades after the conflict. Mine action's assistance programmes alleviate their present victimhood from a temporally distant war. Demining in Cambodia provides a sense of redemption for direct and indirect victims of landmines/ERW. For example, one of the CSHD deminers who lost his arm to a UXO when he was a child later trained to become a deminer.[107] He tells of his dream of raising his own family someday and continuing his demining work until Cambodia becomes free of landmines/ERW. His accident serves as his motivation because he does not want to see his children and the children of Cambodia experience his accident. Income opportunities through demining give victims and their families another shot at life. Demining operators in Cambodia employ people with disabilities. They also ensure that women are given an equal chance of participating in demining activities. Women's participation in demining is changing the perception of women in society. Srey Ven, a field officer with the HALO Trust, said that she never thought she 'could work as hard as a man'.[108] Two female CSHD deminers we interviewed told us how proud they are of their work and contribution to Cambodian society.[109]

This analysis of victim assistance programmes illustrates needs-based, locally informed, victim-centred, and development-oriented approaches to mine action. In addition, mine action is instrumental in the Cambodian people coming to terms with the past. The story of Aki Ra, a former Khmer Rouge child soldier who was forced to lay mines and later served the Vietnamese-backed PRK and the SoC army, best illustrates the link between and the complexity of demining and transitional justice in Cambodia.[110] After the war he began demining by himself using a knife and sticks. His community started recognising his work and sought his help whenever they suspected landmines/ERW. He collected the metal casings of landmines/ERW he found and cleared and displayed

[105]CMAC, 'Achievements of the Program of Integrated Mine Action and Landmine Victim Assistance in the Kingdom of Cambodia, Phase I: January 2010-July 2013', cmac.gov.kh/userfiles/file/Peace%20Building%20Phase%20I%20Achievement%20Jan%202010-Jul%202013.pdf.
[106]Personal interview, 25 May 2018, Phnom Penh.
[107]Field observation, 9 May 2018, Kampong Kdei; Cambodia Landmine Museum visit, 11 May 2018, Siem Reap.
[108]Nic Dunlop, 'Meet the 23-Year-Old Woman Clearing Mines from a War She Doesn't Remember', *The Journal. ie*, December 27, 2017, thejournal.ie/mines-cambodia-demining-diana-3735677-Dec2017/.
[109]Field observation, 9 May 2018, Kampong Kdei.
[110]See also Meghan Wallace, 'Hero Profile: Aki Ra', *The Journal of ERW and Mine Action* 14, no. 3 (2010): 1–3.

them in his house where set up a small museum to attract donations from tourists and to educate his neighbours about the threats of landmines/ERW. He used the donations to support the children he adopted who were victims of landmines/ERW. In 2007, and after a brief closure due to safety issues raised by the CMAA, the museum moved to a larger and safer location, thanks to a donation from the Cambodian Landmine Museum Relief Fund based in Canada. In the same year CSHD, a Cambodian NGO run by and for Cambodians, was officially founded after accreditation from the CMAA.[111] For someone with post-traumatic stress disorder Aki Ra said that clearing the mines, some of which he had laid with his own hands years ago, is his way of coming to terms with his past. Some former combatants from all competing factions have been trained as deminers.[112] They are not only reintegrated back into their communities but have also become part of the solution, serving on a different battlefront – one that saves lives. The integration of former combatants in post-conflict rebuilding activities, such as demining, is instrumental to their rehabilitation and reconciliation with their communities.

Clearing the deadly legacy of war indicates a fresh start, not only for former combatants such as Aki Ra but also for innocent civilians caught in-between exploding lands. After mine clearance farmers can cultivate their lands and children can go to school safely. By prioritising farming, education, and healthcare facilities demining also contributes to socio-economic development. It is linked to poverty reduction by encouraging socio-economic activities on cleared lands. It was emphasised during the 2018 National Mine Action Conference that mine action is not just for ensuring physical security but also for socio-economic development. Removing the threats of landmines/ERW also contributes to healing the memories of Cambodia's violent past. The CMAC, for example, partners with international organisations and private companies in providing development packages to communities after mine clearance. These packages ensure holistic and long-term assistance to communities previously affected by landmines/ERW.[113]

The tangible outcomes of mine action differ from the symbolic reparation that usually comes with common mechanisms of transitional justice. Adopting a liberal-legal norm of accountability for the mass atrocities Cambodia has experienced naturally faces obstacles. The authoritarianism and corruption of the current government, composed of perpetrators of past violence, undermine the legitimacy of transitional justice mechanisms. In addition, the daily socio-economic concerns of everyday Cambodians dislodge transitional justice from the list of prioritised needs amongst individuals. Also, with each passing day the temporal distance of past Cambodian conflicts grows further from the present circumstances of the Cambodian people. Mine action's contribution to social justice and community development becomes even more crucial amidst these obstacles. The form of reparation that mine action provides is needs-based, victim-centred, and locally informed, contrary to the ECCC's symbolic, perpetrator-centred, and donor-driven transitional justice. Even preserving the memory of the conflict through the landmine museums of CMAC and CSHD in Siem Reap showcase, not just the suffering of the Cambodian people as seen in

[111] William Morse was inspired by Aki Ra's story and permanently moved to Siem Reap from the United States. As the international project manager of CSHD he is the primary donor and responsible for finding new funding sources. Morse nominated Aki Ra for the 2010 CNN Hero.

[112] Oum Phumro, deputy director general, CMAC, cited in Japan International Cooperation Agency, 'JICA, Cambodia Help Demine Colombia', May 1, 2017, jica.go.jp/english/news/field/2017/170501_01.html.

[113] CMAC, 'Demining and Development', cmac.gov.kh/en/article/demining-and-development.html (accessed August 2018).

Tuol Sleng Museum and Choeung Ek Killing Fields, but their positive contributions to rebuilding their country and making it safer for future generations. These landmine museums are more than symbols preserving Cambodia's history; they are expressions of the link between that history and the present security and economic concerns of the people. More importantly, they demonstrate the agency and willingness of the Cambodians to end the continuing devastation from the deadly remnants of war.

Transitional justice addresses the massive human rights violations in the past; mine action focuses on the present security threats that are consequences of the past. Transitional justice memorialises victimhood; mine action showcases agency. Transitional justice provides collective and symbolic reparation; mine action repairs individual and collective experiences of harm in both tangible and symbolic forms. These complementary differences imply that the activities of mine action have the potential to meet the goals of transitional justice. The discussion above points to the potential positive contribution of mine action to transitional justice in Cambodia. At the individual and local levels, the involvement of former combatants in mine clearance aids in their psychological rehabilitation and inter-personal reconciliation with members of their communities. The non-discriminatory threat from landmines and the collective effort of mine clearance forge social cohesion among the people and imprint the sense of being a part of a national endeavour. As such, their victimhood from Cambodia's past conflicts is redeemed by their agency to contribute to mine clearance and education. At the national level, mine action, which is less controversial than the trials at the ECCC, encourages the government to exercise bureaucratic accountability and transparency at least within the mine action regulatory offices it built. The government has a cooperative relationship with mine action-related international and local organisations and demining operators, in contrast to human rights organisations, because mine action does not directly participate in political deliberation and temporarily bypasses the guilt of those who placed the landmines by focusing on the immediate threat of landmines. Mine action, therefore, provides a congenial venue for the government and mine action CSOs to test future collaborative efforts towards addressing post-war issues.

Whilst mine action has the potential to contribute to aspects of transitional justice it is not a straightforward matter to include their activities under this label. The work of mine action groups in Cambodia is too complicated to be considered unequivocally as a transitional justice mechanism or a form of reparation, particularly if the ECCC is taken as the frame of reference. The ECCC's mandate is narrowly defined; its temporal jurisdiction is from 17 April 1975 to 6 January 1979, the first and last days when the Khmer Rouge controlled Phnom Penh. The problem of landmines/ERW extends long before and after that period. Many of the mines were laid by the 1980s PRK government, which was led by many of the same people who continue to rule Cambodia. Thus, to consider mine action an element of reparation or as linked to transitional justice presents a significant complication in the narrative of the crimes. The narrative the government builds is one where they are the saviours of the nation, and the most senior leaders of the Khmer Rouge are solely responsible for Cambodia's ills. The government builds on this narrative by leading and regulating all mine action-related activities in the country. Like the ECCC, mine action in Cambodia could be instrumentalised to cement the heroic image of Hun Sen and the CPP and buttress the political legitimacy of the current government all the while omitting the atrocities they committed in the past, including the laying of landmines. Endorsing mine action as a transitional justice mechanism may also embolden perpetrators who hold power in post-conflict societies to downplay retributive forms of transitional justice in favour of mechanisms that do not require the assignment of guilt and accountability, such as a mine action. Thus, although mine action could, generally speaking, be regarded as a form of reparation, it cannot be straightforwardly labelled as such vis-à-vis the Cambodian political environment and the mandate of the ECCC.

The consideration of reconciliation attached to mine action is also complex. Demobilised fighters are often involved in mine action in organisations worldwide; it provides a new form of employment for them and they often already possess at least some of the necessary technical skills, having been involved in laying mines.[114] While this also allows communities that may have been on opposite sides of a conflict to build trust[115] there is also the risk that those who are regarded as perpetrators, those who laid the mines in the first place, are now seen to be benefitting economically from landmine/ERW clearance. Moreover, and in relation to the service delivery mode of civil society, mine action conflates the need to amend the crimes of the past and the government's responsibility to provide basic services to its citizens.[116] When does something like mine action belong to the category of reparations? For the delivery of certain services to be labelled as reparations conveys legitimacy and a victim status on those who are being helped. However, people whose suffering does not fit easily into simplified narratives of the past are often excluded from victim labels, and the services provided to them are less likely to be labelled as reparations.[117] With these risks and complexities, linking mine action to transitional justice is probably best operationalised through the victim assistance schemes of both. This synergy will not undermine criminal trials and condone the perpetrators' guilt. Mine action's potential for individual rehabilitation, local reconciliation, memorialisation, and material and symbolic reparation, in fact, coincides with the objectives of the victim-oriented sections of the court (such as the Victim Support Section of the ECCC).

Conclusion

Mine action and transitional justice are pressing issues in some post-conflict societies, and CSOs have proven to support both at the global and national/local levels. In this paper, we explored the potential and challenges of integrating mine action with transitional justice against the backdrop of state-civil society relations in Cambodia. CSOs have long been engaged with transitional justice, and this has particularly been the domain of CSOs focussing on legal or human rights issues. However, in a situation where the state is actively restricting civil and political rights, the types of CSOs that would normally engage with transitional justice might find it unsafe, if not impossible, to operate fully. In this case, CSOs need to find alternative ways to engage with citizens without presenting themselves as challengers to those who control the state. The case of mine action in Cambodia demonstrates the potential for CSOs working in politically restrictive environments to operate and work with the government in less political spaces and issues (to the benefit

[114]Harpviken and Skåra, 'Humanitarian Mine Action', 814.
[115]Ibid., 817.
[116]Miller, 'Effects of Invisibility', 285.
[117]Michael Humphrey, *The Politics of Atrocity and Reconciliation: From Terror to Trauma* (New York: Routledge, 2002), 121.

of the state) and deliver more practical and immediate services (to the benefit of the people). Mine action could provide a safer and neutral venue outside the transitional justice mechanisms of the ECCC for individual rehabilitation through participation in demining activities and community-level reconciliation through mine action-related beneficiary programmes. The interface where mine action, transitional justice, and civil society meet is blurred at best but examining their dynamics in the case of Cambodia illuminates their underlying relevance to each other.

This paper also unsettles two common assumptions about civil society and transitional justice. First, the case of Cambodian mine action demonstrates that civil society is not separate from the state, contrary to the common conceptualisation of civil society as autonomous. The government regulates CSOs working on mine action in Cambodia. These CSOs also have a working relationship with the Cambodian government to achieve the goal of a mine-free Cambodia. While this arrangement appears to be a form of co-option of civil society it serves the purpose of improving the efficiency and effectiveness of mine action by streamlining all mine action activities. Although the government regulates their activities CSOs related to mine action are not necessarily enmeshed in Cambodia's politics because of the technical nature of demining and their overlapping priorities with the government, except for instances when corruption and international concern over Cambodia's declining democracy affects donor funding. Therefore, mine action can potentially inform the evolution of civil society in Cambodia, although we acknowledge that this is a highly optimistic prediction. Mine clearance and land release mechanisms create venues for grassroots participation and capacity-building in CSOs, which signals hope amidst Cambodia's shrinking democratic spaces. The participatory approach to mine action in Cambodia has the potential to nurture CSOs, venues for public deliberation, capacity for democratic participation, and voices from the grassroots level.

Second, exploring the link between mine action and transitional justice also encourages a rethinking of the common mechanisms of transitional justice. In a post-conflict society where there are limits to the retributive approach of justice mine action, as a collective action, opens opportunities for people to come to terms with their past. Those who laid mines and left other ERW decades ago are involved in mine action, and so are repairing some of the harms they contributed to. Victims of landmines/ERW are encouraged to participate in demining or shaping victim assistance programmes. Mine action, therefore, fills a gap in current mechanisms of transitional justice in Cambodia by fostering a needs-based, victim-centred, and locally informed form of reparation for the harmful legacy of Cambodian conflicts, specifically threats to life and livelihood from landmines/ERW. This is not to suggest that mine action should have replaced the ECCC as a form of transitional justice; it could, at best, have complemented its existing victim assistance schemes. Although the technical removal of landmines reduces physical violence, the pursuit of justice ultimately remains an effective means of reducing structural forms of violence.

In Cambodia the collective harm the people experienced blurs the line between victimhood and perpetration of crime.[118] This blurring is a manifestation of the complexity of Cambodian conflicts and, consequentially, the complexities of transitional justice in the Cambodian context. Therefore, collective efforts such as mine action are more attuned to these complexities. In mine action victims and perpetrators can contribute to clearing

[118]Erica Bouris, *Complex Political Victims* (Bloomfield, CT: Kumarian Press, 2007).

the injustices of the past by assuming the roles of deminers and educators without necessarily denying or acknowledging their victimhood or perpetration. Their efforts in clearing landmines/ERW and raising awareness express local agency instead of passive victimisation,[119] which is crucial in creating a civil society that encourages an empowered citizenry. Furthermore, the intersection of humanitarian mine clearance with socio-economic development and community participation in Cambodia's mine action ensures not only short-term physical security but also long-term and locally informed peacebuilding and development. Although it is unlikely to be formally recognised as a transitional justice mechanism, mine action has the potential to respond to more complex elements of Cambodian conflicts than the ECCC has been able to. It is clearing the legacy of decades of violence without simplifying the perpetrator and victim dichotomy. In doing so it is also repairing an element of the past while assisting Cambodians in creating a safer future.

ORCID

Dahlia Simangan http://orcid.org/0000-0001-9418-969X
Rebecca Gidley http://orcid.org/0000-0003-2297-6971

Acknowledgments

The authors wish to acknowledge the assistance of Sam Oum of the CMAA, Edwin Faigmaine, UNDP-Cambodia Chief Technical Advisor/Mine Action Specialist, Fabio Oliva, UN Peace and Development Adviser in Cambodia, and William Morse of CSHD during the fieldwork in Cambodia.

Disclosure statement

No potential conflict of interest was reported by the authors.

Funding

This work was supported by the Japan Society for the Promotion of Science (JSPS) [Project Number: 17F17780].

[119]Ruth Bottomley, 'Balancing Risk: Village De-Mining in Cambodia', *Third World Quarterly* 24, no. 5 (2003): 824.

Index

Aceh 9, 52–55, 58, 61, 64–65; space and power in 55–58; spaces of memory activism in 51, 68; vs. Timor-Leste 54–55
Aceh Reintegration Agency 62
action agencies 102–104, 106
Action Conference 100–101, 108
activist-led commemorations 53, 65, 67
actors 4, 12, 26, 28, 52, 56–57, 59, 76, 88
Ambon 71, 81, 83–88
Ambon Bergerak 83, 85–86, 88
anti-personnel mines 92
Autonomous Bougainville government (ABG) 39–43, 48

Basudara Stories of Peace 82
Bergh, Arild 80
Bleiker, Roland 78–79
Boege, Volker 2, 4, 7, 9
Bougainville 46–47, 49
Bougainvilleans 24, 39
Bougainville Peace Agreement (BPA) 22
Bougainville Revolutionary Army (BRA) 39–40, 62
Bräuchler, Birgit 3–4, 7–8
Brown, Anne 14

Cambodia 3, 5–7, 9, 90–93, 96–104, 106–107, 109, 111–112; backdrop of state-civil society relations in 91, 110; civil society and transitional justice in 93, 97; conflicts 111–112; government 91, 93, 96, 99–100, 102–104, 106, 111; mine action in 92, 100, 102, 109–111; people 91, 102, 105, 107–108; state-civil society relations in 91, 110
Cambodia Mine Action Centre (CMAC) 5–6, 92, 100, 102, 104, 108
Cambodian Mine Action and Victim Assistance Authority (CMAA) 100–102, 104, 106–108
Cambodian People's Party (CPP) 91
Cambodians 90, 92, 96–97, 100–101, 104, 106, 108–112
Cambodian Self-Help Demining (CSHD) 100, 108
civil society (CS) 2–7, 10, 14–16, 30–37, 47, 58, 60–61, 72, 75–80, 92–98, 101, 104, 110–112; actors 2, 4, 6, 58, 60–61; reconceiving 3–7; religious 95; and TJ 33–38; and transitional justice 93–94, 97, 111
civil society organisations (CSOs) 2–7, 14–15, 21, 31–33, 35–37, 44, 46, 48, 92–96, 98, 102–103, 110–111; conflict-affected societies 34; legitimacy of 37
Comissão de Acolhimento, Verdade e Reconciliacao (CAVR) 44, 55, 62
commemorations 52–53, 59, 61–68; activist-led 53, 65, 67
commodification, of reconciliations 23–24
conflict: affected people 75; affected societies 4, 6, 8, 30–34, 36, 38, 46–49; Cambodian 111–112; and peacebuilding in Maluku 72–73
Conselho Popular de Defesa da República Democrática de Timor Leste (CPD-RDTL) 44–46, 48–49
conventional peacebuilding 34, 36

demining: CSOs 3, 9; operators 93, 100–104, 109
documentary theatre 79
dominant spaces, of memory 64

events, violent 66
Extraordinary Chambers in the Courts of Cambodia (ECCC) 5, 93, 97–99, 103, 105, 108–112

FUNCINPEC party 91

Gidley, Rebecca 3, 5–7, 9
Gready, Paul 4

A History of Democratic Kampuchea (1975–1979) 99
Hobson, Kersty 79, 87
Husain, Rifky 82

Jeffery, Renée 95
Joinet, Louis 58

Kanaks 14
kastom reconciliations 16–17, 20–24, 26, 28
Kent, Lia 3, 5–7, 9, 95
Khmer Rouge 90–91, 97–99, 102–103, 105, 109
killings 46, 51, 61–62
kinship-based societal networks 16
Klinken, Gerry van 82
Konselho Revolucionário Maubere (KRM) 46, 49
Kritz, Neil 94

landmines/ERW 91, 92, 99–101, 104–111; victims of 106–108, 111
legitimacy of CSOs 37

Maarif Award 83
Maluku 7–8, 71–74, 77, 80–85, 87–89; conflict and peacebuilding in 72–73
Mauk Moruk 46, 49
Me'ekamui 39–42, 48
'Me'ekamui Government of Unity' (MGU) 40–41
Melanesian reconciliations 11–13, 17, 27, 29
Memorandum of Understanding (MoU) 41–42, 51, 54
memorialisation 2–3, 7–8, 32, 52–53, 58–61, 110
memorials 56, 58–59
memory: dominant spaces of 64; spaces of 53, 67–68
memory activism 5, 53, 58, 65, 68
Miller, Zinaida 95
mine action 92; in Cambodia 92, 100, 102, 109–111; as instrument of transitional justice 105–110; as a link between state and civil society 101–105
mines 91, 107–111
Moluccan Hip-Hop communities (MHC) 84–85, 87
Moluccans 73–74, 80, 82, 87–88
MoU. *See* Memorandum of Understanding
mourning, space of 67–68
music 7, 80, 83–84, 87
Musingku 41–43

National Mine Action Strategy (NMAS) 101
no-go zone 40–41
non-government organisations (NGOs) 2, 4–5, 14–15, 53–54, 58, 60, 65, 74, 76, 78, 92, 96
Norwegian People's Aid (NPA) 100, 104

Original Me'ekamui Government (OMG) 40–41
Ottawa Treaty 92, 99–100

past Cambodian conflicts 108
peace 5, 11–12, 14–16, 21, 28, 33, 39–40, 42, 47–49, 57, 71–72, 75, 77, 80–85, 87–89; agreement 39, 54–55; disturbances of 16; process 14, 38–43, 48–49, 72; provocateurs 80–82, 86; sustainable 28, 71–72, 75
peacebuilding 2–5, 8, 11, 13–14, 16–17, 20–22, 25, 31–33, 35, 37, 46–49, 72–75, 77–80, 82, 88–89; conventional 34, 36; Melanesia 13–16
Peace Provocateur Movement 82–83
people, conflict-affected 75
People's Republic of Kampuchea (PRK) 90–91
performative justice 8, 70, 72, 74, 79–80, 84, 86–88; Maluku 81
post-conflict peacebuilding 92
post-conflict reconciliation 20–25
Premaratna, Nilanjana 78–79
prosecutions, criminal 2, 7, 58–60, 64

reconciliations 5, 10–11, 13, 16–28, 32, 35, 39, 41, 44, 72, 74, 77–78, 108, 110; ceremonies 18–19, 23; Melanesian style 11–29; post-conflict 25; processes 17–18, 23–25, 39, 71, 78
Regional Assistance Mission to the Solomon Islands (RAMSI) 14
religious civil society 95
resistance: in Maluku 81; Maluku 81
restorative justice 9, 19–20, 27, 76
Robins, Simon 4
Roht-Arriaza, Naomi 95

Sagrada Familia 44–45, 48
Salay, Ali Madi 82
Save Aru movement 8
SaveAru movement 85
Simangan 5–7, 9; Dahlia 3
Sloboda 80
social justice 71–72, 80, 83, 88–89, 92, 108
social media 81–83, 86–87
spaces: intimate 67–68; of memory 53, 67–68; of memory activism 51, 68
state-building process 44
state-civil society dynamics 6
state-civil society relations 91–93, 99, 110
state institutions 5–6, 33–34, 36, 40–41, 44, 47–48
State of Cambodia (SoC) 90
structural violence 8, 71–73, 77, 79, 87–88, 95
sustainable peace 28, 71–72, 75

Tessart 85–87
Timor-Leste 2, 5–7, 9, 30, 32–33, 38, 43–44, 46–49, 51–55, 57–58, 60–62, 64–68; vs. Aceh 54–55; memory and space and power in 55–58; spaces of memory activism in 51, 68
TJ. *See* transitional justice

transformative justice 3, 72, 77
transitional justice: action and 90–91, 94, 105, 110–111; mechanisms 28, 54–55, 58, 60, 90–92, 94–95, 108–112; reconceiving 7–10; and spaces of memory activism 51–68
transitional justice (TJ) 2–111; literature 6, 31–32, 34, 36–37, 47–48, 76; processes 2, 31–33, 35–38, 41, 44, 48–49, 76–77
Truce Monitoring Group/Peace Monitoring Group (TMG/PMG) 14
Truth and Friendship Commission 55
Truth and Reconciliation Commission (TRC) 21–23, 26, 28, 32, 39, 64, 71
truth and reconciliation commissions 32, 39, 71

uncivil society 30, 34–35, 38, 47; in Bougainville 38–43; role of 33, 36, 38; in Timor-Leste 43–46
'uncivil' society, transitional justice 30–33
uncivil society groups 2, 5, 9, 31–33, 35, 37–44, 46–49; role of 32–33, 38
United Nations Observer Mission 14
United Nations Transitional Authority in Cambodia (UNTAC) 91, 96

victims 18–20, 25–28, 52, 58–59, 61, 63–67, 71, 74, 76–77, 92, 97, 99–100, 105–107; assistance 92, 100, 106–107; families of 63, 65; of landmines/ERW 106–108, 111
violence 5, 8, 14, 23–27, 54–55, 59, 61, 64–65, 67, 71–75, 80–84, 88, 111–112; inter-communal 14
violent conflict, Melanesia 13–16
violent conflicts 13–14, 20, 25–26, 58, 88
violent events 66
vocational training 106–107

Wallis, Joanne 2, 4–5, 9, 95